WHEN THE SICK RULE
THE WORLD

SEMIOTEXT(E) ACTIVE AGENTS SERIES

© 2015 Dodie Bellamy

Published by Semiotext(e)
PO BOX 629, South Pasadena, CA 91031
www.semiotexte.com

Cover: Tariq Alvi, *Two Hankies: Pony, The Bandaged Lady*, 2005.
Design: Hedi El Kholti

ISBN: 978-1-58435-168-9
Distributed by The MIT Press, Cambridge, Mass. and London, England
Printed in the United States of America

WHEN THE SICK RULE THE WORLD

Dodie Bellamy

For Kevin, who has held me for so many years.

Contents

What I dislike about a lot of contemporary artists is that they want to be hipsters. They're not willing to be fools.

— Mike Kelley

1

WHISTLE WHILE YOU DIXIE

I hate whistling. When I hear it I feel irritation that glides into panic, and my body clenches like Gregory Peck's when he sees stripes in Hitchcock's *Spellbound*—WHISTLE WHISTLE—my eyes cross, my back arches, and I go all Salvador Dali. Then I'm lying on a tapestry-draped chaise lounge, babbling, "I know it has something to do with maleness, something from my childhood, men and whistling, but Dr. Freud, I just can't remember!" My friend Neil told me how a student whistled in his painting class and the professor went ballistic. I imagine her brandishing a giant paint brush and shrieking, "Stop that whistling!" The brush is dripping red paint, red for anger. It turns out the professor used to live with a guy who would whistle whenever they had a fight, he'd walk about their place whistling as if he didn't have a care in the world, and that would drive the professor insane. If I root out my primal scene of whistling abuse or horror, will I arise, cured of all sorts of symptoms—or like Neil's professor, will I carry this burden around with me forever? To further explore the repressed I study two YouTube videos—Snow White's "Whistle While You Work" number in the Disney film and Billy Currington's dangerously seductive cover of the Bellamy Brothers' country hit "You Ain't Just Whistling Dixie." It's possible for me to watch them because neither contains any actual whistling.

"Whistle While You Work" opens inside a filthy cottage overrun with wildlife. Snow White presses a pointer finger to her blood-red lips and chants:

> Now you wash the dishes
> You tidy up the room
> You clean the fireplace
> And I'll use the broom

The animals look around, wide-eyed and confused. The sink and kitchen table stacked with precariously balanced dishes, clothes strewn across the living room floor, cobwebs, thick patina of dust—the Seven Dwarfs are real slobs. Three blue birds chirp a militaristic call to attention, then Snow White begins to sing, "Whistle while you work ..." and the animals get busy, cleaning in a frenzy. Snow White has cast a spell on them. Even though Disney has given some of the animals opposable thumbs (a chipmunk winds a ball of spiderweb string, raccoons scrub clothes) they prefer to use their mouths and asses. A deer licks dinner plates, and a squirrel dries them with its whirling tail. Snow White corrects, with a high pitched, "Oh! No no no no! Put them in the tub." Stunned, the animals obey. The deer fills the tub by undulating its ass on the pump handle. Squirrels hula their fluffy rumps with zeal, like nothing could be more pleasurable than dusting. A deer and bunny attend to a chair whose backrest is a carving of a rough-hewn humanoid face, hole in the middle for the face's open mouth. The bunny perches on the seat, facing the hole; the deer stands behind the chair, presses its ass to the back, and brushes the top with its tail. The bunny peeks through the hole, right into the deer's asshole, then the deer pokes its tail though the hole with a very intense look on its face, in a gesture that simultaneously suggests fucking and fellatio. The bunny sits upright and excitedly wiggles its own pom-pommed derriere. Outside at the pond, a chipmunk scrubs a shirt on a turtle's ribbed tummy. The turtle sits on the bank of the pond, partially submerged. The shirt extends into the water, between the turtle's legs. As the chipmunk rubs the cloth up and down, the turtle throws its head back, clenches its eyes, gapes open its mouth, and rhythmically moves its bottom legs up and down—a pose of such jouissance it suggests the chipmunk is jerking him off with the shirt. When the chipmunk tries to leave, the lascivious turtle latches onto the chipmunk's tail with its massive jaw and snaps the chipmunk inside its shell. Both animals' heads poke up from the turtle's shell, they look at one another with a startle that quickly melts into dreamy bedroom eyes. "Whistle while you work" means make the most of your drudgery, and the animals have obeyed big time, reinventing domestic labor as bacchanal. Snow White emits high-pitched operatic hums and sighs, but she never whistles. Whistling, the great unutterable, comes from elsewhere, this condensed libidinal energy from which Snow White draws her power. She lackadaisically swishes her witch's broom and sings, "whistle … whistle," and transfixed animals writhe and scour.

If "Whistle While You Work" is the yin of whistling lacuna songs, Billy Currington's "You Ain't Just Whistling Dixie" is the yang. For the acoustic set, Billy stands on a stage that's bare save for two mics, two wooden stools. He's unshaven in worn jeans, white T-shirt, backwards baseball cap, thick wavy hair caressing his neck. A cloth banner behind him and his two band mates reads "96.9 KAT Country." He holds the guitar tenderly as a lover. He closes his eyes, looks pained and sings; he opens his eyes, smiles and sings. When the audience applauds he stumbles about all humble and handsome, effortlessly charismatic. "You Ain't Just Whistling Dixie" is a melody so sweet and lilting it makes my hard heart sappy. And then I start listening to the words. It's about a guy who's left the South and is recalling it through the misty lens of nostalgia. Men go fishing, get drunk, long for the glory days of the Confederacy. Pa comes home loaded with gin and mean as a rattlesnake. Momma not only washes clothes, she has to haul heavy buckets of water from the creek to do so. The sentimental son and the drunken husband cuss the garden hose rather than helping her. To whistle Dixie means to not be serious about something, to engage in idle fantasies, to lack resolve. To not whistle Dixie means to be serious and committed. It isn't enough to simply not whistle—one has to mention whistling, to be in the active state of not whistling. Of not acknowledging the domestic violence and the horrors of slavery and gender oppression implicit in the lyrics. Billy Currington's breathy voice is so sultry and he's so hip and sexy, it's hard not to get sucked into the fantasy of the song. "Here are a few things I'm in love with." Despite my resistance I feel a pervy twinge of wanting the wrong thing.

My dad's family was from Kentucky. While not the Deep South, it was too south for me—I was raised six hours north, in a working class suburb snuggled between Chicago and Gary. My mother called my Kentucky relatives "trash." They had no morals, my Uncle Noah (which they pronounced "Noh-ee") killed a man and never went to jail, they stole, they farted and belched and fucked like rabbits, they had ten kids apiece and our tax dollars paid for them to be on welfare. I remember my aunt's legs thick with crusty red and white psoriasis, naked towheaded children smearing snot on the couch, putrid stench of dark claustrophobic outhouses, holding my breath so I wouldn't retch, chickens with their heads chopped off running in circles on parched weedy grass, blood fountains spurting from their necks, weird foods like fried squirrel brains and pickled pigs feet. Grandpa Bellamy, proud member of the KKK, sitting at the kitchen table sopping up bean broth with a biscuit, curly white old man hairs sprouting from the neck of his wifebeater, hatred spewing from his lips like caustic spittle. Ten years after my father died I was drinking chocolate sodas with my mother and out of the blue she said the reason my father was so mean was because Grandpa Bellamy beat him. "He was always beating on your dad, she said. "One time he threw him down the stairs. He singled your dad out, he was a mean son of a bitch." I've always assumed it was my father who whistled, but maybe it's Grandpa Bellamy. He lived with us for a while, maybe he whistled when he pinched me—hard—little Dodie screaming in pain and him laughing, it was a panting sort of laugh, his thick frameless glasses glinting. Sound of straws slurping ice cream, soda, chocolate sauce. "Your father never knew how to raise kids because of the way he was raised."

When Billy Currington gets to the part of the song about Pa coming in full of gin and mean as a rattlesnake, he looks at his hands picking the guitar as if he's suddenly forgotten how to play. His stepfather beat him, knocking him unconscious when he was ten. Billy acted out by getting in fights in grade school. "When you are taught to hate, you carry that with you," Billy told *People* magazine. "Even today, I call myself 98 percent laid-back, but 2 percent is Little Billy, my inner child that's hurt, sad and furious because he was never taken care of." In 2007 he entered a trauma recovery program and canceled 83 shows. Then he spent a year in Hawaii working with two specialists in childhood trauma. "My childhood did not turn me into an alcoholic or a drug addict; my challenge in life is my anger. I'd be Little Billy for two seconds, yelling and blowing up. And in those instances, that rage can destroy relationships, whether it's with a girlfriend or a business partner or a fan." Two years later, while Billy was performing an outdoor concert in Alberta, a tornado destroyed the stage. Billy suffered a concussion and canceled four shows. Pic of Billy being ferreted away by a handler, mop of curly hair battered by the wind. The handler has an arm around his waist, and Billy's looking back over his shoulder, terrified and innocent, the sky a huge menacing poltergeist. When the rage of the Little Billy breaks through, it's eerie quiet at first, no birds chirp, nothing. Then a hissing like steam or rushing water, then a roar and a deafening whine. The ground vibrates and Billy hears the crashing and cracking of trees snapping and houses being ripped apart. It sounds like a gigantic freight train is coming right at him. Billy relives his stepdaddy's fist in his face and Billy has this gut realization that he's a grown man now, a famous country singer with body guards and fans and gym-buffed abs, and step-daddy can never hurt him again.

Back to me on the tapestry-draped chaise lounge. I remember the folk saying "Whistling women and crowing hens will come to no good in the end," and I roll my head from side to side ranting, "Why is whistling a male thing?" Dr. Freud suggests I look at Anne Carson's essay, "The Gender of Sound." Carson traces Western Civ's attitudes towards the sounds humans make all the way back to the ancient Greeks. "In general the women of classical literature are a species given to disorderly and uncon-trolled outflow of sound," she writes, "—to shrieking, wailing, sobbing, shrill lament, loud laughter, screams of pain or pleasure and eruptions of raw emotion in general." Such female outpourings were associated with "monstrosity, disorder and death." These are the sounds of madness and witchery, and the wild, unruly women who spewed them could make men physically ill. Worst case scenario, they could kill a man. The Greeks saw women as having two mouths—an upper mouth and a nether mouth, connected by one long tube of nastiness. Carson's essay confirms what I already suspected—that high pitched sounds are gendered female, that subarticulate cries and moans are gendered female, and thus patriarchal culture from antiquity to present day has sought to control these savage vocalizations. Carson never mentions whistling. "Whistling is high pitched, yet it is gendered male," I sob. "What's going on here," I lament. "Anne Carson," I shriek, "why haven't you explained this to me?"

Left to my own devices, I think back to Snow White and Billy Currington, I think really hard, and I realize that in both videos a spell is being enacted outside the bounds of the civilized world—"Whistle While You Work" literally takes place in the woods, and "You Ain't Just Whistling Dixie" happens in the backwoods of remembrance. In the Snow White video the boundaries between domesticity and the natural are subverted, releasing bizarre libidinal energies. Snow White is a faker. She hates housework as much as I do, she probably fought with her mother over scrubbing the bathtub just like I did. The animals' writhing, ass-driven cleaning techniques are a hysterical projection of her rage at the lazy-ass Seven Dwarves. She and her deranged animals desecrate their cottage with the sinister pleasure of the restaurant worker who spits in the obnoxious customer's soup. The narrator-singer of "You Ain't Just Whistling Dixie" is under a spell of nostalgia that smokescreens histories of violence and oppression. It is a male evasion of rationality for only in a nonrational realm could one proclaim oneself an heir to the Confederacy, without at least a teeny footnote in there. The whistle is unheard in both songs because it endangers the spell. The whistle's irritating shrill would jerk the participants awake. I try to whistle, which I'm really bad at, and it seems to originate from the throat. Wails, moans, sobs, belly laughs come from deep in the diaphragm, the whole body shakes, and emotional expression seems frighteningly unmediated. But the whistle comes from the throat, high up in the body, right there below the brain, that powerhouse of logic. Whistling is tame and harmonious, the mouth becomes a flute playing melodies at the virtuoso's bidding. The art professor's pig of a boyfriend could whistle dispassionately whenever they got in a fight because a real man can dissociate himself from his emotions and thus control his sound. Whistle, whistle, you ain't getting to me, bitch. The whistle is the piercing blade of rationality, the red-faced cop in the middle of a busy intersection, whistle in mouth, blowing and blowing until rush hour chaos grinds to a halt, and drivers sit erect in their seats awaiting direction. There will be no whistling in this piece. Whistling is as rude as touching someone with your feet or showing the soles of your shoes when sitting in public. Whistling is bad luck, especially on ships, especially when done by women. In *Faust*, the angels sang, but the Devil whistled. Whistling is freakish, like a wheeze that has been unnaturally domesticated. Writing this piece I am actively not-whistling. May the kink of denial and enchantment reign.

* * *

If my mother knew any of this she'd say I was nothing but trash. Late summer, 1974, I was hitchhiking from Sarasota back to Bloomington, Indiana with this guy I barely knew who had strawberry hair past his shoulders, not frizzy curly but soft wavy. He was thin and angular, I was fleshy, but with the hair and freckles we still looked like brother and sister. My freckles were muted due to the tan I'd acquired from going to the beach every day for the six weeks I'd stayed with my friend Dennis at the Selby Botanical Gardens, where he worked as a caretaker. We shared two rooms in what was formerly the servants' quarters of the Selby mansion. The strawberry guy was handsome but bland, he didn't talk much and what he said bored me. When we fucked it wasn't all that great for either of us; it was okay, a friendly, low key release. I'd met him briefly in Bloomington with a girlfriend that clung to his arm, she was younger and pretty with long brown hair parted down the middle—and even quieter than he. I have no idea what strawberry guy was doing in Florida. You could put me under hypnosis, and I wouldn't remember his name—it was something simple, like Greg. Dennis had told me I couldn't crash with him any more, which meant moving from the Selby paradise of banyan trees and orchids to some dumpy studio apartment. I was terrified of being alone. So when Greg said he was hitchhiking to Bloomington, I crammed whatever I could into a backpack and left everything else—two white Samsonite suitcases stuffed with most of the clothes I owned—with Dennis. Dennis was pissed. "What am I supposed to do with all this shit?" "I don't know, send it to me?" What a grouch, I thought, as I scampered to the highway in cutoffs and water buffalo flipflops. I was on an adventure! Greg was going back to his girlfriend; I was going back to a longterm girlfriend I'd split with a couple of months earlier, a sort of boyfriend, Michael, whom I was obsessed with, and a grad program I had no interest in. The Greyhound down to Florida had been a nightmare—I may have been raised in a racist environment but I was unprepared for the hatred of Dixie, you could feel it growing like a dark cloud the further south we rolled—and then it's nighttime and the Greyhound is lit by anemic overhead lights, the seats are blue the floor ribbed charcoal, a black boy has done something wrong and three or four thuggy white men with glasses and short-sleeved button-up shirts, or maybe they were cops, have him in the aisle and are punching and dragging him to the front of the bus, cussing and punching and calling him names, the boy lying on the filthy floor squirming, he's an animal to them, there is no humanity to keep them from beating him to death. Grandpa Bellamy would have eagerly joined them. I turn my face to the open window, take in a deep breath of diesel and jasmine.

We stuck out our thumbs, and a pickup truck pulled over. "Where you headed?" a shirtless young guy shouted out the window. "Bloomington, Indiana." He said he'd take us as far as Indianapolis. This part of the story is true—we hitched from Sarasota to Bloomington, 1030 miles, in two rides. Getting a lift from Indianapolis was always a cinch. I climbed into the cab of the truck and slid into the middle, the seat blistering hot from the sun. Greg followed. The guy had a mop of streaky blond hair and his long dusty body was slick as a whistle, but he was really young, like still a teenager, too young to be taken seriously. I took in his cuteness the way I'd take in a cat's or chihuahua's. He asked me what drugs I liked. I said I no longer did them but I used to smoke grass and drop acid—and psilocybin whenever I could get it—and occasionally I'd down a quaalude. "Have you ever snorted glue?" he asked. In high school back in San Francisco he snorted glue and gasoline, all his friends did. With all the great drugs I'd read about in San Francisco, why would this guy resort to glue and gasoline? I imagined greasy concrete, a sharp chemical stench, a group of hormonal youth sprawled on the ground in front of a gasoline pump, their crazed eyes superimposed with black and white spirals which spin wildly, out of control. The tanned, feral high school boy was kind of creepy, but so fucking easy to talk to. He's also nameless in my memory, but let's leave him that way. He was the first person I ever met from San Francisco. In San Francisco, packs of gay men roamed the streets like antelopes and you could buy strawberries as big as your fist, anything could happen in San Francisco. I sat between the boy and silent Greg, happily sharing intimacies as we sped north through Dixie's sweltering terrain, which pretty much looked like Indiana— evenly-rowed farmlands punctuated by truckstops or cows. "Look at the horses!" Occasionally while performing the machinations of driving, the teen's hand would accidentally graze my thigh, and the heat of his tawny bare-chested body would hit me.

I'd hammer my impulses back to subconsciousness and resume cheery chitchat mode. In rural Georgia we stopped at a farm stand. I'd heard of Georgia peaches from listening to the Allman Brothers, Georgia peaches were like famous, so I bought a sack of them. The teen and I shared one as we drove on, I'd hold the peach in front of his face and he'd take a bite then I'd take a bite overlapping his bite then he'd take a bite overlapping my bite, our saliva mingling on the dewy orange fruit flesh. I wanted it to taste sweeter than an Indiana peach, but it didn't. As the day slid languorously into evening, I found myself giggling a lot, and the frequency of teen hand to Dodie thigh accidents increased steadily, so that by the time it was decided the drive was too long to make in one day, and that in Tennessee the three of us would have to share a motel room for the night, I was feeling like a desperate pervert. I was 23 and he was old enough to have a driver's license—just.

Two double beds side by side, flanking a small nightstand. I'm in the bed on the right with Greg, on the inside, beside the night-stand. Our driver has the other bed to himself. The three of us lying there naked, our sheet-tangled bodies hot and sticky as the hot sticky night. I don't think I'm ever going to get to sleep and then the teen reaches out his arm, takes my hand and tugs. The cheap motel dark isn't very dark, and I can see his head motion for me to join him. I shake my head no. What's going on with Greg? Maybe he's sleeping. He's like Teflon to my consciousness, his presence keeps slipping away. The glue-sniffing teen continues to tug and silently plead. My head shakes no, but my hand holds on to his—I know this reads like a porn story, but I really didn't want him, or at least I didn't think I did—his exuberance was tinged with a frightening unhealthiness, his eyes dull, his tan tinged with gray, like if I really got up close and took a good sniff he'd smell musty like an old person—still my hand holds on—

this cloud of sexuality has overtaken me, like when I was a kid and the mosquito man drove his truck through the neighborhood trailing a thick white cloud of pesticides and all us kids chased behind it thrilled to be running in a cloud, like heaven had touched down in a sharp chemical stench tinged with sweetness, and afterwards we were so dizzy we sprawled on twilight-cooled lawns, in a swoon. When I was in high school, boys either ignored or ridiculed me, the nightmarish ones made wolf whistles and laughed their asses off—and now this high school boy wants to fuck me. My upper mouth is saying no, but my nether mouth is moaning boy meat ... yes ... yes ... now. I suppose I could have seized this opportunity to explode my trauma in a Freudian frenzy, my body drenched in his gasoline-laced semen, and then I'd be a whole person. Or maybe it was that trauma that kept me from going there.

I didn't go there. It's not like I had any commitment with Greg, it's not like I hadn't done similar things before. In Sarasota I had crawled from one guy's bed into another's, and those guys were in separate rooms, and it hadn't turned out well, meaning the first guy, who I kind of liked but who was being a cold asshole, stormed into the second guy's room and told me he never wanted to see me again and I said to him, if you cared so much why weren't you nice to me. A few months earlier, in Bloomington I went to a party with my girlfriend and ran into Michael—he wasn't my boyfriend yet, I'd drunkenly fucked him once and was desperate to do it again—so he and I went into the bathroom, locked the door and made out like crazy, bumping into the tub, the toilet, the sink—my girlfriend on the other side of the door, banging—I waited until she left and I went home with him. When it came to sex I was heartless. When I saw something I wanted, I went for it, I didn't care who was watching or who might be hurting—rejection cut me in two but guilt didn't faze me, I was too desperate to register something as nuanced as guilt. But suddenly, here it was, a line, this chasm between the beds, a decadent boy with raging horniness on one side—me on the other—if I crossed it I would lose something, the last strand of my humanity—somewhere within me I did have the ability to say no—survival instinct kicked in, what if Greg stormed out and I was left alone with the boy, what would become of me, promiscuity had turned out to be disappointing, I didn't know what I wanted, I wanted a guy just like my girlfriend but with a dick, what if that's what boys were like, a girlfriend with a dick, what if I ended up in San Francisco strung out with a gang of demon children.

What I did was to fuck Greg—quietly of course. Whispers, sighs, breathing that escalates to a pant. Streetlight streaked in through the edges of the motel curtain as both beds creaked in unison.

In Indianapolis, the libidinous teen dropped us by the side of the road and sped out of my life. In a perfectly wrought narrative he would have pulled away, whistling—and maybe he did, maybe life is really that kind to future writing projects. I wonder what happened to him—is he still in San Francisco? Have I passed him on the street? Did he turn out okay? Driving cross country in a pick up at such a young age demonstrates a high level of organizational abilities. He was a self starter, I'd say. Was he that toothless old guy panhandling in a wheel chair I skirted this afternoon on Market Street? I didn't drop any coins in his cup. Why didn't I?

When I returned to the filthy house I shared with my four gay roommates—all of us considered ourselves too fabulous to clean—I dumped the bag of Georgia peaches into a colander, opened my *New York Times Natural Foods Cookbook*, and before the San Francisco-bound teen hit Missouri, I whipped up a peach cobbler with sweet biscuit topping. A domesticity joyful and effortless as Snow White's, flour puffing in the air like a cloud. I chant to my animal companions:

> Now you wash the peaches
> You grease the pan
> You light the oven
> And I'll open the baking powder can.

Deer lick the peaches clean with quick pink tongues. I don't reprimand them, I let my animals express their animalistic selves. I slice the peaches as raccoon claws maw 1 3/4 cups of flour and 6 tablespoons of butter until it's all cut together the size of small peas. To grease the casserole a chipmunk sits on another slab of butter and sleds back and forth, leaving a thin trail of chipmunk dung. Turtles carry mouthfuls of milk which they spit in the mixing bowl, I toss in some sugar and baking powder and salt, and a squirrel whips it all together with his big bushy tail. Mice carry the peach slices, one at a time, in their mouths and carefully layer them in the greased casserole. Bluebirds fly overhead and sprinkle the peaches with cinnamon. Nobody whistles. A squirrel pees on the rug, a deer shits on the kitchen floor, bunnies fuck behind the stove—feathers piss shit slobber fur jissom—my animal minions flee before it's time to clean it up. They're no slaves to drudgery.

I fed the cobbler to my roommates, my girlfriend, my sort of boyfriend, anybody who happened to stop by. "I got these peaches in Georgia," I'd say. "They hitchhiked with me all the way from Georgia." Friends and lovers took a bite of sweet cinnamony goodness and said, "Wow." Weeks later my suitcases arrived from Sarasota with an angry note from Dennis.

2

WHEN THE SICK RULE THE WORLD

"And comes from a country far away as health."
— Sylvia Plath

Have you often had to lower the regular dose of prescription or over-the-counter medication or herbal supplements because you were too sensitive to normal doses do you avoid caffeine in the afternoon or altogether because it can keep you up at night have you ever experienced adverse reactions to medications if so what happened do you smell odors when others can't what kinds of odors do you have a sudden onset of symptoms headaches skin rashes nausea shortness of breath etc. on exposure to chemicals mold dust pollens or other environmental allergens what symptoms please list all the chemicals you get a reaction to when do you last remember feeling really great describe your residence when your illness began type age carpets heat source paint proximity to industry etc. describe your work environment when your illness began type of building ventilation toxic exposure neighboring businesses etc. have you ever had to change your residence or job due to health reasons have you ever had a known chemical injury or major exposure have you ever been exposed to chemicals or toxic metals in the course of work of schooling when how long name them have you ever worked where adjacent businesses regularly used chemicals or toxic metals when how long name them have you ever worked in a building where the windows were always closed when how long have you ever worked where you or your co-workers complained about the air quality or smells in the workplace or were injured in any way when how long have you ever heard about any air quality incidents in your place of work when describe what you heard have you ever lived near any heavy industries that regularly emitted waste into the air or water i.e. golf course dry cleaner plant shipyard mine chemical factory dumpsite or landfill what type of pollution when how long have you ever lived in a house built before 1978 how long were you there have you ever lived on or adjacent to an agricultural area what kind of area was it when how long have you ever lived in a home where mold was a problem when how long have you ever lived in a home with a water leak or water damage when how long have you ever lived in a mobile home when how long have you ever lived in a home where turning on the central air or heat caused you or family members to feel sick when how long have you ever felt there were conditions in your home that affected your health use of aerosol sprays chemicals cleaners construction painting etc. when how long are pesticides or herbicides used inside or outside our home have you ever lived near a busy highway street or gas station when how long when were your air ducts last cleaned when were your air filters last changed is your stove gas or electric is your furnace gas or electric water heater gas or electric do you wear dry cleaned clothing if yes how frequently and in which room are they stored are there animals in your home do you have air purifiers or water filters in your home do you heat food in a microwave do you have candles in your home do you regularly get hair coloring permanents or visit a beauty salon have you ever had acrylic fingernails or been to a beauty shop where acrylic nails are done if so when have you ever used scented soaps detergents potpourri perfumes etc. do you still have you ever used fabric softener do you still have you ever used recreational drugs if so when and what compounds have you ever lived with animals that received treatment for fleas or ticks if so when have you ever lived in a home with new carpet new furniture and new construction if so when have you ever lived on or near a golf course or other areas where heavy pesticides and herbicides are used regularly if so when have you ever regularly worked with chemicals in any hobby i.e. solvents paints stains cleaners etc. if so when have you ever had silver fillings put in your teeth if so when do you still have silver fillings in your mouth if yes how many and how long have they been in your mouth have you ever had root canals implants or bridgework done on your teeth if so when have you ever had any implants stainless steel Teflon silicone etc. put into your body if so when and what kind of implants have you ever been given vaccinations if so when have you ever had reactions to any vaccinations have you ever smoked if so for how long have you ever lived with others that smoked if so for how long and how old were you how often do you eat fish what types of fish do you eat?

The wall of questions makes me feel devastated and hopeless. I have lived in and worked in and gone to so many bad places. The naturopath is young, small and blonde, and has a little girl's voice. Based on my answers she says, "You are very sick, your apartment is making you sick. You have to move." She's ordered lots of lab work on me, but she hasn't gotten back any of the results. "If I were to move," I ask her, "what should I look for?" She stares back at me, confused and suspicious, like it were a trick question. Finally she says, "You *can* move, I know you can move. Many patients have moved and they felt so much better. If you don't move, you'll never get better." "But what kind of place should I move to?" She says to look on the internet, there's lots of information online.

I join a listserve for the sick and learn that the monthly meeting of the sick is happening the following weekend. It takes place in a nontoxic apartment building in San Rafael, built especially for the sick. No fragrances are allowed in the building. Those attending the meeting must use fragrance-free soap, lotion, shampoo, hair conditioner, gel, deodorant, laundry detergent. No fabric softener, no clothes that have been dry cleaned. I already do most of this, but my hair products and body lotion have herbal oils in them, so I spend $30 on fragrance free versions. I enjoy the ritual of carefully bathing and dressing myself in preparation for my entry into the realm of the sick. The fragrance-free shampoo makes my scalp itch, so I rub on some locally made, stone crushed extra virgin oil. Driving across the Golden Gate Bridge, I imagine a spa atmosphere, a peaceful, wood-hewn paradise, the crisp air super-charged with oxygen. Instead I find boxy, institutional, white. In the courtyard, a frail, frizzy-haired woman stops me from entering the community room. "You have to be sniffed first," she says, and she places her nose right up to my body and takes deep noisy sniffs. "I smell some-thing," she says. She moves her nose along my arms and shoulders, "No I don't think it's your sweater." She moves her nose across my head. "It's your hair." "Do you smell anything?" she says to a large-breasted woman. "Yes," says the large-breasted woman, "it's in her hair, it's giving me a headache." The frail woman tells me I'll have to cover my hair. "But I did everything you asked," I say. She steps into an apartment and returns with two cotton scarves, a green one and a black one. They're those hanky-scarves that hippies used to wear and gay men put in their pockets to announce what sex kink they were into. "It's just olive oil," I plead. "You're giving me brain fog," the large-breasted woman replies. The other woman holds out the scarves. "Which one do you want." I take the green one and fold it into a triangle, put it over my head and tie it in the back. "Some of your hair hanging out," I'm told. "Put on the other one too." So I wrap the black one around the back of my head and tie it on top, above my forehead. The women joke that I look like Aunt Jemima.

Most sick experience headaches, burning eyes, asthma symptoms, stomach distress/nausea, dizziness, loss of mental concentration, and muscle pain. Some individuals also suffer fever or even loss of consciousness. Motor skills and memory may be impaired. The sick practice calm abiding. They say to themselves, "I feel so nauseous in my stomach, this means I'm alive, I am a living being, that I can feel this, and all these sensations and worries," and they breathe it in and they feel good, to be a living being. When someone wearing perfume lies down next to me in yoga I get up and move. When someone sits beside me in a theater wearing perfume I get up and move. When someone sits at the next table wearing perfume I get up and move. When a student comes to class wearing perfume my nose runs, my eyes tear, I start sneezing; there's nowhere to move to and I don't know what to do. When the sick rule the world perfume will be outlawed. Dealers will stand in alleyways selling contraband Estee Lauder and Chanel no. 5. They will carry tiny capsules of perfume in their mouths, tucked along their gums, and when they open their mouths they'll look like vampires with their extra row of liquid gold teeth.

Later in the restroom I long to snap a picture of Aunt Jemima Dodie with my iphone so I can show it to Kevin and we can share a laugh, but I can't get myself to even peek in the mirror at my round bound makeup-less face. I do my toilet business with my eyes cast down at the stone-tiled floor. At the end of Todd Haynes' movie *Safe* when sick Julianne Moore looks in the mirror and says, "I love you," she looks great, with her fluffy hair and her cheek bones, not like a bloated Bandana Monster, I imagine kids scaring one another at sleepovers: "The Bandana Monster's coming to eat you!" So I don't know what the sick saw as I sat in my chair during the sharing portion of the meeting and told them my symptoms, I've been tired and headachy, with a chronic ADD-esque lack of focus. I've been having allergic reactions to everything, and if I eat the wrong thing I'm up with diarrhea, dry heaves and god-awful nausea for like 7 hours. The sick sympathize with my symptoms. They suggest I carry Alka-Seltzer Gold with me, that Alka-Seltzer Gold will stop an allergic reaction dead in its tracks. I tell them my young, blonde, child-like naturopath thinks I have a problem with my phase II detoxification, and the one sick guy in the group says they all have that, over-active phase I detox and underactive phase II.

The sick rinse their bodies with vinegar and dry off with a blowdryer to prevent mold growth. The sick travel in used cars which they sell to one another, cars that have never been detailed, that have been aired out and cleared with activated carbon felt blankets and zeolite. Behind their used cars the sick pull teardrop-shaped trailers made from steel and non-fragrant wood. Or vintage bullet-shaped trailers made from steel and porcelain. The sick will create new families based not on blood but affinity of symptoms. The sick will travel in packs commandeering porcelain-lined fragrance-free buses. The well will no longer delete the email of the sick. When the sick rule the world hotel rooms will be obsolete, airplanes will be obsolete, new cars will be obsolete. All existing new cars will be remaindered and shipped to Cuba. When the sick rule the world fragrance-free auto shops will keep the old cars running smoothly. All service stations will be full service, the well filling the tanks for the sick. Mechanics and gas jockeys who do not wear gasmasks will soon themselves become sick. The sick refer to people who do not wear gasmasks as "breathers."

The rest of the meeting is about the dangers of cellphone towers. Christy, our guest speaker, tells us that electromagnetic fields— EMFs for short—are slowly destroying us all. Christy, a middle-aged fleshy woman with shoulder-length straight brown hair and bangs, learned about EMFs in a weekend seminar she attended in Encinitas. Symptoms of EMF exposure include dermatitis, burning pins and needles sensations all over the body, pressure/heaviness in the head, arrhythmia, high blood pressure, migraines, insomnia, profound malaise, blurred vision, nausea, tinnitus, tiredness, exhaustion, loss of concentration, loss of appetite, mood swings, tearfulness of eyes, pupil dilation, perspiration, muscular weakness, speech difficulty, convulsions, unconsciousness. Christy warns everyone to disable the wireless in their computers and to keep their cellphones turned off and as far from their bodies as possible. "A microwave oven cooks your food," she says, "but a mobile phone fries your brain." EMFs can lead to cancer, ADD, Parkinson's and even back pain. She passes out photos of camouflaged cellphone towers— cellphone towers hidden in the cross of a church, a flagpole, clock tower, grain silo, water tower, palm tree, fake rock, cactus. The fake rock and the cactus have trap doors, which are photographed open, revealing electrical guts. They look like movie props, but this isn't a movie, this is real life, Christy reminds us. Electromagnetic fields are lethal. During the presentation, I change seats in order to get a better view. The woman I sit next to looks stunned and immediately gets up and moves across the room, as far away from the Bandana Monster as she can get. Christy passes around a swatch of cloth made from some kind of metal—it's a surprisingly soft mesh—that she's using to make curtains to hang from her canopy bed to protect her from EMFs. You have to make sure the bed is completely enclosed, both above and below the mattress, as electromagnetic fields come through floors and ceilings. She gives us a handout listing where we can get the best deal for the mesh and other EMF supplies online. Christy also demonstrates a small box-like contraption, protruding from its top is a two-foot long antenna that's shaped like a mini-Eiffel Tower. I wonder what's hidden in the real Eiffel Tower, what dangerous implements and rays. As Christy walks around the room the contraption beeps whenever it detects an electromagnetic field. Cellphones make it beep like crazy. Wherever Christy goes she checks for electromagnetic fields and thus she knows firsthand how perilous the world is. Sometimes she can't leave her home because of all the peril. When the sick who live nearby abscond with Christy to check for electromagnetic fields in their apartments, I rip off my bandanas and flee. Driving across the Golden Gate Bridge I wonder, am I one of them—I have been sniffed and found wanting, I gave that woman brain fog—would anybody want to be one of them? But if I'm not one of them, what am I, what's going on with me?

When the sick rule the world roses, gardenias, freesias, and other fragrant flowers will no longer be grown. On Valentine's Day the sick will give one another dahlias and daisies to say I Love You. The sick should have sex as often as possible because it's good for the immune system. The sick should lie on their backs and receive rather than deliver the fucking. When two sick bodies come together their desperate hearts open, it is lovely to watch them, the thin iridescent haze of sickness flowing across their skin, when two sick bodies fuck their hazy genitals sparkle and frizzle. The sick and the well should never mingle. The sick latch onto the genitals of the well like carnivorous plants, milking the well of their lifeforce, but the well are too rich, too funky, neurotoxic deodorant off-gassing from pores, the sick's iridescent haze curdles, congealed vinegary bits clinging to sweaty torsos, the sick spasm with so little pleasure, turn away sickened with remorse.

Sick Bonnie is married to a Rabbi. She has moved from house to house but cannot find one she can tolerate. She used to sleep in the kitchen or outside when weather permitted until the neighbors in the cul-de-sac began to spray pesticides. Now she and her young daughter sleep in her car parked at the end of the street. After looking at almost 200 trailers, sick Catherine bought a steel utility trailer with a camper shell to have shelter from the summer monsoons and winter snows. Although she does not see her three sons, she talks to them regularly on the telephone. Sick Rhonda and her husband are homeless and sleeping in their van, which is parked on five acres belonging to a sick friend. They have fashioned a makeshift shower outdoors. Rhonda's husband, a physical therapist, spends his days off renovating an old RV so they will have a place to live that is insulated from the elements and has indoor plumbing. A former psychologist, sick Nina has been living in her van for three years. Homelessness is expensive; there is no place to cook and no place to rest, which has made Nina even sicker. It is her passion to create a homeless shelter accessible to the sick. Sick Patrice used to work as a registered nurse at a treatment center for chemically-dependent teenagers. She spent a couple of winters freezing on friends' screened-in porches. When she overstayed her welcome, she rented an apartment so she could have a bathroom to use though she still sleeps in her tent outside. Sick Tom worked as a counselor in public schools. For many months he slept in the back of his truck because he could not tolerate being indoors. He finally found this Airstream, but he cannot find a permanent safe place to park it. Sick Mary used to be a bodybuilder. She lives in a homemade tent in the desert with her sick baby. The desert will soon be leveled for a golf course, making Mary and her baby homeless.

Sex partners of the sick must wash their hands carefully before sex and avoid touching the genitals with a hand that has had contact with the anal area. For lubricants, synthetics may be a problem; experiment with butter or vegetable oils made from foods the sick are not sensitive to. Incense and perfumes cannot be used to set the mood, but good music, videos or other approaches can work. Organic cotton bedding can reduce coughing and other less romantic symptoms. Muscle spasms and cramps from pesticide exposure may be immediate or delayed by as much as 3 days up to 6 weeks. If fatigue or pain are problems, the sick should remain passive and their partners should assume the positions that require the most energy. Fresh air and improved environmental controls will help the sick gain vigor. Be creative, patient, and persistent. The sick must always empty their bladders shortly after sex. The sick should never be kissed on the lips, as lip-kissing transmits bacteria and viruses.

There is no such thing as a hypochondriac; there are only doctors who cannot figure out what is wrong with you.

When we eat in a restaurant we take in the energy of those who cook and serve it, and their energy is bad energy. When the sick rule the world there will be no restaurants. When the sick rule the world Calvin Klein will design aluminum foil window dressings and our porcelain walls will be decorated by Limoges. Gas masks will be sexy, the envy of every Paris runway.

Sick Mark, a former videomaker, has lived in his car for eleven years. Indoor air is a chemical soup he reacts adversely to. His most frequent reactions are blinding headaches, a nasty metallic taste, tingly face, hoarseness, difficulty breathing, burning lungs, and stinging eyes. Less frequent but much more serious reactions are throat closure, asthma, chest pains, dizziness, and disorientation. Mark's car is twenty-two-years old and long ago has lost that "new car smell." It's Christmas morning and Mark is sitting in his car in a park; the park for the time being is "safe." This could change at any moment with a shifting breeze, bringing with it whiffs of industry, detergent, fabric softener, fertilizers, pesticides, herbicides, burning wood or synthetic logs, exhaust from cars, buses, trucks. When an air problem suddenly arises Mark drives his car to a different area. Mark drives 2,000 to 3,000 miles per month trying to find a safe spot.

Wary of money, the sick use credit cards whenever possible. Upon returning home they empty their pockets of any coins or bills they may have accumulated and immerse them in a bowl of zeolite crystals, which absorb dangerous residues. Placing the crystals outside in the sun will recharge them. When the sick rule the world the well will be servants, and all the well will try to become sick so they too can have servants. Pretending to be sick will be a capital offense. When the sick rule the world the limbs of the well will be chopped off in the middle of the night, the well one still alive, flailing and screaming. The limbs of the well will fetch exorbitant fees on the black market, sold to sorcerers who will dry the limbs and grind them into magic powders to be placed into amulets to ward off blindness and toxins. These amulets will bring prosperity to their owners.

On her all-metal bed and organic cotton blanket, sick Elizabeth lies absolutely still, cradled in the impermeable membrane of her galvanized steel shed. The thin blue filtered air cools her inflamed lungs. The sheen of the porcelain walls and ceiling reflects her image back to her. The clear silky arms of her ghost selves reach out and caress her. "You are totally alone," they sing in an eerie high-pitched wail. They remind her of Antony and the Johnsons, but at a whisper. Twin yellow bulbs screw into the ceiling, like glowing yolks she thinks, like God's testicles. Her naughtiness makes her smirk. She misses curtains and cushions, but she's grown used to the sheets of aluminum foil taped over the windows, the total lack of ornamentation, it gives her eyes a rest, an unbroken meditative line. She falls asleep and dreams a Bandana Monster is chasing her into an ever-receding horizon. When she awakens her ghost selves beckon, "Join us." She tries to ignore them, tries not to think of the organic rope in a ziploc bag hidden beneath her bed. With an organic rope hanging is totally non-toxic. "Elizabeth you don't have to be alone," her ghost selves sing. "We're waiting for you." "But I'm happy," she counters, "living inside my little porcelain house. It's cute as a teacup. I'm happy as a pinafored mouse living in a teacup."

When the sick rule the world mortality will be sexy. When the sick rule the world, all writing will be short and succinct, no paragraphs will be longer than two sentences so we can comprehend them through the brain fog the well bring to us daily.

3

RASCAL GURU

When a student goes to discuss the teachings, the Master opens the door shirtless, with a beer in his hand. On the sofa the Master lunges at the student with sloppy kisses and groping. The Master tells the student she will be strengthened and healed by having sex with him and that to be hit by a Master is a blessing. The student takes it as the deepest compliment that he's interested, and she surrenders to him. This is NOT abuse. The Master is not married and does not claim to be celibate. The student who claims to be a hapless victim is in deep denial about her own role in the incident and her own personal responsibility to herself and the Master. She could, for instance, turn away at the door, refuse to sit next to an apparently intoxicated and frisky Master, or reject his advances and promptly leave. When a student drags the good name of a Master, who never claimed to be perfect, through the mud for making a sloppy pass, it is her own actions that are ethically challenged. Sexual relations with a Master are a means of enhancing spiritual insights. The Master can change alcohol into an elixir. He drinks because it facilitates his ability to teach in the West. He drinks because it allows him to harness more energy. Whether alcohol is poison or medicine depends on one's awareness. The Master blacks out and drives his car into a joke shop. Each night the Master chooses a male student to have sex with. Through butt fucking the Master performs a rectal innerphase on the student. Rectal innerphasing increases the student's aura and allows him to burn off a lifetime of karma in a few minutes. While jogging through a park, the Master urinates in some bushes, where he finds the corpse of a man with a bullet wound to the head and a revolver nearby. The Master returns to the body over several days to meditate over the corpse. He takes the revolver and stores it in the garage of the spiritual center. Five years later, when he is mugged near the center at knifepoint, the Master retrieves the revolver from the garage, and follows the mugger into a housing project. The Master is arrested for brandishing a firearm in public. When accused of giving his daughter LSD and raping her, the Master claims she's a lying drug dealer. The Master exemplifies the qualities of buoyancy, vigor, straightforwardness, simplicity, humility, security, joyousness, uncanny perspicacity and unfathomable compassion. The Master owns ninety-three Rolls Royces. One Rolls Royce is one thing—even two or three—but ninety-three is guts! At a Halloween costume party a student is stripped naked, at the Master's joking command, and hoisted into the air and passed around—all in good fun. The Master is a person without a defect, showing no self-interest, desire, interior calculation, or a shortcoming. The Master is a pure vessel, a man of wisdom, far beyond the questioner's limited understanding and suspicion. The Master drops his monk's robes, marries a sixteen-year-old student, and starts drinking and smoking cigarettes. The Master is found on the bathroom floor, face down, arms outstretched in the position of the cross, saying mantras. The Master plants trees in a circle so that he can work with the surrounding spirits. He invites all the neighboring spirits to come live with him, and decades later the house is still haunted. The Master marries a German princess. The Master marries a Tibetan princess. After US marshals seize the Master's property, he orders his students to break into his deceased wife's heart-shaped marble tomb and remove her casket, which he then keeps hidden in a storage unit for seven years. Several students have sex with the Master while their unsuspecting boyfriends and husbands are out in the desert. If you become jaded and if you become solid into your self, how else are you going to get out of there? You need a Master to help free you, and whatever his thing is, that's his style. Don't cramp the Master's style. He's a drinking madman! How much of a madman are you? How brave are you to really do things? The Master is a warrior. A warrior with the pen. A warrior with the word. A warrior with the drinking. The Master spends $100 on cinnamon buns to scent the air of his hotel suite. He spends $60,000 on gold-plated bathroom fixtures. As the uppity students he's commanded stripped by his guards stand naked, holding each other, sobbing, the Master says, "See? It's not so bad, is it?" The Master could have kicked out the uppity students, but it is kinder to shock them out of their aloofness. Students who leave the path will suffer unbearable, subtle, continuous anguish, and disasters will pursue them like furies. Breaking one's vows to the Master is more harmful than breaking other vows. Compared to falling off a horse, it is like falling from an airplane. The Master drinks in order to determine the illumination of American drunkenness. In the United States alcohol is the main drug, and he wants to use his acquired knowledge of drunkenness as a source of wisdom. The Master is an enlightened being. Therefore he is completely selfless, a completely open person, and acts according to openness. When a student has sex with the Master he will not bring her flowers or invite her out for candlelit dinners. A Master is by definition the ultimate bad partner. The student should not expect her ego to be gratified by a relationship of sharing, mutual enjoyment. The Master does not have to follow rules. It is impossible for the Master to destroy or harm other people, because he embodies transcendental generosity. He has opened himself completely and so does not discriminate between *this* and *that*. He just acts in accordance with what *is*. His mind is so precise, so accurate that he never makes mistakes. He never runs into unexpected problems, never creates chaos in a destructive way. The AIDS-infected Master has unprotected sex with over a hundred male and female students without telling them of his illness. The Master believes that as long as he does his purification practices the students will not get the disease. We must not get trapped in the dualism of good and evil. When the Master keeps us waiting, fails to meditate or is extravagant with money, it is a teaching. The Master teaches that every aspect of human existence—neurosis, passion, desire, alcohol, the dark and the light—is to be embraced and transmuted. The Master is discovered in a steam room naked with three young men. They frolic about, taking turns placing each other on the massage table. Their hands start with the knees, working their way up the thighs into intimate massages—accompanied by schoolgirl giggles and cries of "Whoooeee!" The Master curls into the fetal position when under stress. He's in a fetal position right now, crying and hallucinating and having a fit. His face is buried in the carpet, sobbing. He's kicking the floor. He's writhing. He's retching. The Master opens a bakery, a carpentry business, a retreat center, an organic garden, a restaurant, a high school, an upscale women's clothing store, a temple, a hospice, a press, an antique store, a business school, a software company, a theme park, a hotel in Clearwater Beach, Florida. The Master produces a rock band. The Master is indicted on eight counts of mail fraud, fifteen counts of wire fraud, and one count of conspiracy. The Master sees the throng of newsmen as giant ants with antennae waving. The Master is manhandled, strip-searched and paraded like a freak at a carnival show. Having a nice car, girlfriends, and going out to dinner are implementations of the Master's commitment to lay practice. Critical thought is unspiritual. It means you have too large an ego. Just by hearing your approaching footsteps, by simply seeing you in any activity, with a single glance the Master can divine your state of mind. The teachings are about enlightenment, not personal behavior or ordinary morality. It is well known that sex with a Master will advance a student's spiritual development. Fucking a Master deepens one's understanding and practice, though less evolved students may require psychotherapy for years afterward. In order to radically overturn conventional moral values and social contracts, and to shock students into insights regarding habitual patterns and emotional attachments, the Master directs his followers in public and group sex. As part of the program, they make pornographic movies, experiment with drugs, and eat meat and junk food. The Master has sex with his secretary, who is a virgin. Later he pays her $265,000 in hush money. The Master walks in tipsy and sits on the edge of the altar platform with his feet dangling, but he delivers a crystal-clear talk, which has a quality of not only being about enlightenment but being itself enlightenment. In some instances the Master is too drunk to walk and has to be carried. On a couple of occasions his speech is unintelligible. The Master uses Seconal to come down from cocaine. The Master uses cocaine because he needs to lose weight, and because he feels the pressure of living a physical embodiment. The Master's second wife is brutally murdered by an erratic, antisocial temple assistant. His youngest daughter commits suicide after spending nine years in a mental hospital. The Master and students may be drunk, but they aren't phony. In their drunkenness, they are totally present. Drunk, they build four buildings in ten weeks. Drunk, they take in the Master's teachings brilliantly with raw truth, genuineness and magic. Messiness and ambiguity are part of the Master's legacy. The Master is a complex man. He has no shyness about playing tricks on people or embodying the fantasies people project onto him.

It is part of the Master's wisdom to make students uncomfortable and to trash expectations. Having sex with the Master speeds the student's spiritual development for sex bumps the student up to the Master's energy level. According to the Dalai Lama, it is permissible for a Master to have sex with students, if the Master has reached the nondual insight known as "one taste." In "one taste," all experiences are the same to him: he can enjoy excrement and urine just like the finest food and wine. If you put urine in the mouth of a Master and he does not enjoy it, he should not have sex with his students. During the drug bust at the spiritual center, the Master hides in a stable. Though supposedly on retreat, the Master is seen golfing on the Cape. The Master pays himself $3.4 million in bonuses. The Master lectures brilliantly, yet is so drunk that he has to be held upright in his chair. The Master has transcended the limitations of a human body, thus he is immune to the normal physiological effects of alcohol. The Master has nine polygamous partners he calls his wives, including a *Playboy* centerfold who entered the community as a student's girlfriend. The Master puts a coke bottle in a student's vagina and the bottle breaks. The Master instructs another student to take a vodka enema. Whatever the Master does is a teaching, even giving his wife a black eye. A Master does not apologize for his actions, a Master says obey me or leave. The Master is the final arbiter of reality. He comments on and judges every aspect of the student's daily life. The student will progress at a much, much faster rate if she sleeps with the Master. Through sex the Master empowers the student with his high vibratory energy. The Master is a rough lover, ripping into his students without lubrication. The Master says that in order to understand and transcend ordinary life we have to live it intensely. The Master gives a student some pills, assuring her they're just Benadryl. The pills keep the student in a dreamlike state. She feels like she's wrapped in cotton candy, and can barely talk. The walls are melting around her. Weird sexual things happen to her, and the Master yells at her for hours. She hears him as if he were speaking in a tunnel. By the third day she's reduced to hysteria, and the Master reprimands her for crying in front of an enlightened one. When the Master's indiscretions are exposed he throws himself on the ground and curls up like a pill bug. Devotion, when you really analyze it, is nothing more than trusting the logic of cause and effect. If you cook an egg, putting it in boiling water, you trust the egg will be boiled. That trust is devotion. The Master performs miracles, including levitation, teleportation, projecting light from his hands, and transforming into an old, bearded man before his students' eyes. The Master has the ability to heal people by touching them, control the weather, uplift people by sending them light, and pass through alternate dimensions. The Master needs to sleep with two or three students at a time for a single student has too little energy to stimulate him. "Purity has nothing to do with what you eat or don't eat and who you sleep with," the Master says to his student. "If living in a bordello and doing whatever every night is what helps you do it, that's fine, too." They step into his bedroom, and the Master's orange T-shirt, baggy black sweat pants and bikini briefs fall to the floor. They make love. Enlightened space doesn't create space free of confusion; it is not separate from it. The Master's bodyguards wear blue blazers and receive specialized training in haiku composition and flower arranging. To test a student guard's alertness, the Master hurls himself from a staircase. The guard is inattentive, and the Master lands on his head, requiring a brief visit to the hospital. The Master keeps his HIV-positive status a secret, even from his lovers. He infects a young man who then unknowingly transmits the virus to his girlfriend. All three die of AIDS. Dying of cirrhosis of the liver, the Master lies in bed, incontinent, his skin discolored, his belly distended, the veins in his esophagus swollen and bleeding. Though he appears to be hallucinating, the Master is, in fact, surrounded by emanations of enlightenment, by female cloud fairies who have come to protect him. The Master drowns at his estate after taking a massive drug overdose. He is wearing a suit and tie, with a dog collar around his neck. With him are three terriers drugged with Phenobarbital, and a student who is covered with bruises. AIDS. Alcoholism. Suicide pact. Heart attack. The Master can read his students' minds. By staring into their eyes during meditation the Master penetrates the core of their beings. The students the Master has had sexual relationships with over the past 30 years have been mature, consenting adult women. Those criticizing the Master will invariably get hit by a car or contract cancer. Every authentic Master you ever meet will be a total rascal.

4

BARF MANIFESTO

MLA BARF

Eileen Myles' "Everyday Barf" is impossible to summarize, and that's the point of it. Myles opens her autobiographical essay with: "I don't mind today, but the everyday makes me barf. There's no such thing. Puking would put something on the sidewalk of the everyday so it could begin to be now." The everyday makes her barf, and for the rest of the piece Myles spews recountings and opinions that frequently devolve into onomatopoeic grunts, such as "urp, wha wha wha, harrumph, blah, splat." "Everyday Barf" argues against essentialism, generalizing, pinning things down, forcing experience into predetermined form. It is a manifesto of complexity, ambiguity, indeterminacy, layering, contradiction, blurring of boundaries, in which Myles tracks how the personal intersects content intersects form intersects politics. The first anecdote Myles relates centers on a political sestina she wrote for *McSweeney's*. An editor there rejected it because Myles hadn't followed the rules of sestina building exactly enough. "It simply strikes me," she counters, "that form has a real honest engagement with content and therefore might even need to get a little sleazy with it suggesting it stop early or go too far. How can you stop form from wanting to do that." Comprised of a mere four paragraphs, the form of "Everyday Barf" gets sleazier and sleazier as the piece progresses. The first three paragraphs are brief, less than 600 words total; the final 2000-word paragraph is relentless. Three gags followed by a tour de force rambling gush that twists and turns so violently, it's hard to hold on to it. These twists bring us into the present tense of Myles' piece, lock us into the claustrophobic intensity of her now.

The site of the final paragraph is a commuter boat that runs between Provincetown and the mainland. Myles is feeling sad and a bit guilty about her failure to convince her 83-year-old mother to return to Provincetown with her. It begins to storm outside and the boat rocks violently, provoking the passengers into waves of serial vomiting. In the midst of the vomiting and rocking Myles writes her mother a poem: "From this primal scene I wrote my mother a poem. The puking I do. This. Dear Mom. Blah. My whole life shooting all over the windows of the boat. Dear Mom Blah. The stuff streaming word by word across the lines dripping down the page of my notebook." Throughout her abrupt disruptions and free associations, Myles returns over and over to the body, her mother, vomiting, death, the beauty of movement, the now, how the incessant movement of the now leads us from dead words to living words. Through a sleight of hand the poem Myles remembers writing on the boat becomes a poem she's writing in the present—the fourth paragraph, perhaps the entire piece, becomes the poem she's writing to her mother. Including "Everyday Barf" in her poetry collection *Sorry Tree*, with no break from the poems and with the same title layout, suggests that Myles is, indeed, presenting it as a poem.

December 9, I'm putting on my coat at Eileen's 58th birthday party in Los Angeles. Matias and Caty and I are at the door about to leave, when Eileen grabs a broom and a hammer and announces she's going to crack open the pony piñata. The dozen or so of us remaining gather in the living room and a guy and a woman who look like college students loop the broom handle through the back of the pony and hoist it into the air, it takes both of them because the piñata is giant, practically the size of a real pony, like three feet tall. I cringe as Eileen raises the hammer, the pony all pink and white and dumb, its eyes unsuspecting. Eileen lurches forward and whacks the pony's midriff, she pounds it and pounds it until a hole gapes in its belly, she yells "take that, you fucking piece of shit pony," throws down the hammer and rips it in two with her bare hands, candy spills over the couch, the floor, the coffee table covered in birthday cakes and gifts, Eileen grabs half of the pony, tucks it under her arm and poses for a camera, legs spread, hips thrust forward, she gives a thumbs up and an exaggerated wink, like a victorious frat boy. Eileen's breaking of the pony broke something open in me. I went back to my hotel room in Culver City and frantically scrawled out a draft of this paper longhand in my journal until 4:00 in the morning.

Myles first delivered "Everyday Barf" in 2004 for the panel "Absolutely Ordinary—Writing the Everyday" at CalArts' *Séance* conference, the first of their yearly conferences on experimental writing. *Séance* was held at the Redcat, a small theater attached to the Disney Center in downtown LA. The walls of the Redcat are black and spending the weekend there was grim, like being trapped in a big black box. Myles sat with other panelists behind a long table and read from a legal pad covered with loopy handwriting, the yellow of the legal pad practically glowed against the black black walls, she read quickly in that enthusiastic way she has, pausing every now and then for a deep breath, then rushing on, I was stunned and I wondered did she write it straight through in one rush, or did she agonize over it. Myles is brilliant at speaking extemporarily. I once asked her how she did it and she said she spends an hour planning the transitions, for if you have the transitions down, you can say anything. Three years later when they moved the CalArts conference across the street to the Museum of Contemporary Art, its focus was on feminism. I went to the Friday night opening, incredible women were reading, but I got sick and had to duck out to the bathroom and throw up. In between bouts of puking I lay on a couch in the lounge outside the auditorium and watched a looped documentary of Richard Tuttle, I don't remember the details, just that Richard Tuttle was very careful in the choices that he made, Richard Tuttle was like the opposite of vomit, and then I'd rush to the bathroom. Bleh. In "Everyday Barf," Myles is thankful she didn't bring her mother on the rocking spewing boat for her mother wouldn't have been able to handle it. The last month of my mother's life I got sick at her house and was puking for hours and my mom got upset, thinking it was somehow her fault, and I'm all no no no bleh it's not you, it's me, my fucked up body. I keep thinking about Raymond Federman's description of his course for Naropa's 2008 Summer Writing Program: "As an experimental writer, I do not teach anything because experimental fiction does not try to say anything; it tries to be something. To be rather than to say, experimental fiction always talks about itself, it exhibits itself, it is always self-reflexive, that is to say, it tells what it is doing while doing it." I wrestle with that puppy, I totally resonate with it and I totally disagree. I email Eileen, "While I'm drawn to the whole issue of being rather than saying, I get hung up on 'experimental fiction does not try to say anything.' So that's why straight guy experimental writing can be so fucking boring." "Everyday Barf" says so much. It says too much. Meaning is so surplus it decimates form—or is it the other way around, its form is so vicious it beats the fucking pony of content to bits.

The pony explodes and chunks of content bob about, collide with one another in the great toilet bowl of memoir.

Last February when Kass Fleisher invited me to be on this panel, she wrote, "just in case you visit your mother for Christmas … MLA being in Chicago this year (12/27–30) … would you be interested." I emailed back, gotta visit Mom sometime, okay. But my mom died in November, so now I'm here for no good reason, I don't have any interviews, I didn't even apply for any jobs, and on Sunday I'm taking the South Shore train to stay in my mother's cold, empty house. They don't even have a Starbucks in Hammond, Indiana. The night before Christmas I kept tossing with those horrid mental nightmares, *your paper has no thesis* my nightmares screamed out, *you have to fix your paper right now, you have to take the seven pages of vomit you typed into the computer and hammer it into logical order,* but I couldn't do anything about it because I was sleeping, it was like when I was an undergrad and took LSD when I had a paper due, and I sat there staring at the paisleys undulating across my friend's legs, panicky and abject because in my fucked up state I was incapable of doing school work. Eileen surveyed the candy guts strewn across her living room, lollipops and lurid pink and white mouths called gummy fangs, and said, "I'm leaving this. I'm going to have coffee here in the morning. It's going to be a good year." The pony, she said, was for her sign, Sagittarius, the centaur, half horse, half human holding a bow and arrow, the hunter. She joked about having internet sex among the gummy fang carnage, telling an unsuspecting partner, you have to come here, right now—the dating site would be called fuckupyourpony-dot-com.

San Diego, summer 2006, when I arrive at Eileen's house it's late and there's no toilet paper, so Eileen brings in a roll of paper towels from the kitchen, this'll have to do, she says. I tear off a sheet, then rip that in half, trying to use the smallest piece possible, but the next morning when I have a bowel movement it won't go down, the toilet water fills to the brim, precariously quivering, then Eileen's handing me a plunger and telling me to pump and to keep pumping until all the water is gone, it's first thing in the morning and I haven't had coffee, and it's hot as hell, I'm wearing this thin white organic cotton nightgown, with peach and white embroidered vines on it, and I'm sweating and as I pump my breasts are bobbing crazily for all the world to see, the water finally goes down and I flush and the toilet fills up again with my horrible smelly poo, my shame, and Eileen's in the doorway barking, keep pumping, pump until all the water's gone, and I argue that's not going to work and Eileen argues that's what she did in New York, and I'm flopping about and sweating and pumping, on the wall beside me hangs the black and white Mapplethorpe photo of a young Eileen, it's such a bright morning, keep pumping Eileen barks and I'm feeling like this miserable worm, I want to shout it's not my fault, but it is my fault, my crap clogged her plumbing and she's showing no mercy, outside grow all these weird tropical plants imported from Hawaii, I took some photos of Eileen in tank top and shorts watering them, John Granger, who teaches nature writing, told me that the landscape of San Diego is all fake, some rich woman at some point liked the look of Hawaii and that was that, I doubt John used the word fake, fake is my word for sure, the way my mom called nonindigenous plants "foreign plants," she said it with a scowl, "those foreign plants," which so perfectly sums up the conservative Midwestern America I grew up in, for hours I watched my mother gasp then jerk her head to the left, each breath was like this big event, gasp jerk pause gasp jerk pause and the nurses assured me this was a peaceful cancer death and I believed them—gasping and jerking my mother was at peace—I had to believe them. The last time I taught "Everyday

Barf," a paralyzed woman in a wheelchair said people don't want to think about the body because it reminds them of their vulnerability, the woman breathes through a tube that she closes her lips around like a straw. So I'm pumping, pumping, but the water's going down way too slowly, my crap's all wrong, too much for Eileen's plumbing, I'm begging her this isn't working, jiggling breasts, pump she says, that same trip her ancient pitbull Rosie pissed on the dining room floor, and Eileen cleaned it up so tenderly, petting Rosie, telling her it was alright, and I hate that she's treating me worse than a dog. The vulnerable body subverts the forward propulsion of the narrative arc, that fantasy of progress, resolution. As Julia Kristeva posits in *Powers of Horror*, bodily emissions nauseate because they aren't alive yet they come from us, bodily emissions point up our mortality, our impending thingness. Over and over I find myself asking people, have you seen anyone die, and surprisingly most of them have— I bet you have—all these people walking around with this intimacy with death, only one person found it scary—David whose father died of a heart attack—and then there was my brother who saw somebody gunned down, but these slow deaths were somehow comforting, my curiosity to witness death enormous. My mother was unconscious, she couldn't defend herself against my ravenous voyeurism, her body turning blue, shutting down. "Everyday Barf": "Death is so great because it's the attachment you can never open." Finally I have my grand moment of rebellion and I'm all "No more pumping!" Eileen calls the plumber and I'm vindicated, it wasn't my poo, it was the paper towels in Eileen's crotchety plumbing. The plumber says Eileen's plumbing needs a major overhaul. This incident, which we've never spoken about, so traumatized me I removed Eileen's name from the dedication page of my book *Academonia*, something I regret. Her name belongs there. I posted a picture of Eileen's toilet on my Facebook page, the Mapplethorpe Eileen looks so young and smug with her long shag, toilet paper has been placed in the holder so this must have been taken after the plumber. The offending roll of paper towels is still sitting on the floor. Since none of the creative writing departments I teach in are members of the MLA, I had to purchase my own membership. I asked Kass if I could at least wait until after the proposed panel was accepted. "As for MLA," she replied, "no, of course the fuckers won't announce whether they took the panel b4 we pay up." When it was time to choose my MLA password online, I typed in "fuckers," in Kass' honor. Eileen never called the piñata a horse, it was a pony, this weak despicable thing that had no resources to fight back. As she ruthlessly beat the shit out of it, snarling and thrusting, we the spectators guffawed and hooted, holding our bellies, doubling over, laughing until it hurt, we were no longer ourselves but the extended, pulsing body of Eileen's fury. We were glued to the now, we were alive, delighted to be alive, and I love Eileen for giving me that. I remember someone shouting, "Hit it in the head, in the head!"

CCA BARF

I've written a number of essays the past few years, and I keep vowing to quit. "No more essays," I told myself when my book of essays, *Academonia*, came out December 2006. But then I found myself writing the introduction to Christine Wertheim's treatise on "litteral poetics," +|'me'S-pace. Again, I said to myself, "No more essays—time to finish your novel!" And then the beginning of January I found myself making notes for this talk. "Stop writing a talk, you don't have time to write a talk," I scolded myself. "Joseph Lease assured you no talk was necessary—stop borrowing trouble, just read some fiction." But I kept making notes, pages of notes in my journal. I knew I was really addicted when, a week or so ago, I started interrupting my work on *this* talk with notes for a catalogue essay for the Tariq Alvi show opening in March at [2nd floor projects]. "What's it with you and essays," I ask myself. "Why can't you let go?"

The essay is a form I've always found oppressive, a form so conservative it begs to be dismantled. In the San Francisco avant garde feminist poetic circle of the early '80s, a sort of patchwork personal essay was de rigueur. The feminist poetic essay was riddled with collaged texts and vulnerability. It switched person at will, "I" flipping to "she," inside magically flipping to outside, and back again. I didn't know what to make of all these anti-logocentric Theresa Cha/Cixous/Irigaray inspired poetic prose things, spastically shifting and disrupting before my eyes with no apparent rhyme or reason. '80s avant garde feminism produced lots of self-indulgent, sloppy work, but still it was exciting—and important—to undermine the patriarchal hegemony that created the MLA Style Sheet. Around the same time I discovered Kathy Acker, who in some novel had a character shit on a priest's altar—which I'm sure she got from Bataille. Even though desecrating Catholic icons is so old school, has been so done to death, the zeal with which Acker does it is infectious. Passion in writing or art—or in a lover—can make you overlook a lot of flaws. Passion is underrated. I think we should all produce work with the urgency of outsider artists, panting and jerking off to our kinky private obsessions. Sophistication is conformist, deadening. Let's get rid of it.

I used to write reviews pretty regularly for the *San Francisco Chronicle*, and even though my editor Oscar Villalon was a joy to work with, the form was killing me, the suppression of the self, the tidiness, the pretense of objectivity. Perception is about framing; when it comes to doling out opinions, I am the frame.

To deny that framing feels so—I don't know—dishonest. I have a similar problem with attitudes that some students in fiction workshops have absorbed, the ideology that fiction is supposed to be fictive, that fiction isn't about me, and that's a good thing because I'm the god of this made up world, and the further I can push characters and plot away from my own personality and experiences, the greater the writer I am. I always want to say put some of yourself in there and maybe you can pump some life into this stuff—but I don't because I know me being brutal and cranky won't help anybody.

My first foray into writing an essay that transcended my stilted college offerings occurred in 1985, when I wrote a piece on Dennis Cooper. This was slightly after the feminist poetic essay phase, which I never actually tried. Experimental feminism felt too watery for me. I wasn't into watery, I was into libidinal. I was marginally employed, I had no real personal commitments, and I was young enough to get away with it, so I made everything I did libidinal. And the queer writing scene I'd shifted into encouraged that. In the essay I recount my first meeting with Cooper, how like a buffoon I nervously babbled that I'd heard his next book was about eating shit. My anecdote excited me, to be so transgressive in an essay with such a Take Me Seriously title as "Digression as Power: Dennis Cooper and the Aesthetics of Distance." Twenty years later, when the essay was reprinted in an academic anthology, I edited out the shit eating passage. Fear of appearing juvenile. I'm pissed at myself for that, for not just going there.

I felt really nervous about writing a paper for the MLA Convention—one of the most snooty pockets of being in the US—think interview suits, briefcases, tense jaws, and the occasional sexed-up star academic oozing power like ectoplasm. The title of the

MLA panel was "*Intimate Revolt: Recognizing Liberatory Forms of Documentary and Life Writing.*" In her panel proposal, moderator Kass Fleisher argues, "If some documentary and life narratives concern themselves with *the means* (the form) of producing the effect they desire *as much as* they concern themselves with the *ends* (the content, the injustice), might these works possibly augur a more communal form of knowledge-making?" Kass' proposal goaded me into going all Robert Smithson and diving wholeheartedly into the site-specific, by confronting the form of the MLA panel presentation itself. And when I found out my panel was scheduled for a horrible time—8:30 on a Friday morning—it freed me. The audience would be small, an insider collection of friends of the panelists, meaning I could do whatever the fuck I wanted. And what the fuck I wanted to do was to shit on academic pretension. Envisioning an insider audience is essential to me; I've been infested by Jack Spicer's doctrine of the local, which he took so far as to declare that San Francisco poets shouldn't publish outside the Bay Area. Jack Spicer was like the father of narrow-casting.

After I agreed to the panel, the obvious question came up—what do I have to say about form and life narratives? A panicked voice inside me screeched: nothing nothing nothing nothing noting. In September I taught "Everyday Barf" in a class at San Francisco State, which forced me to reread it closely. I again was blown away by it, but I couldn't really get a handle on it—a crappy place to be when you're having to teach something. I managed to fake my way through the class—"What do you think she's doing here, students?"—but I was determined to spend more time with Eileen's piece, to get inside it, figure out how it ticked. I had my paper topic. I wanted the form of my essay to somehow reflect its content, I wanted to grapple with the points Eileen was making through her wall-of-sound style, I wanted to apply some of her techniques in my piece. I wanted to start out like Eileen in short straightforward paragraphs and let things unwind from there. Like Eileen I wanted my last paragraph to be the longest, and I wanted it to twist and turn. Like Eileen I wanted to pull the reader into the present through these twists and turns. And I had to do all this without mimicking her, for when I tried to mimic her, I churned out adolescent garbage. In the background was my failure to write a feature story on Eileen for *The San Diego Reader*, my embarrassment at my flakiness. The whole project was a disaster—there was my procrastination, the tension that blew up between Eileen and me, and then the death of my editor, Judith Moore—with Judith gone I did not find myself in such friendly hands at the *Reader*—but mostly on some primal, Freudian level I was unable to stomach writing in newspaper style about Eileen, who I'd known in a complex way for twenty years. I couldn't bear to write about her in a way that hid or denied that complexity. To deny one's lens is corrupt. Immoral even.

When I was grappling with Eileen's essay, I remembered my husband, Kevin Killian, had written about it in his contemporary report, "What I Saw At The Séance Conference Los Angeles, Halloween, 2004." "Eileen Myles began," Kevin wrote,

> by quoting the old Groucho show, *You Bet Your Life*, as though to show how the ordinary words are sometimes the words that are hardest to project, and she denied that there was no such thing as the ordinary. From Bridget Riley Eileen learned the lesson of how to avoid getting blamed for things and also how to avoid the shame of having your work distorted into something you never intended, how to escape from these two catastrophes. In that the everyday might have happened to other people but only seems to happen to oneself under extremely close scrutiny. "If you write while you're moving,

it's good." I was typing so fast that halfway through I had a moment of panic wondering if Eileen had referenced Bridget Riley (the UK op artist I remember from the 1960s) or Bridey Murphy (the Irish girl who was reincarnated from the 1950s)? Thinking deeper into the reasons for my confusion I tremblingly make out several similarities between the two ... Kind of scary—the way the mind works, trying to make connections everywhere.

What's this Bridget Riley business, I thought. I'd read "Everyday Barf" many times and I didn't remember anything about Bridget Riley, so I looked again, and sure enough she was there. Eileen lists Bridget Riley as one of the topics covered in Pamela Lee's *Chronophobia*: "A woman Bridget Riley going to see a collector who turned her work into a dress. I thought you'd like it, he said. She got blamed for Op Art which they continually tried to link to her being some kind of Irish domestic servant, and she responded by negating her sex. Feminism was splashing up around her like vomit and obviously that's the problem." A reference for me too offhand to sink in, but here was Kevin placing it center stage.

I saw Bridget Riley give a lecture right here, in Timken Hall. It was the year I met Tariq Alvi, the year he came to San Francisco on an extended residency as the "Capp Street Artist." I was thrilled to see Bridget Riley, the legend. It was like when I was a kid and I'd watch the story of the white buffalo on TV—it was the Christmas special for a Western series, and the white buffalo would only appear to the pure at heart. There she stood before me in all her brilliance, Bridget Riley, the white buffalo. She did a great job of pulling off old yet hip, with her short brown kind of spiky hair, jeans, tucked in shirt, and this cool little scarf tied around her neck. The part of her talk that intrigued me was her discussion of Seurat's "La Grande Jatte." She'd been to the Chicago Art Institute on some rare occasion when they removed the glass from the painting—and Riley seemed so pure, such an artistic soul to be excited by this. I grew up around there and had seen "La Grande Jatte" a zillion times with a sort of casual indifference—but here was Bridget Riley having an epiphany before its unglassing. I felt so shallow. She discussed Seurat's use of contrast in the laying down of his dots—how does the Pointillist delineate the edges of objects with all these micro blobs of color. Riley projected a slide of the painting and she pointed out that when the edges of a figure met the background, the dots of the figure would subtly get darker and the dots of the background would subtly get lighter, and so the gist of this portion of the talk was the importance of contrast in art—and this idea shot through me and through Kevin as well and through Tariq, it sparked excitement in all of us—Bridget Riley's artistic soul was infectious. I've applied her theories of contrast repeatedly in critiquing student work, for fiction students are taught that change is imperative in fiction. "If your piece is about the character's move from rigidity to spontaneity," I say to them, "you have to show more of the rigidity first, so the text has some place to move to." "It's all about contrast," I add with great authority. After Bridget Riley's talk a group of enthusiasts were standing outside swooning, and it became clear that half of the enthusiasts had been invited to the Bridget Riley dinner and half hadn't. Ralph Rugoff, then the head of the Wattis Institute and thus the sponsor of Riley's talk, trying to separate the sheep from the goats without anybody noticing. But of course the uninvited always notice.

A couple of weeks after the MLA I finally mustered up the nerve to e-mail my paper to Eileen. She was great about it, complimentary, and she even magnanimously apologized for the toilet incident. She joked that my depiction of her birthday party made her sound like Lynndie England. Since I'm so bad with names I had to google Lynndie England. The first hit was prisoners.com: "Lynndie England, the vicious slut employed as a guard at America's notorious Abu Ghraib concentration camp in Iraq." Eileen went on to give some intimate anecdotes about family members who had recently died. She ended the email with, "I dunno. I love you Dodie." So we were fine, but since she was going to be in town for the opening of the George and Mike Kuchar show at [2nd floor projects], we agreed to meet for dinner to catch up and further clear the air. At the Sunflower on Valencia Street, over vegetarian crepes and sweet and sour soup, we talked about our mothers, how "Everyday Barf" was inspired by Eileen's guilt about not urging her mother to come stay with her at this fabu place she was renting in Provincetown. Eileen said she could see herself living with her mother, how that wouldn't feel like a loser thing at all. I talked about the last few years of my mother's life, how I looked forward to visiting her, how I savored our closeness. The life of a working class widow was so relaxing, I said, lunching at Old Country Buffet, watching reruns of *Frasier* on TV. Eileen and I agreed it was bizarre and amazing we'd both come to this place of tenderness with our mothers. Eileen mentioned the lesbian vibe in the coupleness of her sister and mother, and I went on about how my mom's excitement at seeing me and the intensity of our caring had lesbian overtones, which was doubly odd given the unspoken lesbian past of mine hanging in the air—and then at the end when my mother was needing me to hold her and touch her, it felt so much like we were in a lesbian relationship, and I had nowhere to put that. Eileen said, exactly—and nobody talks about it—she said this looking for an erotic relationship with the mother was all over the lesbian community, causing lots of tension because nobody wants to be the mother, they want to be mothered, that mothers tend not to mother their daughters the way they mother their sons so there's all these women out there desperate for mothering. Eileen said she wrote "Everyday Barf" straight through in a rush, she said she didn't know herself as she wrote it how or why it worked, but she was on a roll, she knew it was good what she was doing, she knew to just keep on going, to not stop, to let the rush flow through her.

Kevin wrote a play for Tariq's 40th birthday—it was called "Tariq Alvi's Nightmare"—we performed the play at Tariq's birthday party in Lee and Erik's backyard in the hills above the Castro. In the play, Tariq Alvi is trying to return from London to CCA, and he's held up at US Customs—a real concern of Tariq's, as a Muslim artist, of Pakistani descent, in the States on a limited work visa—and *San Francisco Chronicle* art critic Kenneth Baker, artist Kota Ezawa, and Bridget Riley come to his aid. Kevin played Kenneth Baker, Kota played himself, Tariq played himself, and I was Bridget Riley. To play her I wore a black and white diagonally striped skirt, a black knit top, with a yellow and white striped scarf around my neck. Ralph Rugoff was present and I remember feeling uncomfortable playing Bridget Riley in front of Ralph Rugoff. As Bridget Riley I say, "What we artists do *[pause]*—what we great artists do is we work in mistakes to make a piece seem alive, to add energy. The tapestry makers of old Persia would put in a knot where it didn't belong, just to avoid competing with God. For only God is perfect. Except for myself naturally. I'm so glad you like my scarf, it was a present from *[pause]* Seurat. Love those dots."

As a teacher of writing, I keep trying to figure ways to encourage risk in student writing, but it sometimes feels like a losing proposition. Here's an Amazon review of a novel by one of my former colleagues in another creative writing department:

This novel, which I looked forward to reading, was somewhat of a disappointment. It's one of those novels in which a cloying MFA-driven writing style gets in the way of what could have been a riveting story. The novel follows too many of the precepts of what is expected in "quality" fiction: quirky characters, an intrusive and forced writing style (sentence fragments abound), and a general sense that most of the material in the novel was researched, not lived. The novel seems more like a response to an assignment than a work of art. As a response to an assignment, it, of course, earns an "A." As a novel, it's a "B-."

Let's call the author of this novel Professor X. Professor X teaches a structural approach to writing a short story, with lots of shoulds and should nots. [I realize only now the deep subliminal connection my mind must be making with those "knots," the knots of mistake, that Bridget Riley told us about, encouraged us to put in our rugs, as it were—and here's that other word, the "should nots," of Professor X.] Students who'd worked with X turned in formulaic, dead stories—it's like they'd memorized a series of steps but were stomping around all rigid, like the zombie dancers at the beginning of Michael Jackson's *Thriller* video. I'd come in and try to get them to tune in to the beat, to flounce around and sway their hips, and not worry so much about what their feet were doing—to get some kind of visceral connection going with their writing. So I said to Kevin, cattily, that Professor X destroyed students' souls. Professor X is really charismatic, which I've never understood. She's a total Midwestern frump. One student told me it was like this sexual thing with Professor X, all the power she exuded. Since I'm not charismatic, I always thought that if I could only dress a little hipper, that would help—if I buy that $300 sweater people will sense I'm someone to be reckoned with. But here was Professor X with her bad haircut and split ends, with her ill-fitting pants, her sloppy print blouse, exuding power and sexual allure. I haven't seen Professor X in years, but the thought of her instills this primal jealous rage—I can't spit out that it's unfair that that bitch is popular but I'm not, so I complain about Professor X's aesthetics. Objectivity is such a lie. When Kevin was writing his Spicer biography, there were all these rifts among the poets in Spicer's group that they'd claim were aesthetic differences, and they'd attack one another, subvert and plot against one another with pit bull zeal. Invariably the real story that Kevin unearthed would boil down to sexual jealousy or betrayal. Y slept with Z's long-term boyfriend, etc. I hate this petty, jealous, territorial part of myself, and I'm always thinking, maybe if I meditated regularly I could get rid of it. Just last weekend a friend told me about holly, a Bach Flower Remedy, because my cats are all jealous of each other. "Give them some holly," she said. On the bottle it reads, "Encourages a more generous nature when you feel jealous, envious, vengeful, or suspicious." And Kevin said I should take some myself. Plenty myself. Dollops of it.

Since the MLA was in Chicago and Kevin had never been to the Art Institute, we skipped the Saturday afternoon panels and headed over to the museum, bundled up in the down coats we'd gotten for our December trip to the Midwest. We saw *American Gothic*, we saw that self portrait of Van Gogh with the little red beard. I'd forgotten about Seurat's painting, but we stepped into a room and there it was. I marched up to it and stuck my nose into the dots, wanting to absorb in person their splendid contrast. I stood before it, the glass covering the painting reflecting me, reflecting the room, and in real life it was hard to pick out the subtle darkenings and lightenings that Bridget Riley so masterfully pointed out on the slide. I'd lost my Bridget Riley vision. I stood there grazing on high culture with the rest of the

Midwesterners who ambled about the room, families in puffy jackets, the older ladies with their museum shop jewelry, and I said to Kevin, "I never would have noticed this, would you?" After dinner in San Francisco Eileen and I walked over to the Sex Worker's Art Show at the Victoria Theater. One of the performers did a piece about how for her stripper name she used her sister's confirmation name—Bridget. She sat on a chair in a demure stripper outfit, a little blue halter-style dress with a flounce skirt, crossed her legs, and sang a sweet little song about Saint Bridget's humility and virginity. Then she ripped off her clothes and leapt onto the tall pole-dancing pole behind her, climbed up the slippery looking thing with the ease and strength of Dracula climbing up the side of a castle, her naked muscles bulging and flexing. This woman, I thought—this woman really knows about contrast. When the edges of a figure meet the background, the dots of the figure subtly get darker and the dots of the background subtly get lighter.

Now I've dived into "Everyday Barf" yet another time, and my perception of it keeps changing. With each iteration I could write another frame recontextualizing Eileen's and my Barfs, and the piece could reflect and expand ad infinitum, like one of those drawings where a person is looking at a reflection of a reflection of themselves in a mirror or holding a box of cereal and on the box of cereal is a picture of themselves holding a box of cereal and on that box of cereal is a picture of themselves holding a box of cereal and on and on. Cereal—why am I thinking of cereal? It's like that knots and nots thing, and my mind wants this hidden reference to seriality, to the serial, to resurface. In this, my third generation Barf, I'm inaugurating the Barf as a literary form. The Barf is feminist, unruly, cheerfully monstrous. The Barf comes naturally to women because women like to throw up *fingers down throat, one, two, three, bleh* ... The

Barf is an upheaval, born of our hangover from imbibing too much Western Civ. The Barf is reflective, each delivery calls forth a framing, the Barf is expansive as the Blob, swallowing and recontextualizing, spreading out and engorging. Its logic is associative, it proceeds by chords rather than single, discrete notes. Hierarchies jumble in the thrill, in the imperatives of purge. Chris Tysh once said that the difference between French and American feminism of the '60s and '70s was that the French feminists wore sexy shoes. The Barf invariably wears bad shoes, it is gender-confused, a state of trans, of flux. The Barf is not so much anti-logocentric, anti-dichotomy, as outside the whole fucking system. The thing people always said about Op Art, curator Jill Dawsey reminds me, is that its assaultive patterning made them want to throw up. The Barf is messy, irregular, but you can feel in your guts that it's going somewhere, you can't stop it, can't shape it, you've just got to let it run its course. In my fourth generation Barf I could talk about how I wore my Bridget Riley outfit to this Barf—see what I'm wearing?—and how clever I thought that was, and on and on.

5

GIRL BODY

Along her lashes she paints a thick white line, then a thinner black line, but the brush in her chubby hand wobbles it always wobbles, in the mirror a smooth white horizon, row of black blobs in the foreground, pale blue shadow. Some girls would wipe it all off and begin again but she leaves it unscrews a tube of Maybelline slips out the wand sucking sound faint chemical odor she brushes her lashes wet and spidery. She'll be too lazy to wash her face that night, her mouth open snoring and drooling on the olive green pillowcase, black mascara grit pooling in the corner of her eye, the other girl in the bed is all mouth and fingers sucking her budding tit lifting the hem of her flannel nightgown streetlight from the alley graining the darkness she pretends she's still sleeping, the expressway at the end of the block roars unceasingly like an ocean she thinks but she's never seen an ocean. The girl bites her lower lip clenches her eyes nobody fucks in her fantasies fucking is two dogs stuck together in the neighbor's front yard two mongrels on spindly hind legs heaving and tottering, her fantasies are flat as leaves pressed between a book, no touch no smells, they're all excited vision and narrative drive. Sometimes body heat. In ratty thrift store fur the fantasy girl races her Schwinn from adventure to adventure. The fantasy girl is super smart but reckless, she hurls off her bike and lands on the pavement outside the apartment of a stern sexy man, he's tall, dark-haired, boyish, the man boy wraps his arm around her takes her inside dabs her scratches with a tiny glass wand of mercurochrome, it stings like crazy, stains her palms and knees neon orange, the man boy smiles as she screams—body is elsewhere throbbing ravenous body will stop at nothing to come and come and come the icy white of street-light filtering through bedroom curtains roar of expressway down the block saliva and mucous cramped legs pushed-up flannel nightgowns, brush rollers in hair nauseous stench of Clearasil—the fantasy girl's been raped or almost raped the man boy chases after her assailant, gives her a glass of whisky wraps his arm around her and takes her to the ER, the calm radiant heat of his armpit calms her—furtive orgasms in the dark—the fantasy girl is effortlessly brilliant, wears a tight sheath skirt with tucked-in white blouse, her hair in a long single braid down her back. She wears cordovan-colored penny loafers, her name is Sally, after the little blonde sister in the Dick and Jane books. Sally is vulnerable, mysterious, other. She's smarter, more bohemian than other girls. She oozes erotic but never has sex with the boyish men who service her. She titillates them. Fingers in the dark enter her vagina, a mouth sucks on her tit she pretends to be asleep as she bucks and gasps and sweats. Her favorite song is "Teach Me Tonight." The sky's a blackboard high above you/ And if a shooting star goes by/ I'll use that star to write 'I love you'/ A thousand times across the sky. Sally takes LSD and wanders through Central Park, she's beckoned by a massive oak tree, the man boy is leaning against it, she floats over to him stands too close light streams from his fingers she touches his hand—you're too young to be doing this he says— you speak she says, giggling—then the trip turns bad/she freaks out/he wraps his arms around her, the full weight of her body falls into his like an animal's would a domesticated cat or dog but still an animal, he takes her home to his bachelor pad and holds her until she calms down. They fall asleep, fully clothed atop his bed, which is covered by a quilt his grandmother made, a chink of tenderness beneath his stern sexy demeanor. In the morning scent of strong coffee and the promise of barefooted conversation at the kitchen table. Sally is frisky, vulnerable, fearless, surrounded by animals, totally present. Open armed she chases a butterfly *look up look up up up run run run jump run jump up* dog familiar leaping at her side, the butterfly flutters over a hedge, Sally continues chasing it and tumbles into the bushes with Chaplinesque slapstick ease. She dunks her bear familiar in a fountain, throws him down the stairs, her puffy minidresses barely cover her hairless pubes. We never get to see her panties, even when she's standing on her head, but we know they're white or pink with ruffles across the ass. She's a stowaway on a pirate ship the only girl in a sea of men, she's a frisky Maid Marian, Robin Hood carrying her off for her own good as she clings to his neck kicking and huffing, she breathes easily in her tight medieval bodice red pus dripping down her thigh her insides are rotting a finger slips inside her all sensation rushes to it sensation so dense it explodes. At night things she puts in her mouth: Chianti from a straw-wrapped bottle cigarettes liverwurst sandwich slathered with Miracle Whip and onions sloppily rolled joint. Fingers. She's nuzzled between two man boys in a Corvette straddling the stick shift a blond one and a dark one the heat of their bodies sizzling her sides as they hurl down the highway can go can go can go look look see can go she's in trouble and they're taking her some place to save her the body takes over the body clenches thighs together the body holds its breath gulps for air hips roll forward and back forward and back cunt muscles squeeze and release tension building go go down go go go, go down the girl has a crush on a boy in her math class, he has short cropped flaming red hair and his name is Bill, she dances with him at a party soapy scent of his crisp pin-striped shirt pinching her nose, she wraps her arms around his back tracking the compact heat of him he stiffens and she grinds her groin against his—he pulls away—his translucent freckled skin blushing in hot pink circles. He doesn't talk to her after that. Body oozing blood jiggly breasts this body cannot be real metal garters bruising thighs fat belly scaly patches on feet the sound comes from elsewhere enters her throat cries gurgle out no stopping them, she feels like a ventriloquist's dummy, finger wigging in vagina controlling guttural puppet voice. Ohhh. Ohhhh. Oh no. Sally peers at herself in the dresser mirror, she says "I see something." She orders her cat familiar "jump up!" then her dog familiar "come come jump up!" then her bear familiar "jump up see jump jump up!" The animals obey. She stares in the mirror: girl bear dog cat: cat dog bear girl: the four of them are now eight of them: the doubling sends chills down her arms, she says, "I see something something and something. I see something I want something." Sally breathes easily in her thigh-length girdle, garters do not leave steer-head indentations in her leg flesh, her feet look dainty in cordovan penny loafers, the straps of her primitive white cotton bra— pointy with circular stitching in concentric rows around the cups—do not poke out of the neckline of her blouse. She does not leave bloody puddles on the back of her skirts, no hot stinky ooze, no mother in cafeteria lady uniform finding her bloody panties at the bottom of the hamper, yelling, "I told you about this, you have to wear a kotex now." No hobbling with thick flat wad between legs, damp and chafing. The girl does not want to end up in a job where she has to wear a hairnet. She cuts out pictures of animals and pastes them in scrapbooks, underwater creatures bright as Crayolas, translucent veils extending from their bodies, undulate in turquoise deep sea silence. The girl colors all people with the crayon labeled "flesh." A mouth sucks her tit through the nylon of her apricot baby doll top, clit twitches as if there were a cord stretching from tit to clit, body squeezes thighs together and clit jumps harder jump jump jump clit jump funny funny clit jump mouth sucks voraciously large circle of wet on the front of baby doll hand slips between clamped thighs body wants to clench the hand until it breaks but body relaxes, finger slips inside vagina and body explodes. The man boy does not sit at the dinner table smoking and farting, man boys do hold belching contests at the dinner table, flick ashes into cold mashed potatoes, man boys do not get up to piss in the middle of the night, their huge cocks pale in the blue glow of street light dick is big, big big dick. Bear familiar between her legs pressed tight against her clit, Sally covers his eyes with a yellow bandana, her own eyes with a blue bandana, she's wildly drunk and making a scene either alone or in public, the man boy would never think of taking advantage of her naughty banter her slithery indecencies, he wraps his arms around her and drags her into an icy shower, she's so drunkenly limp he has to hold her up, her hair's drenched her arms flail, her nipples are hard beneath her soaked blouse. The scent of strong coffee brewing in the kitchen. "Come on, let's get you out of these wet clothes," he says. Sally throws her little red car in the pond, drops her bear familiar in a pit, drops him also in lake. Cat familiar and dog familiar jump off the stairs can jump can jump look see play, Sally eagerly follows look see jump see jump down down down down, then she's sitting on the stairs again, her hair in disarray, the right strap of her pink overalls undone, the front bib gaping open to her waist, her head's turned in the direction of the gap, her gaze totally focused on the bear familiar who's hovering in midair oh see funny little see, the gap has changed her has given her powers, dog familiar crouches, cat familiar's tail is erect. Sally throws her head back raises her arms spreads her fingers and chants, "Jump up jump jump jump

jump up jump!" A storm of paper cutouts twirls in the air bear boat bird Corvette bandana cat dog. Lacy white pinafore strains across heaving breast, mouth gapes open mouth clamped on tit lips sucking tongue flicking and licking saliva nipple teeth nibble tongue swollen and itchy clenched thighs spasm clit she wants to push it away this endless flesh devouring mouth she wants to dissolve into it oh oh go come come come go oh body clenching spasms in clit hand goes down she squeezes and grinds her clit against it she wants to break it in two I want I want I want cookie's too high to reach bear familiar is drowning in lake I want I want help the body legs part help the finger slips inside help I want help I want I want. Sally is undomesticated, toys litter her bedroom floor, so many toys it looks like toy slaughter—when it's time to clean up she and her dog familiar shove the toys under the bed, in blue minidress she bends over, ass up in air, dog ass also up in air funny funny oh oh oh.

6

THE BANDAGED LADY

"Ownership is the most intimate relationship that one
can have to objects. Not that they come alive in him; it
is he who lives in them."

— Walter Benjamin

We hang on the wall side by side, Pony on the left, me on the
right—Pony with his red carousel flesh, me with my red shoulder
flesh. I am all orifice, greedy mouth and eyelids emerging from my
bandages. My eyes are closed because I have X-ray vision. Strip of
cumulus behind me—I am a woman with her head in the clouds.
Kevin thinks I'm a burn victim but I say, look at my lavish mas-
caraed eyes, my meditative aura—I am both eager and patient for
my facelift to heal. The oversized safety pins on either side of my
neck add a note of humor, emphasizing the scarfness of my neck
bandages. One can't do the face without the neck. Some women
forget the neck when moisturizing, for instance, but I never did.
Tariq Alvi created us in summer, 2005.

Kevin dials Tariq in London, but the connection doesn't go
through. Dodie: "Try pressing 'one' first." Doesn't work. Dodie:
"How about pressing 'zero' first?" Doesn't work. Dodie: "I know—

google 'how to phone England.'" Kevin finds a site and enters Tariq's number into a box and then a string of new numbers appears in front of it. Kevin: "Wow, look at all those numbers!" Clumsy, side-blindered Americans who know nothing about city and country codes. When they finally reach him, Tariq tells them about an image he found on the web of two teen boys with their heads in nooses. "They were hanged," he says, "because they were gay." "Who hung them?" Dodie asks. "The entire community." "So they were lynched," Dodie says. Then the line goes silent as Dodie waits for Tariq to say something, anything—the silence is too long, the silence seems to say "what?"—Tariq says softly, "They were executed, Dodie," and she wonders if "lynched" is an Americanism—did they lynch witches, or did the word enter with a later form of hate crime? With Tariq and Dodie words frequently pop up the other one doesn't understand, a cultural gap both sexy and frightening. Back in 2005, when I was no more than a concept, a plan, Tariq showed Dodie a picture of a red pony and a blue pony. "I want to print this photo on a handkerchief," said Tariq. "Which color should Kevin's pony be," he asked, "red or blue?" Dodie can no longer remember if she had a preference. And then it proved to be impossibly difficult to find white linen handkerchiefs in San Francisco—Tariq looked in big department stores, Brooks Brothers and other high end men's stores, to no avail, and presently he found them in an Irish shop, a shop devoted to everything Irish. When Dodie was a child women bought their white linen hankies at Woolworth's or at Goldblatt's, the locally-owned department store—her grandmother taught her to embroider flowers in the corners and to crochet lace around the edges, the fine thread grooving her chubby grade school fingers. Kindness—we are gifts of Tariq's kindness.

Kevin commissioned our vitrines at FastFrame. The vitrines are airless, sepulchral—and the UV glass doesn't keep anything out—

death surrounds our white Irish linen fields, death and capitalism pile up around us.

Even though you don't believe in black and white, in good versus evil, even though capital punishment appalls you, there's always that one person who has behaved so abominably towards you, who has schemed and plotted, betrayed you with a smile, that person who brings out the vigilante in you, a person at whom— even though you know better—you would gladly cast the first stone. Dodie saw our enemy at a poetry reading. Our enemy was wearing this creepy black leather jacket, hip length, kind of shiny, her hair was pulled back and up with a barrette, the last few inches of hair cascading over the top of the barrette like a hair fountain. Despite the youthful way her hair flopped when she moved, she looked old, fleshy, her skin powdery. Our enemy watched Dodie from across the room, hungry for information she could use to destroy us. To evade her gaze, Dodie scanned the rest of the audience, most of whom she's known since the '80s, the whole room of them aging, the floorboards buckling under the weight of their aging. All of them moving forward on an unstoppable conveyor belt, like the TVs in the RCA factory Dodie worked at for four days one college summer. Entire families labored there, in Bloomington Indiana, generation after generation, Dodie was an outsider to their close-knit community, a college student (having lied on her application, saying no I'm not just seeking summer employment, I want nothing more than to make a career at RCA), and the other workers snickered at her pathetic job performance. The Elvis records blasting from loud-speakers are almost impossible to hear over the roar of the machinery. TVs relentlessly flow by and she has to tighten several screws and bolts on each of them. Dodie cannot train her limbs to move fast enough—her wrench catches on a screw, but the TV keeps on going, pulling the wrench with it, twisting her arm.

One woman loved Dodie's hair. "That strawberry blonde sure is pretty, how'd you get that color, doll?" she said with a Southern twang. "It's natural," Dodie replied proudly. That's the only dialogue Dodie remembers—a compliment on her looks—she was young, she needed to be beautiful, but she wasn't. Her hair was nice though.

I just got back from Indiana, my first trip since I was bound and framed, I sat on the nightstand in Dodie's childhood bedroom, watching her propped up with a pillow, writing in a red journal made from the cover of a funky old hardback book. The cover reads MISS PAT: thus Dodie writes: *MISS PAT—which I didn't relate to at first—obviously a woman's name, a school teacher I imagine, a dyke-y one—but now I see it as a cryptic message about needing to be touched—MISS as in missing—PAT as in touch—my own need to be touched but also my mom's need at the end—over and over her saying about the stray cat—'all he wants is some human touch'—and my pathetic attempts to touch her, my pathetic patting her on the head when she was dying—but a nurse or somebody, it's such a blur, I can't remember, telling me how she held her mother's hand the whole time she was dying. So MISS PAT comes to me as a message from my mother, her missing my touch. I miss her.* At night Dodie's afraid of the empty house, with its lingering energy of her dead parents—what if that energy has somehow changed, flies out at her—to ward against it she takes Ambien—but we both know ghosts could give a hoot about prescription drugs. It snowed in Indiana, the smooth white yard refracting the morning sunlight, sparkling like diamonds, but.

Flying to Indiana has made me thirsty for adventure. How I long to be a hanky tucked away in a pocket or purse, to go on daily trips. It is unnatural to be trapped in this frame, this cage. Children confined during their formative years—imprisoned, for instance, in a house of indescribable filth for seven years—exhibit psychosocial dwarfism. An infant with bones as fragile as crystal, a seventeen year old boy the height of a nine year old, a thirteen year old girl who looks like a seven year old. Gonadotropic secretion from the pituitary can also be suppressed, meaning the children never reach puberty. Confined children finish all sentences with the word "but." If only Tariq had kept me for himself, but. I'd be an international adventuress, exploring Europe and Asia, and even Las Vegas from a pouch in his gray camouflage backpack, but. Tariq doesn't lock his art in frames, he lets it sprawl across walls and floors and wheelchairs, all those glorious naked bodies tumbling and overlapping, butt, butt, butt. Tariq is the great liberator of prices—$29.95, $5.00, $1799.00, two for $10.50—he scissors them from their newspaper ads and sticks them on the white expanses of galleries. The narrow-minded see this merely as a critique of consumerism—when really it's about emancipation, unleashing the beauty of a block of numbers preceded by a curvaceous dollar sign—or in England, a lithe pound sign, but. Dodie didn't fly on a plane until she was 23 or 24, it was to Jacksonville Florida, she felt so cosmopolitan—finally—with her ivory hardsided Samsonite luggage her parents gave her as a high school graduation gift. Dodie didn't get a driver's license until she was 48.

Confined children communicate using primitive whimpers and whines—and short high-pitched squeaks that are hard to understand. If you were to give a toy to a confined child, she would feel it gently first with her fingertips. Then she would rub it against her mouth and face, using her lips to feel the object. The confined child does not seem to know when to use her eyes and when to use her sense of touch.

We look up "lynch" at dictionary.com:

The administration of summary punishment, esp. death, upon a suspected, accused, or convicted person by a mob acting without legal process or authority.

[Origin: 1805–15, Americanism; after the self-instituted tribunals presided over by William Lynch (1742–1820) of Pittsylvania, Va., c1776]

So witches weren't "lynched," as they didn't have the word yet. We type in "gay teens hanging" and in .66 seconds Google offers us over a million hits. I'm surprised to discover the hanging occurred in Iran. Since Tariq hadn't specified, Dodie and I assumed it was England or the US. The boys, like Tariq are gay Muslims—that familiarity, of course, would make them just boys, where as to white ladies, unqualified boys would never be Muslim. Muslims are never unqualified. We find several variations of the same image: against a flat blue sky two blindfolded boys, two hooded men, two thick ropes with nooses. The bottom of the frame cuts them off at the waist, the boys' pale short-sleeved shirts are ordinary. The blindfold on the left is dirty muslin, the one on the right looks like a necktie, gray with diagonal stripes. The hood on the right also looks recycled, a khaki T-shirt or sweater with holes cut out for the eyes. The executioner on the left's head and face are wrapped in a black cloth, leaving a slit for the eyes, in a fashion I've seen Muslim women wear, the sleeve of his red shirt is a clot in the middle of the scene. From what I can see of their faces the boys are handsome. There's a stillness to the picture, as if a superhero has frozen time and will jump up on whatever platform they're on and free the boys. In the mock-ups for his show at [2nd floor projects], Tariq disrupts the stillness with saturated color. Now the boys' shirts are corn-flower blue blobs, the executioners and their ropes are raincoat yellow, the sky hot pink. Around the boys the ropes the hang-men, a thick white aura whooshes. Over it all in pale blue Tariq has painted: BE CALM. I have never seen such outrage emanating from the word CALM.

The confined child's first words are "stopit" and "nomore."

When Dodie was in her 20s she never used kleenex. Instead she kept vintage hankies stuffed in the pockets of her jeans or 1940s jackets or sloppy shoulderbags. The hankies were brightly colored cotton with elaborate floral patterns, or white linen which her grandmother embellished with embroidery and crocheted lace. Dodie's favorite hankie was plain white, with an inch wide border of white cotton lace that her mother carried on her wedding day in 1949. Dodie's snot dried on her mother's wedding hankie. I know not if that hankie still exists, but I dream of meeting her some day, befriending her, absorbing that sense of history and perspective that an older hankie can give. Or would she see me as her enemy because I'm perky and starched, not wadded like her for years in the back of a dresser drawer. I shudder at her wrinkles, her stains.

On the way back from Indiana we flew above the clouds, blinding white mountains of billows and the blue blue sky—it all looked so primordial, like worlds were being formed in those clouds, that sea of blue air—I thought men—meaning myself—weren't meant to see this—within these swirling soupy masses, earth gels then hardens, then within its briny deep, elements collide and life appears, then evolution fastforwards, one cell morphs to many cells which morph to reptiles birds mammals apes Neanderthals and then the woman with the wrapped face sits above it all on a plane bound for San Francisco, Japanese flute music piped into her headphones. Disney probably already did this— no new thoughts in this bound head of mine—Disney would have made it playful, thrilling—within these swirling soupy masses earth gels then hardens, lightning flashes and suddenly there's Life—for eons there's nothing but one-cells blindly absorbing nutrients, and then bam! two cells stick together—this is the beginning of love—then there's three cells—community— then four cells then an animated frenzy of more and more cells—Mussorgsky clashing on the soundtrack—joining and joining, together and together, whole nations of cells, galaxies of cells—and then a slug inches across the ocean floor, beautiful flower-headed anemones sway gracefully to Brahms, then cute little fishes with bulgy eyes and puffy lips dart about, one of them sprouts feet and crawls upon the land, giants arise, the mighty Tyrannosaurus Rex roars, the wide-winged pterodactyl flaps through antediluvian skies, the Ice Age spreads across the land, wreaking havoc to the tune of "Sorcerer's Apprentice"—a dark dark frozen time—silence—then the drip drip drip of melting snow, melting ice—cherry blossoms bloom, adorable chipmunks and mice scamper, bees pollinate lascivious buttercups, wide-eyed deer bat long luxurious lashes, a pair of bluebirds touch beaks and hearts spark in the air—"L'Apres-midi d'un Faune" in the background—in the next scene the bluebirds are feeding worms to a nest full of baby birds—life goes on—and then there's ponies and apes and hunch-backed Neanderthal families, then upright man—then Cinderella in her ballgown, mice with spectacles and measuring tapes, bluebirds fluttering about with ribbons in their beaks—then the Classical Era, then the Modern, Oppenheimer builds a bomb so big it looks from a distance like new worlds are being created—Angelina Jolie leaps forward as action figure, the twin towers of the World Trade Center collapse, then flashes of talking fish and donkeys, headless gay porn figures tumble across the screen on a diagonal, a fountain of pumped-up naked pink and brown male bodies, two queer boys hang in the Iranian heat, rats cook delicious French soup, and then we zoom out to the wrapped woman with her head in the clouds on a Southwest flight to San Francisco, sipping cabernet from a plastic cup, surveying it all.

Confined children speak in shrieks grunts growls and snarls. If confined with other children they may have developed sign language or other strange languages that sound like German but aren't. The confined child is brilliant at nonverbal communication. When frustrated at not being able to say what she wants, she will grab a pencil and paper and in a few strokes, illustrate fairly complex ideas and even feelings. The confined child achieves the highest score ever recorded on tests that measure a person's ability to make sense out of chaos and to see patterns. In later images the hanged boys are swinging—their blindfolds have been pulled down and their hands are bound behind their backs, their ankles bound as well. Their full pants balloon out—I imagine them filled with helium, lifting the boys, relieving the weight of all that death. The boys look serene, with their heads cocked to one side, as if behind their closed eyelids they're just sleeping. One white slipper on the boy on the left, otherwise bare feet. Mobs of spectators in the background. Julia Kristeva: There are lives not sustained by *desire*, as desire is always for objects. Such lives are based on *exclusion*. I spoke to the blindfolds, and they're grief-stricken. "It's not our fault," they wail. "We had no choice, the hangmen stole us from our homes, tugged and twisted and knotted us. We were just following orders. We weep with the sweat of the boys' terror." My head, like the hangman's, is bound—slit for eyes—but my bandages are white. I am the good guy in the Western, the cowboy with the white hat. See me ride my Pony into the sunset, but. What was Tariq thinking, giving me to Dodie, who's afraid of surgery, afraid of anesthesia—including novocaine at the dentist's office—who lumbers out of bed smelly and old, who glances at her makeup mirror and thinks *why bother*. When there are so many reasons to bother. I was young, I had good genes, I deserved to be beautiful. I wasn't. My bandages wipe away all that messiness. Soon I shall emerge smooth and tight, too tight for a full range of facial expression, but I have my spidery lashes, pillow lips—and my wit—don't underestimate that—I'll dazzle the world with wit and smoothness—no need for muscular tics that any baboon could read as Happy or Sad. Neanderthals invent fire—they scamper away frightened at first, then their eyes pop right out of their heads in delight—then agriculture is invented and primitive man plants soybeans corn and wheat, laying the foundation for American agribusiness—but they're too primitive to know this—barebreasted women with hair long enough to cover their nipples grind masa by hand—rope is invented and then money, happy merchants in togas, golden coins stacked to the sky, thieves in the background hanging from trees—then Modernism and the rise of factory farming—a conveyor belt of happy chickens and pigs and cows glide into a gleaming factory—and on the other side of the factory emerges a conveyor belt of Chicken McNuggets, hot dogs, and steaming burgers—children of all races and nations stand round, sniffing the air in delight.

New Years Eve Kevin and Dodie went to see *Charlie Wilson's War* in Schererville, Indiana. Dodie thought the movie was reactionary *let's get together a vigilante squad and kill us some A-rabs*, while Kevin saw it as a Brechtian saga of government dysfunction. Midway through the movie Dodie has to pee—inside the women's room a small boy races past her a woman with a blown dandelion perm shouts at the boy "Not that way!" so the boy spins around runs into Dodie and falls to the ground. The dandelion-headed woman bends over to help him, so Dodie continues into the stall. As Dodie sits on the toilet the boy's cries turn to screams, he's screaming as if he were dying out there and with each "That's all right, honey" his screams get louder. "Shit," says Dodie. When she opens the stall door, yet another dandelion-headed woman confronts her—she looks like the other dandelion woman, so they must be related, but Dodie can't tell if they're sisters or mother and daughter, the perm wipes out age distinctions. The boy's still screaming. She yells at Dodie, "You knocked over my child." Scream scream. Dodie: "No I didn't, he ran into me." Scream scream scream. Dandelion Head: "Why didn't you tell me you knocked him over!" And then she raises her arm, points a finger at Dodie, and shouts, "What kind of woman would walk away and leave a wounded child." Scream scream scream scream. Then the original Dandelion Head is also pointing at Dodie, "What kind of woman," and all the other Indiana women in the restroom are staring at her, appalled—scream scream—and Dodie begins to feel scared. Dodie wants to shriek, "Stopit nomore!" Instead she walks quickly towards *Charlie Wilson's War* and the anonymity of darkness, too afraid to look back to see if they're following her or pointing her out to security.

What kind of woman! What kind of witch. In 1692 the following women were hanged in Salem: Bridget Bishop, Martha Carrier, Martha Corey, Mary Easty, Sarah Good, Elizabeth Howe, Susannah Martin, Rebecca Nurse, Alice Parker, Mary Parker, Ann Pudeator, Wilmott Redd, Margaret Scott, and Sarah Wildes. No mercy was given to the condemned. As they were driven to their execution they were mocked by a huge crowd that walked and ran alongside the cart. The mockery continued even as the witches climbed or were carried up the ladder that leaned against a high branch of the hanging tree. The executioner lowered the noose over the witch's head, pulled it tight around her neck, then he pushed her off the ladder so she fell downward and swung sideways. A clever witch would jump upwards while being pushed, making the drop violent enough to break her neck. Most died of slow strangulation—similar to being suffocated with a pillow pressed against your face—that could last five or ten minutes. Should the knot of the noose slip to the back of her head, it would take her even longer—up to fifteen minutes. Artaud: The dead little girl says, I am the one who guffaws in horror inside the lungs of the live one. Some witches gave a faint scream and moved their arms up and down, some witches convulsed. A hanged witch's face swells, distorting her ears and lips. Her eyelids turn blue, her eyes turn red and project forwards, sometimes partially forced out of their cavities. A bloody froth sometimes escapes from her lips and nostrils; sometimes her tongue protrudes. Her fingers clench. It is not uncommon for a hanged witch to expel urine and feces at the moment of her death.

I am the masked white woman, the executioner, Time streams from my eye-slit my mouth hole monotonously there is no stopping Time's forward momentum—Dodie tries to steer her students away from writing about Big Concepts like Time, but here we are—Time is the prison treadmill that destroyed sodomite Oscar Wilde—Time is the hellish conveyor belt Dodie worked beside for four days that one summer in her bell bottoms and Indian hippie shirt embroidered with tiny mirrors that reflected TV guts as they flowed on by, muffled Elvis above the roaring machinery *wise men say only fools rush in*. There's the politics of death, and then there's just death. Dead Elvis. Time streams from my mouth and eyes there is no stopping it. Ever since the Dandelion Head incident, Dodie's been afraid of children, like what if she knocks another one over—when to look at—when to pat—the living—the dying—the proffered object—Dodie dials Tariq in London, but. The connection doesn't go through. She's typed in all the country and city codes, but. A woman's voice comes on the line, with a thick recorded British accent: You have insufficient funds to complete this call. It takes three redials for her to realize it's Tariq's cell phone that has insufficient funds—a frequent occurrence the six months in 2005 he lived in San Francisco. Ownership is the most intimate relationship that one can have to objects. Not that you come alive in us; it is we who live in you. Dodie woke up remembering Tariq telling her about a near death experience—not like he was out of his body, entering a tunnel, but. Somehow he confronted death, was in a mortal situation, but. Survived. It's driving Dodie crazy she can't remember the specifics. The situation changed Tariq, it opened the beauty of life to him, inspired him to embrace and savor each moment. In the midst of a fucked up, violent, homo-phobic, racist world hurling toward extinction, a world teeming with enemies, Tariq has found the key to happiness, but. What is it?

7

THE FEMINIST WRITERS' GUILD

"I don't know whether we were feminists. We did establish
political positions in our class by picking best friends."
— Kathy Acker

In her book *Intimate Revolt*, Julia Kristeva argues that the "new
world order," which Guy Debord characterizes as "the society of
the spectacle," is not conducive to revolt. "Against whom can we
revolt," she asks, "if power is vacant and values corrupt?" In order
to nurture a healthy questioning of the status quo, she proposes
"tiny revolts." "[W]e have reached the point of no return, from
which we will have to re-turn to the little things, tiny revolts, in
order to preserve the life of the mind and of the species."
Addressing the feminist movement, Kristeva suggests that "after
all the more or less reasonable and promising projects and slogans,"
feminism's great contribution has been a "revalorizing of the
sensory experience." Of course we could argue with this, we
could say "how patronizing," we could shake our fingers at
Kristeva's lengthy analyses of Barthes, Sartre, Aragon, and ask,
why doesn't she add at least one woman to the mix. We could
mutter about her stilted, abstract style—like how sensual is that?
But in her own way, Kristeva approves of feminism here. She

lauds the sensory intimacy that arises out of "the universe of women" for it offers "an alternative to the robotizing and spectacular society that is damaging the culture of revolt."

Reading the first couple of chapters of *Intimate Revolt* got me rethinking the Feminist Writers' Guild, the short-lived US-based political action group. I'm not sure exactly when the Guild was founded, but its national newsletter was published from 1978 through 1987. Whenever I've written about my late '70s involvement with the Bay Area chapter, I've presented the group as rather dopey. Here's an example from my essay, "Low Culture":

> When we published an anthology of members' work, we held our editorial meetings naked in a hot tub in Berkeley, and we collated the printed pages, naked on a deck in Marin. I got sunburned on parts of my body that had never before seen the light of day. Compared to these lusty gals, I was a bit of a shrinking violet. My first poetry reading was arranged by Gloria Anzaldúa. It was with the owner of the Marin sundeck, a woman who went by the name of Abigail Tigresslily. Abigail began with a rather ecstatic piece about her big dog going down on her—and then when she got to human-to-human sex, she used the word "slurp." I was horrified, more by slurp than the dog.

Publishing collective, uptight me naked with a bunch of women, bestiality, my inauguration into the public sphere—reading this now through the breathless lens of French theoretical nostalgia, I'm struck by the radical potential of these "lusty gals," how in the culture of the Guild the business of writing, marketing, group process itself is shot through with sensuality and the body. I wonder if what I've been seeing as dopiness isn't in fact the epitome of Kristeva's tiny revolts.

In 1979, six of us formed a publishing collective. We took a 10-week course in offset printing, and for our class project printed an anthology of our work entitled *Danaid*, whose name comes from the Latin for monarch butterflies. In Greek myth the Danaids are the daughters of the Earth and the moon goddess. We were struck with the notion that "although there were only three, their might was such that mythology called them fifty." The cover sports a wrap-around photo, printed in purple ink, of a zillion monarch butterflies. In publishing the anthology, we too were mighty, shedding our cocoons. Even though we were publishing ourselves, in forming our collective, "we would be able to promote the writing of *all* women: lesbian and straight, women of all colors, ages, backgrounds." I'm quoting from the mission statement we published as the introduction to *Danaid*.

Before the collective settled down to just the six of us, when it was still an amorphous group of maybe-I'm-interesteds, each meeting would devolve into long, heated arguments over whether or not quality of the writing should be a concern in editing a feminist publication. Feminism was about promoting and encouraging all women. Editing for quality would reinscribe patriarchal hierarchies. And who dare define what's quality and what isn't, anyway? Someone would invariably say something like, "Come on, get realistic, we don't want a crappy anthology," and then came the racist and classist accusations. Women would spurt tears of frustration, anger, hurt. These arguments bored me at the time, as I sat on the floor drunk and stoned, but now I look back on them with awe, the overtness, the trying to work through differences, the belief that classism was bad.

At the back of *Danaid* there is a group photo of the six of us sitting in front of a printing press. I'm on the far right, my hair falls to my shoulders and I'm wearing my Tibetan wrap-around, maroon-colored, or perhaps cranberry in today's parlance. My eyes are round and vacant, I'm staring but don't seem to be seeing anything, so caught up in my own interiority I'm impenetrable. Such withdrawal is my knee-jerk response to group situations. One therapist told me I had "reverse charisma." Abigail sits beside me, her arm resting on my thigh, laughing, looking at me with delight, suggesting that just before this photo was taken something amusing transpired between us, that I was present for a moment, then the lens clicks and I'm gone.

At 28 I hadn't been civilized yet—I was a blur of raw emotions, ranging from the ecstasy of encountering a particularly beautiful day to panic attacks that left me doubled over. "It's like there's this horse inside my solar plexus," I said to Cindy over the phone, "bucking to get out." "Dodie," she said, "let me come over and get you." We weren't lovers, but when I was frightened or lonely, Cindy would take me into her bed and hold me. I've parodied Cindy more than once in my writing. She appears as a straight woman with a penchant for lesbian spectacle, toying with my hair and coming on to me in public. She wore her Southerness, too, like a gaudy accessory. A product of private schools and psychotherapy, even though she was raised in New Orleans, she never tasted gumbo until some guy served it to her in San Francisco, then she was all over filé powder. "Dodie, let me come and get you." The generosity of her body pressing calmness into mine, heartbeat, breath, arms, in out, in out. In our group photo, Cindy's gaze is locked on the camera, as if to say, "All mine."

Memory: Finally breaking up with my on-again off-again long term lover over the phone while spending the night at Abigail's. Crying and shivering—it gets cold at night in Marin—on the futon in the guest room, which was lined with books and thus called "The Virginia Woolf Memorial Library." When Abigail and her lover get up the next morning, I'm still awake, red-eyed and sniveling. "Why didn't you wake us," she says in exasperation. I didn't trust her. She had all this money, she called herself a Dianic priestess, she used to write speeches for Nixon, when her lover became involved with Susan Griffin, the way she would say with relish, "Susan Griffin stole my girlfriend." Susan Griffin—I remember her standing near a staircase with her blonde bangs, the chandelier in the foyer beams down on her and she glows like a goddess. This was the first time I'd been in the same room with someone famous who I hadn't paid to see. Beneath Abigail's affectations, I sensed a deep and abiding craziness, a white hot radical core. She and the other Guild members led me into a feminist dreamscape. In those wood-laden living rooms in Berkeley and Marin, behind the bay windows in Gloria Anzaldúa's San Francisco commune, Bloomsbury reawakened. We were feminists, we were larger than life, our actions, our words mattered. We would go down in history.

How did it all end? I got involved with some students from the San Francisco Art Institute, I started taking workshops with more experimental writers. I was voracious for experience and sophistication—the artists and avant gardists seemed hipper, more exciting, and they did encourage me to write—but never again would I receive such uncomplicated acceptance from a community; never again would my vacant stares, weirdness, social dysfunction be held with such tenderness; never again would I experience an arts community whose mandate was inclusivity.

Memory: Thanksgiving at Abigail's, picking baby lettuce from her garden, filling her sink and swishing the dirt from the tiny leaves, smoking really good grass, so good the food felt foreign, sitting at her long rough-hewn dinner table, staring down at thick, foreign cream soup. Memory: Walking with Abigail and her big dog, whose name was Artemis, along a hilly dirt road in Tiburon. It's a hot day, not quite twilight, lush vegetation folds in on us in every direction, wild life scampers, Abigail whips off her T-shirt and takes in the gorgeousness bare-breasted. I feel both irritated with her staginess and envious. There's no fucking way I could do this, but Abigail creates within me this little kink, I want to display my body with her ease, want to ram it down my readers' throats, rather than always hunching over, hiding, hiding.

Need the success of a political group be measured on its impact on a larger social order? What about the ways it transforms the lives and psyches of its members—these tiny revolts—are they not profound? As Macy Gray sings in her anthem "Sexual Revolution, "Time to be free amongst yourselves" for your "freak" is "a beautiful thang." I pick up *Danaid* and read my author bio. My clichéd rhetoric embarrasses me. I proclaim myself, for example, "the daughter of a carpenter and strong woman." Then I get to, "She has been writing poetry since the age of 14. While writing has always been an important part of her life, it has often been pushed in the background in favor of more 'practical' considerations, such as the monotony of graduate school or full-time labor. In the past year, Dodie has made the decision to make writing her top priority." After toying with writing for 14 years, I was finally wrenching it from the black hole of hobby. What I learned in that hot tub, sun deck, those Arts and Crafts houses, was possibility, commitment. I was young, fucked up, frightened, working class, I was faking it as a graphic artist, a job I had neither training nor aptitude for, I was a misplaced Midwesterner, maybe I was lesbian or maybe I wasn't, but first and foremost I was a writer and come hell or high water the world would listen to me. When we published an anthology of members' work, we destroyed the capitalist system from within. Naked, gloriously wet, we blazed like jewels, our tiny spasms of revolt burned the sun, boggled the mind. To you it may have looked like a hot tub but to those blessed with feminist vision it was a coracle floating down the river Canaan, we were violets, we were tigers, we wrote and fucked like dogs, we roasted turkeys stoned out of our minds, we read poetry, brought roses, curled in bed together like shrimp, double breasted, double fisted, we slurped up patriarchy in our lily-throated cunts. Moonfaced, smeared with purple butterfly ink, we answered the phone for one another, we were open to all.

8

PHONE HOME

E.T.'s chest glows red with fear as faceless agents chase him through the forest. My mother and I sit in her living room and watch. A week ago she called me in San Francisco and said she couldn't breathe right, that she felt like she was suffocating. The doctor was going to stick a long needle in her chest and drain out the fluid from around her lungs. "I'm afraid," she said. And then she started crying. "Please come home." The procedure didn't help. My mother's breaths are loud, a jerky bellows over the movie's soundtrack. Compared to the swimming-pool studded terrain Elliott crazily peddles his bike around, our Indiana neighborhood is modest. Still, I'm reminded of my recurring dreams of racing my blue Schwinn down Oakdale Avenue. I'm hungry, so while Elliott scatters a trail of M&Ms in the woods, I dart into the kitchen to make a salad. Washing my lettuce I stare out the window at the apple tree in the front yard. The tree looks like a man bending forward with his arms outstretched. Like in a fairy tale, I think. "Dodie!" my mom calls out. She's having an anxiety attack. She had one yesterday and the day before. I give her a Xanax and sit beside her on the couch. She's gasping for air. All through my visit she's been talking about a neglected neighborhood cat—Fred—my mother lets him in when it's cold and feeds him. Last night when Fred came to the door scratching and meowing, she said, "All he wants is a human touch, he's craving a human touch," and I knew she meant herself. She's hunched over in her sleeveless nightgown, shaking. So frail. I awkwardly put my arm around her. She lays her head on my shoulder and holds my hand. My mother's lung cancer has returned. We don't have an official diagnosis yet, but we both know it. She calms down a bit so I nod to the TV and say let's watch E.T. Elliott's just lured E.T. into his bedroom. Elliott places his fingers to his lips, then E.T. places his fingers to his own lips. Elliott sticks one finger to his ear, ditto E.T. Elliott smiles, then holds his left hand up with all five fingers spread apart. E.T. raises his left hand with his three fingers spread apart. Elliott makes a fist and points his forefinger up. E.T. does the same. They both wiggle their fingers. My mom says, "I love this movie."

Nothing about my reaction to my mom's situation is unpredictable. My mind is frazzled trying to figure out what to do, I rehearse one scenario after another, I couldn't possibly drop everything and move here—but who else would take care of her—and if I did who would teach my classes and how could I abandon Kevin. I feel overwhelmed, swallowed. I'm compulsively task oriented. I'm numb—then tears well up. I take a walk during a tornado warning, the sky is a chiaroscuro of white clouds fluffy as cotton candy jammed against ominous dark patches, I'm elated by the drama of the light flickering between sunny and shadowed, the intense cool wind tousling my hair about. I go to a supermarket, the place is huge and unintuitive—too many things too many choices—tears get caught in my throat. For the lung fluid removal my mother is hooked up to a heart rate monitor, I watch as the LED number continuously changes from the upper 80s to low 100s—it's like her heart is convulsing—and I try not to let her see how freaky her arrhythmia is. I drive over to Walgreen's to pick up her prescription and feel tenderness and compassion for each sad, fluorescently-lit person standing behind a cash register or idly wandering the aisles. The horror of old age and illness and being alone surges, I call Kevin and wail, "I want to go home, I can't do this, I'm too weak." My mother panting, my mother gasping, unable to walk more than a few feet at a time. First thing in the morning, I've been up for like two minutes and she wants me to feed her cats, I'm so groggy and she's directing me like I'm a puppet—not that dish, the other dish, and don't forget to rinse the can and wipe up the floor around their bowls, don't stack so many dishes in the drainer and the litter needs to be changed, and when you do that take the garbage out to the alley—and I want to scream "Be quiet!" so I can make some tea and wake the fuck up—I say "okay" with a bit of snippiness in my tone, and she starts crying, saying I'm getting irritated with her, saying "please don't be mad at me," and apologizing. I sit next to her on the couch and put my arm around her—it's not you, I say, it's me, I'm always grouchy in the morning, ask Kevin—and she puts her head in her hands and says she knows why people want to die. It's almost impossible to focus on anything outside my buzzing thoughts.

E.T.'s turned whitish gray and he's lying on the bathroom floor. The soundtrack fills with the labored in and out of his breath. A windy rattle. My mom and I grow silent and stare at the screen. Then E.T.'s in the hospital tent, hooked up to oxygen and machines that monitor his vitals. Elliott's lying on an adjacent table, desperate, reaching out for E.T. "You're scaring him," he cries as the E.R. team frantically prods and pummels E.T.'s body. "Leave him alone, leave him alone. I can take care of him." But E.T. keeps slipping away. Some version of this is going to happen to me and my mom. Soon. The only question is, how soon. Of course Elliott's devotion eventually brings him back to life and E.T. ascends into the night in a spaceship that looks like a many-toothed Murakami beastie. The night sky in *E.T.* is never black, but a vibrant dark blue, an ink-stained cerulean. As the closing credits roll, my mother tells me about my grandmother's death. Even though it happened eighteen years ago, this is the first time I've heard the story. On a Wednesday my grandmother started to whistle when she breathed. My mom took her to the hospital and they kept her there. On Saturday they told mom she was breathing her own carbon dioxide, meaning she was poisoning herself. My grandmother complained—where's my breakfast—and the nurse said they were afraid she'd choke on it. Grandma kept staring at the right corner of the ceiling when she spoke. Aunt Squee came into the room and my grandmother stared at the corner and said, "You are so beautiful." Squee said, "Thank you." "But," my mom said, pointedly, "I don't think she was talking to Squee!" Then Grandma went to sleep and died five hours later—her breathing slower and slower. On the phone that evening Kevin reminds me that the one time he met my grandmother we watched *E.T.* with her. I think back, squeeze my eyes to focus my memory, and exclaim, "You're right!" There were so many of us back then, moving in and out of the living room, Mom, Dad, Kevin, so many people talking over the movie, throbbing with life. It was summer and Grandma was sitting in Mom's chair wearing a purple muumuu. Her soft liver-spotted arms, her I love you unconditionally smile. She hugged me good bye and said, "This is the last time I'll see you." She said it so matter-of-factly, never stopped smiling, and she was right, she was gone in a month or two.

My mother is nauseous and fluish but has to sit upright because any kind of incline tightens suffocation's vise. Her foot is huge and puffy with edema. Numb. I fetch her a chocolate milkshake and drive home though a glorious sunset, the sky rippled with grays and yellows and then at the bottom a sharp edge of azure blue. My own needs feel petty, selfish. When I bring her home Chinese take-out she makes a face and says, "Why'd you get me so much food." Tears swell, but I don't cry—it's like there's this dam inside my head that the tears bounce up against and then fall back. I try to produce more compassion, but remain detached and listless. Hard to sleep. Mom has a panic attack, she tells me she doesn't feel right in the head. I give her a Xanax and fix her tomato soup and egg salad. I have one of those primal "what the fuck is existence all about" moments—which haven't changed much in quality since I was a child. The fact that we are here at all makes less sense than that we will no longer exist—and that thought is still terrifying to me. The results of the labs on my mother's lung fluid are dire. The pulmonologist says she'd never handle chemo and suggests hospice. My mother calls her friends. "The cancer's back," she says, panting. She can't breathe and talk at the same time. When I arrived she could fix food but now she can barely pour out a bowl of cereal. I feel guilty and guilty and guilty and guilty. She shows me where her will is. I can't quit thinking about *E.T.*, the coincidence of it being on TV right before my grandmother died—and then when my mother takes a turn for the worst it reappears. I'm afraid that because we watched the film, this will be the last time I'll see my mother alive. In my journal I write, "E.T. is the angel of death."

Thursday I return to San Francisco to prepare for an extended stay in Indiana. Sunday my mom's taken to the hospital in an ambulance, and the following Wednesday morning the pulmonologist calls and says to come home—immediately. It's Halloween. Six hours later I'm sitting on the plane, wearing velvety orange and black cat ears. No other passengers are in costume except two little girls in matching satin dresses and purple capes. The headband of the cat ears presses into my skull, a dull soreness, but I leave them on. The cabin's oddly empty—

I have a whole row to myself, with no one in the row in front of or behind me. I feel ridiculously lucky, turn sideways with my back to the window and my legs luxuriously spanning all three seats. Nibbling on a spiced sugar cookie in the shape of a pumpkin, I open my journal. "In the mad dash to get washed up and packed this morning," I write, "I couldn't quit thinking about *E.T.* Watching it with my grandmother then watching it with my mother, it feels like I'm living a variation of *The Ring*, that film where you watch the videotape and then in nine or ten days you're dead. In my version you watch *E.T.* on TV with someone you love, then E.T. harvests their soul and you never see them again. The Halloween scene in *E.T.*—in clown shoes and white sheet with eye holes cut out, E.T. the ghost hobbles in plain sight among the living. And now I find myself—unexpectedly—flying home on Halloween—the parallelism is laughable." I look out the window. Darkness ahead, glowing vermillion strip of sunset behind us. No turbulence, no sense of movement, it's as if the plane were being absorbed by the night. "The cabin is dark," I write, "and I'm sitting in a halo of light—like the beam from the spaceship's open chute. E.T. phone home. When my mother dies, home will no longer exist." Then I try to take cute pictures of my cat-eared self on a Boeing 737, but the digital images look old and haggard, like the flesh of my cheeks and jaw is melting.

It's well past midnight by the time I get to the hospital. The room is blurry—a couple of nondescript chairs, something turquoise—on the far right by the window my mother pops out in a focus so sharp it pinches the eyes. I stand beside her bed and watch her sleep. The nurse taps her shoulder and says, "Winnie, look, Dodie's here." My mom opens her eyes, confused and remote, as if the inside of her skull were enormous and she was peering out from very far away. The left eye's glazed over and her head wobbles. She doesn't recognize me. She doesn't recognize anything. When I called her that morning she was still *there*. I told her I was coming, and she said, "Good." You're such a fuck-up I think, why didn't you come home yesterday, and when you got here why didn't you rush right over instead of dawdling at the house, unpacking. Her lips have disappeared—a thin band around a mouth drooping into an O-shape, never closing. She noisily gulps in air and then her head twitches back and to the right—gulp/back/right—pause—gulp/back/right—pause—her movements mechanical and rhythmic as an antique wind-up toy, the circus monkey banging cymbals as his tin head swivel-jerks left and right. Clear oxygen tubes drape softly from each nostril. The nurse says, "Touch her, talk to her. That's still Mom in there." I take her nonresponsive hand and say, "I love you Mom."

An aide brings in a cot for me. I take off my shoes and lie on my back. Millions of holes in the ceiling tiles. The dimmed bulbs cast a yellowish aura, there's the expected mechanical beepings, voices from the nurses' station across the hall. On the other side of a thin cottony curtain, my mother's arduous breathing. My eyes produce their own light, flash spangles of pixilated gold pink and green—no lines, no sharp edges between figure and ground, image and memory, thought and vision, it all tumbles together in a gravity-free frenzy until my mind grows woozy. As I anxiously toss in and out of consciousness, my mother radiates aliveness, her aliveness tingles the air like the scent of roses, the bouquet of yellow roses I bought her on my last visit, a gesture she took to heart, the roses said you're not a pain in the ass, the roses said I'm happy to be here, the roses sat on the coffee table in the living room as she hunched over in panic, a superfluous flush of beauty, she had me put them in the closet at night to protect them from the cats. I'm seized by this primal love a mother has for her child—it's not directed at me, it doesn't even feel personal, it's roaring through me, this vicious, unreasonable, gut-love—a love that would rip apart predators with its bare teeth—and it becomes clear to me that nothing could stop the violence of this love, that it was always there, every second of my life it was there, even when she acted like she didn't like me. Then the atmosphere switches to calm—no transition—the turbulence of the racing mind clicks off. Click. Calm. Behind my mother's struggle to breathe lies a seductive stillness, she's ushering me into that stillness, and I feel ecstatic lying there beside her. Time lurches rather than proceeding with its typical metronome—bleep somebody comes in to check her vitals—bleep I'm sitting cross-legged on the cot in the middle of the night, the nurse has pulled up a chair and is telling me about her own mother's cancer death, we have the intimacy of adolescent girls at a sleep-over, sharing secrets—bleep she's putting a hot towel on my mother's waxy blue feet—bleep I'm lying down again—bleep another nurse says we can roll her on her side if you'd like, rolling them on their side fills their lungs with fluid, it makes them die faster, I stare at her without answering—bleep I'm home taking a quick shower—bleep I'm patting her head saying "I love you" over and over, her hair's thin and scraggly, a few wisps that feel soft to the touch, her smooth head beneath it, so small—bleep the breathing therapist puts a clear plastic cup over my mother's nose and mouth, flips a switch, the machine makes a loud whooshing noise and pressurized steam bubbles and billows within the cup with such force my mother's head shivers with it, her eyes remain closed, her mouth slack and open—bleep my mother's love blankets me—bleep the pulmonologist arrives and offers morphine to speed up her dying—bleep I'm calling my brother and saying come right now—bleep I sit in a chair at the foot of her bed, blankly watching her convulse for air. I've seen this before, I think—the cramped O-mouth, the gasps and head jerks—but where. The relentless spasming is exhausting. On the phone Halloween morning the pulmonologist said, "I don't know how long anybody could go on like this." Anybody. Any body. And so I flew home. My own breaths become deep and irregular, as if my autonomic system were in upheaval, trying to realign itself with my mother's. Where did I see this before. It must have been in a movie, but what movie. I observe her for maybe an hour when I realize it was E.T., the part where E.T. turns white and is dying—and all the kids are sobbing—E.T.'s round lipless mouth gasping for air— this is what my mother looks like, E.T. dying. Spielberg must have based E.T.'s death scene on someone he observed dying, I think, someone he loved, dying. I'm stunned how accurate the film is, how graphic. As my mother continues to die the flesh around her mouth stiffens and her lower face wrinkles a bit, so she looks even more like E.T. Her gasping eventually gets slower and more shallow and the jerking less pronounced. Her hands turn cold, and then her head, purple mouth. She stops breathing and I think it's all over, but then there's these waves of tremors on the left side of her neck and underside of her chin. It looks like little animals are scurrying about there. Her body absolutely still, her eyes closed, round mouth open, and these scurrying tremors. It's the Day of the Dead, I think. November 1, 11:05 a.m. Bleep.

I was worried about staying in her house, that it would be macabre. But it's calming to be among her things, I can feel her energy—in the walls, in the air, in her stained Pyrex coffee pot, her Italian blown-glass clowns. I try to log-on to the internet but a dialogue box says "No dial tone detected." I check my mother's cordless phones. The screens on both handsets read LINE IN USE. I turn them on and off, remove and return them to their charging docks, but the screens still read LINE IN USE. I give up, brush my teeth, take some Ambien, lots of it, so I pass out. I wake up in the middle of the night to a pulsing green circle—it's coming from the desk, from beneath my bathrobe, a lime green ball of light expanding and contracting—I realize it's just my iBook under there in sleep mode—but I see this luminous respiration, the same size, the same shrinking and swelling rhythm as E.T.'s glowing red chest when he comes back to life. His love, his magical thump thump always honing in on home. The space heater's power light glows orange. E.T.'s belly button. Breast on desk, belly button on floor—everything's fractured and jammed back together. When I was growing up I couldn't wait to get away from here—but now I cling to the hush of its wall-to-wall carpeting, its dust-free surfaces, its doors with locks I was always given keys to. In the morning I reach into a cupboard for a bowl and find that someone has stacked the dishes differently than how my mother did it. This is all wrong. I take them all down and put her plates, her saucers, her bowls back in her order. I pick up after myself, I wipe the counters. On my last visit when I suggested throwing away her battered Tupperware measuring cup, my mother said, "No, I've always had that cup." She paused to breathe. "That cup is a part of me." I stick the measuring cup in my suitcase. As I walk through her living room, as I boil water for tea in her kitchen, my mother's love is freed up, can circulate through me unhampered by the aging, gasping shell I was afraid to touch—but I did touch it, I held her in my arms. My mother's radiant green heart still throbs, I glimpse her in the periphery, these green trails of light. Phones begin ringing. Constantly. In the hospital, at the funeral home, the credit union, the Mexican restaurant I go to with my brother, in the car. Sometimes the ring is faint, like it's in my head. Other times it's clamorous but muted like it's a cell phone buried in my purse, but when I dig mine out, the phone is silent with no messages or missed calls. As I stand in front of the cat food section of the supermarket, I'm plagued by a ringing so shrill and insistent I look around to see what idiot it belongs to, but find I'm alone in the aisle. Sitting at my mom's kitchen table I hear a voice coming out of my closed cell phone, very distinct—it sounds like my mom—"Dodie pick up the phone." Even though I know it makes no sense, I open my Samsung and say, "Hello." No one answers.

A spray of yellow roses crowns the coffin, dozens of them. My mother's stringy deathbed hair has been set and styled just like in the picture I provided. I smile at the playful crystal cat pin on the neck of her sweater. I'm wearing its mate. She loved animals, volunteered at the thrift store for the local humane society. The crowd is small, but devoted—neighbors, a handful of relatives, former cafeteria ladies my mother worked with, other thrift store volunteers, a couple of carpenters from my dad's union. Everyone says she looks really nice. My mother was losing a pound or two a week. Her clothes hung on her, but she was too weak to buy new ones. She told Linda that in the coffin they'd have to bunch the clothes up under her. So I went to Carson's, where I'd shopped with her many times, and bought her a pair of comfortable Laura Ashley black stretch pants and a cornflower blue mock turtleneck sweater—blue was her favorite color. I also brought to the funeral home a bra and underpants, socks, slippers for her feet—and her new diamond earrings, her splurge from hitting a $1000 royal flush on the poker slot machine. My mother cherished those earrings, but earlier that day, in a burst of greediness, I had decided to wear them myself—and I set aside a pair of gaudy emerald teardrops for her. The emeralds instantly disappeared. After searching room to room in vain, I was stricken with the conviction my mother had spirited them away. She was always so stubborn. A favorite story from her childhood: she was walking somewhere with Grandma, and Grandma wouldn't give her what she wanted, so my mother threw herself down on the sidewalk and held her breath, she held it until her face turned red, until she was about to pass out, until Grandma finally "hauled off" and slapped her. "I'd cut off my nose to spite my face, "my mother said, laughing. In the chill of the funeral parlor, the blue of her sweater adds a cheerful note—I feel proud of how nice my mother looks. But I also tell Kevin that isn't my mother. "That not her in the coffin that everyone's interacting with," I say. "It's a big doll." I don't touch it.

The Lutheran funeral service is stern. We're all sinners in need of salvation. The satin-robed pastor remembers visiting my mother in the hospital on Tuesday. "I told her that I knew her cancer had returned. We both acknowledged the reality that the Lord was calling her. She said being baptized and becoming a part of the church was the best decision she had ever made. And I told her that I knew that when the Lord was ready for her, that Winnie was ready for the Lord. And she said without a moment's hesitation, 'I'm ready now.'" My mother was telling everybody she was ready to die. Her friends say, "Winnie willed herself to die." The pastor continues, "That was the last I saw Winnie Bellamy on earth. But I know that because of the faith that was hers, I will see her again in heaven." He gets to see my mother again, but I won't because I'm such a miserable heathen. In *E.T.*, Dee Wallace, the mother, reads *Peter Pan* to Drew Barrymore. Tinkerbell is dying: "She says she thinks she could get well again if children believed in fairies." Drew and her mother clap and clap, just as I clapped in 1960 for Mary Martin on our round-cornered black and white TV. Whenever you clap Tinkerbell glows brightly. After the doctors have given up on reviving E.T. and they've packed him in cold storage, Elliott cries out, "I'll believe in you all my life. Every day. E.T.—I love you." E.T.'s heart glows crimson and he reawakens from the dead. I'd do anything to see my mother again—anything short of becoming a Lutheran. The pastor points out she died on All Saints' Day. "Very early the Christian Church recognized the need to remember and give thanks to God for all the humble saints who lived and died in the faith whose life and witness are not remembered by many but are known by God. How fitting it was that Saint Winifred Bellamy should be called by God to His presence on All Saints' Day." I turn to Kevin with this look of "what?????" on my face. I thought saints were these special ultra-holy people with miraculous powers, not widows with cancer in Hammond, Indiana. "And now she is in the presence of our Lord worshipping Him and singing His praise with all the saints in glory."

After the service I walk up for my last look at her. The mortician, bizarrely, has painted her fingernails the same Crayola "flesh" color as her skin, and he's stuffed her oversized bra so these huge showgirl boobs poke up beneath her blue sweater. My mother swam in her bras. Last summer I was with her when she bought some. She didn't try them on, she just grabbed D-cup underwires because that's what she always wore. She pointed at her chest she said, "There ain't nothing but skin there anyway." When she sat topless on the pulmonologist's examination table, not just her breasts but her entire torso sagged, waves of it bunching up at her waist. The nurse said, "You two look alike," and I winced. The pastor is planted beside the coffin, his hands clasped together in front of him, like a bodyguard. I feel self-conscious and frozen, the three of us cast together into a tableau. I blurt out, "Bye, mom." He gives me a look that says, "That's it?" The weather was unseasonably warm when my mother died, the trees still green—then suddenly the temperature dropped and overnight the leaves burst aflame with oranges and reds. We drive to the cemetery through a palette of glorious excess, as if all of nature were celebrating the new saint, Saint Winifred.

That evening Kevin and I go to see *Lars and the Real Girl*—to lighten up. Lars has a life-size sex doll that he thinks is real—and the entire community goes along with it. Somehow this is supposed to be good for Lars. His sister-in-law dresses the doll in sporty Midwestern slacks and shirt, and the hairdresser gives her a more contemporary bob. The doll gets a job modeling at the local department store, visits children in a cancer ward, gets elected to the school board. The doll develops such a busy social life, she has a schedule on the refrigerator door. Lars gets jealous and declares she's dying. The doll is rushed to the hospital in an ambulance. It takes days for her to expire. The funeral service is Lutheran. Neighborhood women visit the grieving Lars. "We brought casseroles," they say. The food Lars scoops on his plate—fried chicken, lurid red pasta, coleslaw, squishy rolls—reminds me of my mom's funeral lunch, catered by the local supermarket. Kevin leans over in the theater and says, "He's eating the same food. This is awesome!" My tacky comment about my mother's corpse being a doll is literalized on screen—her rush to the hospital, the deathwatch, the Lutheran funeral I'd been to eight hours before. I sit in the theater weeping.

As soon as I return to San Francisco, I order a DVD of *E.T.*—the 2-disk collector's edition. Four months later I still haven't watched it. It's February, and I have to return to Indiana yet again—to open an estate bank account and to finalize plans for putting the house on the market. I take the DVD with me—its cover is playful, the iconic shot of Elliott in hooded cape, flying his bicycle across a giant full moon, E.T. resting precariously on the handlebars. I'm planning to watch the film on my laptop in my mother's house, on the last night I'll ever sleep there—an eerie ouija-type invocation—I'm planning to fan my grieving to a frenzy and write about it. The house is gradually shutting down. The newspaper and cable TV have been cancelled, the phone disconnected. My brother has emptied the cupboards and scavenged anything he thinks is valuable. After this visit, he's planning to put up a notice on the bulletin board at Inland Steel, to sell what's left over to fellow steelworkers, who are always on the lookout for cheap furniture and appliances. Linda, the next-door neighbor, has been coming in periodically and running water so the pipes don't freeze. Her husband's been snowblowing the sidewalk. It snows my entire visit and everybody says it's the coldest week of the winter. Just darting to the car is brutal, yet exhilarating—crisp, muffled, slippery, eye-clenching white.

It's below zero outside as I sit in the phoneless, TV-less, newspaperless living room and sift through my mother's photographs. She sits in an armchair, our pet squirrel beside her, hanging from the curtains. She found him in the front yard, a starving baby, and nursed him back to health. She's a grinning ten-year-old in a drop-waisted dress, freckle-faced with blonde bangs cut ruler-straight. A little girl with Ds on her report cards and an alcoholic father, a little girl with scrapes and pleasures she took to her grave. She's toasting the camera with a glass of champagne, her huge pregnant belly full of me, who she's planning to name Nancy. She's sitting on the couch, her chemo-bald head covered with a triangular scarf. I went with her to chemo—once. Patients sat in easy chairs in a circle, IVs dripping into their arms. People chatted casually, the Game Show Channel blasting from the adjoining waiting room. Mostly she would drive herself there and back. And be sick all alone in this house. "What if I fell in the bathtub," she'd say. "Days could go by before anyone would find me." So much of her life had nothing to do with me—I always knew that, and I resented it. Her hair's teased into a '60s bouffant as she stands in a white uniform at the far left of a long line of cafeteria ladies arranged from tall to short—she was five-foot-eight back then—the photo is a glossy black and white, printed in my high school year book. She was popular among the cafeteria ladies—because she was a hard worker, because of her sense of humor, her willingness to take part in zany cafeteria pranks. She's the prettiest cafeteria lady. Did the male teachers flirt with her? Did she have secret crushes? Since birth I've judged her by how well she did or did not fulfill my needs, my tremendous need. I pick up a snapshot of her wedding day—she's stepping down the church steps, eighteen years old in a suit and corsage, holding my father's hand, ecstatically smiling. My father was a biker. Was she worried he wouldn't settle down? Did she fear his violence, his moodiness? So much of my mother's life is obscure to me, there were so many questions I could have, should have asked her. In the '70s when it was in fashion to "rap" with the old folks, I asked her if she had orgasms—she said she did, but she was married for six months before she had her first one. I think of the octagonal mirror Kevin pointed out at the foot of my parents' bed. "That could only be for one thing," he said, with a look that implied his ever-imaginative head was filling with sex kinks. She asked me questions too, but I lied. "Yes I tried marijuana, but only once." These photos, which I've glanced at many times before, have become charged with mystery. In them my mother pops out with the radiant otherness of a celebrity. When I was a teen I read that existentialists compared a person's life to a sausage—each instant, each choice is a slice of your sausage—but you don't know what the whole sausage looks like until you die. Looking at the boxes and half a dozen albums of random, jumbled moments, I think *there is no sausage.* Just flash upon flash, slice upon slice, of loss. I give up my sorting and haul all the photos to the car, along with a set of letters she and my father hand-wrote to apply for gun permits, her loose-leaf notebook of recipes, her blown-glass clowns, the engraved tray she kept on her dresser, and the Christmas and birthday and Mother's Day and Thanksgiving and Easter cards I made for her in grade school. I drive over icy roads to FedEx, and pay $300 to ship the stuff to San Francisco. I never take *E.T.* out of my suitcase. When I think of watching it my emotions say *no fucking way.*

In March I choose a night Kevin's out, rush home from yoga with a take-out salad, and load *E.T.* into the DVD player. I need to view it alone, in secret, because of my mother and my grandmother. It would be too dangerous to let Kevin see it. He doesn't even know there's a copy in the house. Elliott meets E.T. and falls in love. E.T. gently touches Elliott's tears, brushes the hair from his forehead. Elliott wraps a scarf around E.T.'s neck in a tender embrace and their eyes meet. I'm nervous Kevin's going to appear unexpectedly. He's having dinner with Raimundas—what if Raimundas doesn't show up, what if Kevin comes back early—what if he barges through the door before I can click off the movie. He can't glimpse even a second of it, for *E.T.* could cast one of its death spells and I'll never see him again. Finally what I've been waiting for yet dreading—E.T. falls ill and wastes away. But he does it like Ali MacGraw in *Love Story*, gently, beautifully. It's 10:00—I should have heard from Kevin by now, he always calls on his way home. When I dial his cell phone, voicemail picks up immediately. I leave a message. E.T. lies on the bathroom floor, grayish white. Elliott: "I think we're dying." E.T. slowly rolls his head from side to side, he groans, he screams, he whispers, "Home." No gasping, no jerking. It's nothing like the merciless spasming of my mother. The sounds of labored breathing come from the government agents lumbering about in their bulky bubble-headed space suits. Maybe this is the wrong scene, maybe it's the next scene, in the medical tent. Cut to E.T. on a hospital bed, oxygen tubes drooping from his nostrils. The doctors run about manically, but E.T.'s movements are subtle, elegant, his mouth closed as his chest silently lifts and collapses, lifts and collapses. Again, he doesn't gasp or jerk. Where are the images I remembered in my mother's hospital room? Where's my mother's death? I press down number 5 and speed-dial Kevin. No answer. My stomach is tense and queasy, and my heart's beating faster. What if something's happened to Kevin, what if my watching E.T. in his home, in his absence, is enough to destroy him. E.T.'s spaceship has arrived. E.T. and Elliott face one another, eyes locked. E.T.: "Come." Elliott: "Stay." Pain on both their faces. E.T. lifts his fingers to his lips: "Ouch." Elliott: "Ouch." Elliott touches his pointer finger to his chest then his lips, then he flips his finger outwards as if throwing E.T. a kiss of ouch. Tears in eyes. I leave Kevin another message. E.T. and Elliott hug, cheek to cheek, E.T. massages Elliott's back, puts a glowing finger to Elliott's temple. "I'll be right here." E.T.'s come back to life, but death wafts off of him like steam, like the scent of yellow roses. In the aura of death all the bullshit dissolves— the one dying is vulnerable, aching for touch, the dying body pulls both of you into the present moment. Fear drops out pretty quickly. Your emotional life is reduced to grief and love, to waves of clinging and letting go, your heart spirals open, a sloppy vortex in the center of your chest. Glowing red. Kevin calls—he's fine, they went to a bar afterwards—but the tension doesn't leave. I'm lightheaded, my breathing's shallow, my jaws clenched as E.T.'s spaceship ascends above the spiky fairy tale forest. By the time Kevin gets home, I'm on the computer looking up E.T.'s death scene. I discover there are two *E.T.*s—the original from 1982, which I've just watched, and a slightly longer 2002 edition. In the later version, E.T.'s facial expressions were computer generated to give a broader range, the government agents' guns were replaced with walkie-talkies, and the word "terrorist" became "hippie." Fifty shots were digitally tweaked. So maybe I watched the wrong one, maybe the death scene does match my memory. "Did you write tonight?" Quickly I quit Firefox as Kevin walks into the room. "Did you work on your piece?" He thinks I'm writing about Vietnam, as seen through the lens of *The Deer Hunter* and *Coming Home*. "I did research," I answer, vaguely.

The next evening, as I pull out of the San Francisco State parking garage, I think about my class, how when I mentioned I was writing about E.T., a collective shudder rippled around the room. Ali: "*E.T.* was the scariest movie ever." Matt had an E.T. doll. "It was too creepy," he said. He looked down at the floor as if his childhood doll were going to materialize out of the ethers of memory, and squinted his face in disgust. "I never played with it." Though celebrated for his cuteness, E.T. gave my students nightmares. At a red light I take out my journal and start jotting down notes. I scribble at the next stop and the next, and when the light turns green too quickly, I continue writing while steering with one hand and I wonder if I'm breaking the law—is it against the law to write while driving?—probably not because the idiots who make the laws wouldn't imagine anyone doing it—night comes on—the moon is huge, round, opalescent, the sky a vivid fake computer-generated blue. I imagine my Subaru lifting off of 17th Street, hovering for a moment, shooting up and flying across the neon bright moon. I am the Wicked Witch of the West on a broomstick, I am a hooded boy on a bicycle racing to get E.T. home. I sleepwalked once as a child—in the living room I opened the front door and walked into a space ship—I stood in the cockpit with all its dials and knobs and circular gauges and looked out on the serenity of space—then my mother grabbed me on the curb outside our house and dragged me back inside.

As E.T. runs through the forest, a ghostly woman is superimposed over him, huddled on the couch, drinking tea. I pull down the shades—my reflection in the TV screen is too distracting, too fertile for bad symbolism. Other than the added bathtub scene, the film looks pretty much the same. Including the death scene. It's still hard to accept E.T. didn't die the way I remember it— some irrational, desperate part of me is still hoping to find a third version of the film where E.T. does gasp and his head does jerk back and to the right, his lipless mouth and my mother's lipless mouth, one. I'm more relaxed this time through—Kevin's at work, he's reachable, he's not going to barge in. I get a little erotic frisson from sneaking, like I'm having an affair with E.T.—like Elliott, I'm hiding him in my closet. The darkened room is making me drowsy. My eyelids droop as these pictures I shared with my mother flutter in the subdued afternoon, her sitting across the living room, snared in cancer's slow terrifying suffocation, her saying, "I love this movie." I click to the bonus features. The scenes were shot in chronological order. This created more tension, provoked reactions from the child actors that were spontaneous, unrehearsed. Real doctors frantically try to revive E.T.—Spielberg's internist and his doctor buddies. E.T. convulses from the shock of their electric paddles. Startled, Drew Barrymore jumps back, tears streaming down her face. Clip of Barrymore after the scene is over, still bawling, Spielberg trying to comfort her. E.T. is a collage of fragments. He's rarely seen as a whole—bits and pieces of him pop up unexpectedly, his head peeks out from among the dolls, his long knobby fingers crawl up from under a table. His hands were performed by a woman mime, hired for her unusually long thin fingers. His puppet-self was operated by a dozen men, who sat in a separate room, watching E.T. on a video monitor as they expertly synchronized his movements. The sets were built on a platform so E.T.'s cords and wires could run under the floor. Spielberg: "There was no full movement except when we had our little people and our young boy without legs inside the E.T. costume." Clip of E.T.'s body topped with a woman's head. The woman makes a goofy face for the camera. She/E.T. are wearing a plaid bathrobe. Clip of legless boy in a blue T-shirt and larval-looking padded vest. A handsome, dark-haired boy. He's sitting on a flesh-colored pillow, so it looks like his body has melted and he's sitting in a puddle of flesh. His hands are on the floor in front of him. The boy winces as helpers begin to lower E.T.'s floppy purplish body over his head. Drew Barrymore: "E.T. was absolutely real to me. I understood that it took mechanics and some people being in his suit and a woman doing his hands to make him manifest and come alive, but I just thought that he was a guardian angel. And a good friend. He was a very real, tangible being." That evening when I go to hear Linh Dinh at UC Berkeley, I'm still sleepy. I've been looking forward to the reading, but I keep dozing off, right there on a wooden chair in the drafty auditorium, my head drops forward then jerks upright, I have to pinch myself to stay awake. It's as if the movie has thrust me into unconsciousness, a narcoleptic spasm of too much meaning, the way Elliott passes out the first time E.T. enters his bedroom. Afterwards in the California cuisine-y restaurant, Linh Dinh sits across from me. Kevin's asking him if he's written any poems about boxes. The walls are decorated with original art, bold black ink washes in frames. I point at the one above my head, a blobby face wider than it is tall, with big hollow white eyes, and say, "Look, it's E.T. It looks like E.T." Lytle Shaw says, "Yes it does—but an academic E.T., with spectacles." I twist around, craning my neck upwards, and indeed he does have glasses, the thinnest of wire rims. Bits and pieces.

I walk down 9th Avenue sipping an "I Am Worthy," a juice blend the bluish red of vein blood. I have the urge to write down everything, to embalm the trivial against the onrush of death. It's a beautiful day, sunny with a hint of distant ocean, a moisture verging on scent, I approach a bottle brush tree, pruned compact and round with dense red brushes, it's perfect, I think, and I don't even like bottle brush trees. I want to capture atmosphere, the quality of light like in a bad Iowa poem, the crisp glare of cool and breezy at three o'clock in the Inner Sunset. I remember walking through the park in Indiana, what an odd fall it was, the weather shifting and shifting. My mother said we might as well spend her gambling money on groceries because she'd "never go to the boat again." She was telling me she was dying, but I didn't listen. I should have stayed with her, should have said fuck to my responsibilities in San Francisco and stayed. I'm on the couch, my arm around her—so frail and angular—she awkwardly puts her head on my shoulder. After a few minutes I move to an armchair across the room. She flinches when I get up, and that flinch keeps playing in my head over and over, my pulling away from her in that moment of need—and in the hospital, I sat against the wall at the foot of her bed, every once in a while walking over, squeezing her unresponsive hand, patting her head, but not lingering too long—I could have pulled my chair up, could have leaned right in, could have held her while she passed. It was enough, I rationalized, for her spirit to know I was in the room. I wasn't perfect. I wasn't perfect. It's like my mother's death is a tape I long to rewind, do over, get it right. But every time I rewind it's always the same—me fucking up, getting it wrong. I swallow a mouthful of "I Am Worthy." It's thick and bitter but cloyingly sweet. I'm wearing her diamond earrings—after the viewing, the funeral home removed them from her ears. I soaked them in saltwater by moonlight and cleaned them with alcohol, still I hesitated to put on a corpse's jewels. Spears of light bounce off the diamonds, cool, breezy light. I wear them every day.

My iBook's battery has become sluggish, so I unplug it. I've heard that if you totally drain the battery, its charge will last longer. As I type, the bar of the battery icon grows shorter and shorter, then turns red. I'm wearing headphones, listening to iTunes. During Midnight Oil—how can we dance when our earth is turning—a staccato, affectless male voice talks over the music, I can't understand his words, but he speaks one sentence, intent as a command. It's eerie. Is iTunes/my headphone acting as some kind of receiver? I'm reminded of an art installation I once saw, headphones mounted on the wall, you put them on and listen to recordings of ghost voices emerging from static. This is called Electronic Voice Phenomena. "The voice or voices of the dead are embedded onto magnetic recording tape by a process that we do not understand." The voices spoke German, crackles emerging from another world. I listened to them for like 30 seconds and ripped off the bulky headphones. The voices sounded demented, like Artaud in hell. They scared the shit out of me. "If the speech is difficult to understand, remember that the spirit talking may be talking in a language or dialog that is not in common usage today. The voice can also be in reverse, you would need a computer to reverse this to hear it." I replay Beds are Burning. No ghost voice. The battery icon bar is a mere slice of red. My computer's death watch makes me nervous. Really. I can feel my heart. A dialogue box appears: You are now running on reserve battery power. I have to pee, my colon's rumbling, but I sit here, not wanting to miss the event. It's going to die during Phil Och's "Crucifixion." I await its final words. The screen collapses to black. My iBook's final words are "So dance." I plug in the power cord, push the On button and the machine bounds back to life. In *E. T.* love equals resurrection. E.T.'s love heals Elliott's cut finger, E.T.'s love perks up the dying potted plant. When E.T.'s dead and packed in cold storage, Elliott delivers a show-stopping soliloquy of mourning: "Look at what they've done to you. / I'm so sorry. / You must be dead / because / I don't know how to feel. / I can't feel anything anymore. / You've gone someplace else now. / I'll believe in you all my life. / Every day. / E.T. / I love you." Then E.T.'s heart beams red and his eyes spring open.

To avoid doing class prep, I fart around with my cell phone, deleting obsolete entries from the address book. So many contacts are from Hammond. I leave in my mom's next door neighbor, her housecleaner/companion, the estate attorney, my brother. I remove Commander's, our favorite Greek diner—their chicken soup was all she'd eat at the end—and Community Hospital, where she died. Each number I expunge feels like a mini-death—and then there's the brutal finality of erasing her home number from speed dial. At any time I could grab the phone, hold down 4 to contact HOME—the most ancient voice I know would answer and love would flow towards me through thousands of miles of wires or it would beam to me from satellites orbiting the earth, huge towers broadcasting love to me. The original voice, hands on either side of her big round belly, speaking to me when I was still floating inside her. Kevin doesn't excise people from his address book when they die—he just types in DEAD, all caps, bold. DEAD is a tombstone beside their name, a remembrance. Writing this piece is keeping my mother alive for me, when I finish it I'm afraid she'll really be dead. I don't remember her last words to me. We were on the phone, 24 hours before her death, almost to the minute—I was coming, the conversation didn't seem important enough to remember. Did she tell me she loved me? Normally she would have, but she was breathless and terribly weak. She told me she loved me so often those last few weeks, she said my love meant the world to her. I wonder if she suspected how much I'd miss her. E.T. points to the sky with his long knobby finger and croaks, "Phone home." If human emotions developed to promote the survival of the species—attraction and its ensuing horniness ensures we propagate—what possible use is mourning. Mourning slows us down, draws us inward, takes away our will to go out and club a wooly mammoth for dinner. Time is no longer linear—it's more like a chord that flashes in and out of being.

In the film's original opening sequence, E.T.'s flight from the government agents is created by a light bulb that zooms in a straight line on a rail. In the 2002 reanimated sequence, E.T.'s glowing red chest bobs up and down through the forest, to show "these things *can* run." But do we really need the bobbing? Some viewers dislike E.T.'s computer-generated face lift, claiming that his lack of expression added to his character, his adorable alien stiffness. We need so little to believe. Before the enormity of death, meaning implodes and fractures—rationality buzzes out of the room like a swatted fruit fly. One walks around in a daze, stumbling upon clues. Phones ring, computer lights throb. *E.T.*, with its surplus symbolism, is loaded with clues. Online I read that the title credits are purple because purple is the color of spirituality. I read that black and red are associated with the antagonists, while the colors of innocence are blue and white. Over and over E.T. is wearing a white hooded cloak like a holy person. Drew Barrymore: "E.T. was like a guardian angel watching over us—there to teach us deep meaning about people and a way of life." Throughout the film Elliott and E.T. wear blue and white, Elliott's blanket is blue. Right before Elliott's brother Michael becomes an ally he takes off his red football jersey to reveal a blue shirt beneath. In the hospital scene, when government agent Peter Coyote switches from antagonist to friend he dons—surprise—blue and white. With Coyote sympathetic, a new antagonist must now be created in order to maintain conflict in the story. In this scene DEATH itself will serve that function, DEATH, which threatens the life of E.T. Elliott: "Look at what they've done to you. I'm so sorry. You must be dead. I … I didn't know how to feel. I can't feel anything anymore. You've gone someplace else now. E.T., I love you." E.T. dies with his head resting on a piece of blue cloth. When E.T. and Elliott hug good-bye they're surrounded by blue and white lights. Of course I'm thinking of my mother's blue sweater. The clues don't add up to an answer or solution—*there is no sausage*—they just echo and reverberate. *E.T.*, the text of my mother's and my grandmother's deaths, infiltrates everything. It melds with and mirrors my life the way E.T. and Elliott become mirror images, one being. E.T.'s frightened, Elliott gasps; E.T. drinks beer, Elliott belches; E.T. falls asleep, Elliott passes out; E.T. turns whitish gray, Elliott says, "We're sick. I think we're dying." E.T. is always a "we," never an "I." Inside E.T. is twelve-year-old Matthew De Meritt. De Meritt, a lively boy who skateboarded around the set, was born without legs. Since he had to walk around on his hands, he couldn't control the arms of the costume—still Spielberg liked the legless boy's "alien, unnatural gait that always looked as if E.T. were on the verge of being off-balance." One of the funniest scenes is when De Meritt as a drunk E.T. waddles around the kitchen and topples backwards with the slapstick ease of a round-bottom doll, the kind that when you knock it over, it pops right back up. His performance so impressed George Lucas, he offered De Meritt the role of Admiral Ackbar in *Return of the Jedi*, but he turned it down. At first Spielberg was resistant to dwarfs—he wanted to stick with legless people. To convince him, optical effects put the young daughter of one of *E.T.*'s lawyers inside the rubber suit. "She hated it. She was screaming and crying during the whole time. But the videotape looked great." Inside E.T. is Pat Bilon, who was 2'10" and weighed 45 pounds. Bilon wore the fifteen-pound latex suit three to four hours at a time inside. His head barely came up to E.T.'s chest, he couldn't see, and it was sauna hot in there. Between scenes assistants removed E.T.'s radio-controlled head and cooled Bilon off with a hair dryer. Bilon died suddenly on January 27, 1983 of complication from pneumonia—eight months after *E.T.*'s premiere at the Cannes Film Festival. He's buried in Calvary Cemetery in Youngstown, Ohio. My mother never visited my father's grave. "Why should I," she said. "He ain't there." Inside E.T. is 2'7" San Franciscan singer Tamara De Treaux, who also played Greedigut in *Ghoulies*. De Treaux's close friend Armistead Maupin based his novel *Maybe the Moon* on her *E.T.* experiences. She died of respiratory and heart problems on November 28, 1990 and is buried in Forest Lawn Memorial Park in Los Angeles in the Courts of Remembrance, wall crypt 5542A, above Andy Gibb. My mother's buried beside my father. Not there. Inside E.T. are Tina Palmer, a legless girl; Nancy MacLean, who played an Ewok in *Return of the Jedi*; and Pam Ybarra. E.T.'s voice was performed by Pat Walsh, a 65-year-old speech teacher who smoked two packs of cigarettes a day. She was paid $380 to record for nine-and-a half hours—with her dentures removed to make her raspy vocalizations sound more alien. Fifteen minutes after the fact, the doctor pronounces my mother dead. Her lips have shriveled, exposing the perfectly even white teeth of her dentures. Her mouth is too small—everything about her—except her swollen feet and legs—is too small. E.T.'s scream is the electronically-altered cry of an otter. Designer Carlo Rambaldi modeled E.T.'s eyes after the eyes of Ernest Hemingway, Carl Sandburg, Albert Einstein, and Rambaldi's Himalayan cat. E.T.'s hands shake because mime Caprice Rothe drank too much coffee the first day of shooting. "I made a joke about E.T.'s D.T.s, but Steven liked the tremor and asked me to keep it in." My mother's hand too shaky to sign a check. "You do it for me," she said. "Sign my name." Caprice Rothe puts on her E.T. gloves, lies on her stomach and cants her arms upwards and out, like the arms of a praying mantis. The position is grueling to hold. E.T.'s going home. Rothe/E.T. hugs a tearful Elliot goodbye. My final visit—as soon as I opened the front door my mother was there, wrapping her bony arms around me, reaching up to me—how did she get this short—clinging to me like a child or my cats, like she never wanted to let go. "I'm so happy to see you," she said. I wish I had spent the entire ten days hugging her, absorbing the last drops of her. E.T. puts a glowing finger (a tiny quart lamp in its fiberglass tip) to Elliott's temple. "I'll be right here." Death entrances like a lover, like an ex-lover you can never quite get over—wherever you go you see fragments of the lost one in others—that person has their eyes, another their laugh, another that quirky cock of the head, another says "whatever" with the same intonation. You cling to those slivers, heart speeding with excitement, even though they're never going to add up to anything. Dee Wallace, with her short blonde hair looks like a younger version of my mother, especially in her gray sweatshirt sweater—time shatters and fragments—when she sits on Drew Barrymore's bed reading *Peter Pan*, she's not Barrymore's mom, she's mine sitting on my twinbed reading a Golden Book, *The Little Engine that Could*, to chubby little blonde me. Before the enormity of death I can no longer synthesize a whole, I can only marvel at reflective flecks, I wait for them, expect them. Kevin and I settle down to watch a DVD of *Mr. Brooks*. Kevin Costner and Dane Cook drive around in a car looking for someone to murder. Costner looks over at Dane in his hooded sweatshirt, and says, "You look a little bit like that E.T. guy—you remember that movie—he flies on the bike." Dane Cook: "Yeah yeah. Yeah, I like that movie." E.T.'s death *is* my mother's death, whether he gasps or not—the film and life exist simultaneously, each dipping in and out of one another. The cat ears I wore on the plane, the cat ears Dee Wallace wears for E.T.'s first Halloween. My mother directing me in the kitchen—do this do that, not like that, do it exactly this way—as if I were a puppet. Inside E.T. it stinks of sweat and silicone. It's airless, sweltering. And so heavy. Soft whirring from the mechanical head up above. I can't see a thing it's so dark in here, so tight, like being buried alive. My mother lying in her bright blue sweater, putty make-up, too angular face—from the waist down, dark wood-grained coffin, giant spray of yellow roses my brother and I picked out at Solan's Florist. E. T. / Stay with me. / Please. / Stay. / Together. / I'll be right here. / I'll be right here. / Stay. / Stay. / Stay. / Stay. / Stay. Flash of myself in my bedroom putting on the turquoise dress I got for my eighth grade graduation. The heels were white satin, which I dyed turquoise to match the dress. Even though my mother was there, orchestrating the scene, paying for it, I have no memory of her. She's white noise in the background of the grand opera of Dodie. Nauseating scent of cigarettes and Estee Lauder emanating from the bathroom as she stood in front of the mirror in her white cafeteria lady uniform, smearing on blue eye shadow. I'm in the kitchen, yelling, "I don't want to wash the dishes, why do I have to wash the dishes." I'm yelling at her, but I can't see her, she's an incidental prop eradicated by my rage. Glimpse of her on the porch, making a face and mouthing to me as I walk by, "You're fat." Glimpse of her running barefoot across the front yard, soaking wet, throwing another water balloon at my friend Ralph. She rarely drank—but here she is, drunk as a skunk with me and my girlfriend on New Years' Eve. She pulls over to the side of the road, jumps out and squat-pees in the snow. Janis and I buckle over with laughter. As I lie on my stomach on my bed, writing in my diary, I can hear her in the living room telling my father she thinks I'm mentally ill— because she found a cache of my poems and all of them were about death. My last visit, sitting at the kitchen table, she complains about the Chinese take-out. I get all silent and stiff, like she's a pain in the ass and she starts crying, saying don't be mad at me—or maybe that was when I acted irritated with her first thing in the morning. Like a scolded child she sat there eating fried rice she clearly found revolting. I should have said that's okay, Mom, what do you want—I'll give you anything you want. Anything. The antagonist is death itself. Elliott frees the chloroformed frogs in the school science lab. "Back to the river, back to the forest," he cries. "I gotta save you." Elliott doesn't analyze, he lets the moment wash over him, possess him. E.T. watches a man and woman kissing on TV, Elliott grabs a girl in his science lab, spins her around and kisses her passionately, their movements choreographed to match the movements of the couple on TV. Dee Wallace: "I truly never thought of E.T. as a puppet. He was very real to all of us." No matter how much I research, remember, shred, E.T. is still real, death is still real, still everywhere. Cutting up a dead frog into little bits and pieces will never contain it. The bits blow apart and scatter like a dandelion puff. E.T. calls us back to the pre-symbolic, the burden of otherness we've carried ever since we left the primal ooze of our mother's body. *I-think-I-can! I-think-I-can! Choo, choo! Choo, choo! Choo, choo!* As we watch *E.T.* fragments coalesce and point in one direction: Home. Home is a place of perfect belonging, wholeness. Home is an instinct, a yearning that has never, ever been satisfied, that can never be eradicated, an itch we will scratch until the day E.T. comes to harvest our souls, until we walk with him into the blinding light of his spaceship and ascend into the heavens to join Saint Winifred and all the rest of God's minions. Into your hands, O Merciful Saviour, we commit Your servant Winnie Bellamy. Acknowledge, we humbly beseech you, a sheep of your own fold, a lamb of your own flock, a sinner of your own redeeming. Receive her into the blessed rest of everlasting peace, and into the glorious company of the saints in light. I'll believe in you all my life. / Every day. / Mom / I love you.

9

THE CENTER OF GRAVITY

Steel is an incredibly cooperative substance, I read in an art review. Mark di Suvero's mammoth creations won't tumble or crumble under their own weight, I read. He loves to sneer at gravity; he creates joy of spirit out of steel. He's like an acrobat feeling for that invisible point, a steel whisperer, madly in love with the brawny alloy, coaxing it into graceful forms, Tyrannosaurus-sized, carnival orange, energetic and muscular, yet seeming to defy gravity like a multi-ton dancer who has lighted on the lawn. Steel geometries connect earth and sky, space and time. Primordial elements, physics, music, poetry, philosophy find their way into the mix, di Suvero's wizardry melding the monumental and the intimate, humanizing steel. Over and over I read *feisty, gravity-defying, bright.*

In the Rust Belt where I was raised there was no poetry in steel. No art. No music. Steel meant *money.* Steel meant *hellish,* smokestacks spitting fire and black clouds. In grade school they showed us a movie about the making of steel so that we would understand where our fathers and uncles went to all hours of the day and night, returning with blackened hands impossible to clean. At 3000 °F the air turns a hazy orange and the solidest things—automobiles, box cars—melt and seethe. Molten metal flaring in huge cauldrons, molten metal glowing white, coronaed by yellow, coronaed by orange. The skin of goggled men liquid with sweat, men wincing like marshmallows at a friggin' campfire. I sat there in my gradeschool deskchair staring at the pull down screen, terrified by the mill's liquid fire, terrified of the molten center of the earth, the molten beginning of the universe, of the unremitting fires of hell they told us about every Sunday. Hell was a steel mill that boiled through all eternity, grimy men prodding an unimaginably hot vat of vile bubbling goo.

My brother operates a crane at Inland Steel, which means he uses levers and dials to lift and move things that weigh many tons. I imagine him hovering above the mill in a small windowed box. Through the window he looks down at the glowing, spitting, steaming vats—the hinge that holds the box cracks and my brother's cage plummets into the thick frenetic brew, incinerated as it's sucked into a lurid orange and yellow downward spiral. This isn't accurate but I can't eradicate this image of my brother hovering precariously above a raging inferno. Yellow and white sparks white clouds tons of hot danger red and yellow smoke. I feel my face melting. That's why you go to college, so you don't have to do stuff like this. Orange yellow white glow spark. The crane my brother operates is a bridge crane. Parallel rails are attached to elevated wall structures. The bridge is a beam that runs between the two rails. A trolley with a hoist mechanism moves back and forth along the bridge. My brother sits in the trolley. It's air conditioned in there, so it's considered a cushy job. My brother got bladder cancer when he was 40, a disease, he tells me, that old men get. He blames the steel's toxic fumes. My brother is used to working double shifts for weeks on end—and the huge double time salary that brings in. (It's cheaper to pay the overtime than hire more people, because of the cost of benefits.) Now that his mill has been bought "by the Japanese," his hours and his benefits have been cut. Regardless, he remains a staunch Republican because Democrats kill jobs. At the mill, only the blacks and Hispanics vote Democrat. Men enter the steel mill clean and exit roasted exhausted covered in grime. Men take their paychecks across the street to the casinos who await them 24 hours a day. Most of the mills in Northern Indiana have closed. My brother works in the sole remaining mill. He's a crane operator, I keep trying to make this more poetic, but I can't *a mind like a steel refinery, prosaic and terrible* I had the tackiest of childhoods but it was not poor. The steel of nails and hammers and organized labor kept our family in Sears Roebuck abundance. *Reaches for gravity-defying feats. Feisty, gravity-defying, bright.* Gravity does not bend. Art writers lie. Art lies. It was the lie of art I wanted more than anything else as a child. I lived in notebooks, lying on my bed writing feverishly along their cool blue lines, while in the living room my father the carpenter smokes and cusses and Mom's in the kitchen and my brother is out engaging in the juvenile delinquent behavior that will make him a high school dropout. In my notebooks I dreamed I knew Latin and I lived in the Alps, where I hovered above the world craneless, educated and beautiful, with a mind lofty and brilliant enough to defy.

10

DIGGING THROUGH

KATHY ACKER'S STUFF

"Fashion is a dream haunted by dresses."
— Christian Dior

All I wanted was a piece of her jewelry. Kathy's executor, Matias Viegener, promised it to me a couple of years ago, so when I found myself staying in his Los Angeles home for four days in February, 2006, all I could think about was getting that jewelry. Matias' living room is an airy trapezoid sparsely furnished with a modernist sofa, chairs and coffee table. Russel Wright vases and pitchers crowd the mantelpiece. Across from the seating area a wall, lined with art, juts into the room at a dramatic angle. There's a mixed media piece by Steven Hall, a stark white canvas with candy-colored plastic flower heads stuck on it in even rows. A couple flowers are missing, their impressions remaining in the white background. Ghosts of flowers. I keep meaning to ask Matias if that's part of the piece, or if some of the flowers just fell off, but I never do. The living room opens onto a kitchen and dining area which open on to a garden overgrown with shiny green leaves. The garden is cool and shady, and as I move toward it, I feel I'm tunneling into the dark gnarly roots of nature. Matias is working at the dining room table. "Hey, Matias, remember when you promised me a piece of Kathy's jewelry." He calls me "honey." "Of course honey, you can have one."

Matias tells me I can hook up my iBook to the DSL in his ex-boyfriend's office. I search through the upstairs office, but can't find an ethernet cable anywhere. The room is overflowing with books, discarded electronics, boxes. There's an open door along the back wall, I climb over stuff and peek my head into a bathroom that has been ripped apart, with dusty Home Depot materials littering the floor. Forsaken. Since I'm up there, I snoop around in the rest of the rooms. I go into the master bedroom and lie down on the bed and stare at its sharply angled ceiling, imagining what my piece of Kathy jewelry will look like, ornate amethyst-studded silver like the piece I saw on the table at her memorial ceremony. I wanted it so bad, I almost snatched it. To the left of the bed I notice a door. I get up and open it to find an irregularly shaped, and teeny, concrete patio scattered with photo lamps wrapped with aluminum foil, cheap flaring lamps bigger than human heads, the kind the AV Department lent out when I was in college. The aluminum wrapping is comically low-tech, like props from an Ed Wood movie. "We from planet Zeron come to you in peace." I cross the hall to the guest room, I've slept in this room before, and even though the desk obscures them, I know there are steps at the back which lead to a dressing room. I check it out, the dressing room's still crammed with men's clothing. At the back of the dressing room is a door, but I don't open it. Shooting off of every room is another room, as if the house were continuously spouting new limbs. But where's the fucking ethernet cable—I flash back to my last visit, get a vague image of Andy waving out of a tiny office, startling me as I climbed some stairs. I go down to the landing by the front entrance. The room's no larger than a closet, but with a high ceiling, books and shelves and boxes, even the electric radiator, loom precariously above my head. The room is so vertical that when I sit at the desk I feel like I'm at the bottom of a well. No windows, odd slanty angles. I check my email quickly because the room is so cold, so *Cabinet of Dr. Caligari* off kilter.

I have a recurring dream where I discover a hidden room in my apartment. Sometimes the room is welcoming, sometimes the room leads to an elaborate basement maze full of dusty, decaying uninhabitable rooms I'm desperately trying to inhabit. Matias' house resonates with both these dreams. I feel grounded and comfortable there, but amidst its Gothic angles and secret rooms, my unconscious bubbles, and I slip into a state of mystery and suspicion. When Matias informs me he's moved into the guest room, so I'll be sleeping in his bedroom, I'm taken aback. I stayed in the guest room on my last visit, its double bed that gave me a backache. Why is he putting me in the master bedroom with its comfy king-sized bed? And then it comes to me, the room must be haunted. Like what is with that closet? Its sliding mirrored doors have been flipped backwards, so the mirrors face the clothing, and panels painted flat white face outwards. The paint is fragmented in an elaborated stratified design. Matias says the paint has cracked on its own, is still cracking. What other renovations is the house making on its own, I wonder. I think of the cobweb in the bathroom with the big ass spider crawling around it, the rats in the attic Matias complains he has to get rid of—I'm convinced the house is alive, that it has a mind of its own. I feel fortunate that the house seems to like me. I putz around its kitchen in my bathrobe as if I owned it. Matias fixes breakfast while working the phone, we shout back and forth between the kitchen and dining room, between the living room and the dining room, sometimes I sit with him at the table, or we stand together in the kitchen sloppily eating mangoes and oro blancos. We sit in the living room on his boxy green sofa and he tells me that even though Kathy slept with many women she really wasn't a lesbian, and even though she was into SM that wasn't her thing, not really, what really mattered to Kathy was to be fucked really well. I say, "Don't forget about that jewelry." "No, honey, I won't."

In 1992 New Langton Arts invited me to present a talk for an evening on "Eros and Writing." As I stood up to give my talk, a gushing tribute to the erotic charge I get from reading David Wojnarowicz and Kathy Acker, I surveyed the audience and noticed that Kathy herself was sitting dead center in front of me. "Oh shit," I said to myself. How embarrassing, what if she hated it, what if she thought I was like this total idiot. It was hard to concentrate on what I was reading, I was trying so hard not to look at Kathy. When my gaze did stumble across her, she seemed to be smiling, which was good, as I'd seen her at another panel scowl dramatically when she didn't like what Earl Jackson Jr. was saying about her. I finished my paper to moderate applause, determined to slip out of there without confronting Kathy, but Barrett Watten blocked my escape. He said something like, "I really liked that," and kissed my cheek. I practically raced across the room to gossip about Barrett's unexpected salute. I interrupted a conversation, pointed to my cheek, and said dramatically, "Barrett kissed me here. I'm never washing my face again." And then I walked up to another friend, pointed to my cheek, and said dramatically, "Barrett kissed me here. I'm never washing my face again." I was looking around for someone else to do my cheek routine for when I saw Kathy approaching. "Oh shit." But she was very sweet. She brought up the long passage I'd quoted from *Empire of the Senseless*, where the narrator has sex with a toy dinosaur. Here's a snippet:

Stray sprays of sperm streamed down the stuffed animal's left leg. Our fucking had made her less fearful for the moment. She actually touched my arm and left her paw there. Then this paw pulled my arm to her monstrous body, lifted it and placed it on her swollen belly. Then she stuck the hand in and squeezed it between her two hot wide thighs. I thought that my hand was going to break.

"I love that passage," Kathy said, "Juan Goytisolo wrote it. He's great, isn't he." She said it so nonchalantly, with no sense of discomfort about owning or not owning the passage. I could have used some of Kathy's entitled complacency three years later when my novel *The Letters of Mina Harker* finally came out. Inspired by Kathy, in it I stole from anything and everything that crossed my path. When *The Bay Guardian* reviewed *Mina* I was thrilled—until I realized the passage Traci Vogel quoted to illustrate my genius was lifted straight out of Gail Scott's novel *Heroine*. To make matters worse, Gail happened to be in town that weekend. Gail was amused, but I was appalled. "*The Guardian* just thinks I have good taste in picking out Gail," I moaned. "Big deal. I feel more like a shopper than a writer." As I wallowed in self pity and despair, I forgot all about the tantalizing intimacy of wearing Gail's text, how it was a tribute to her.

My sophomore year at college, I had a Liberian roommate named Sarah, who was always railing against our foolish American ways. One time Sarah went up to a woman at a party and said, "I like your blouse," and the woman said, "Oh, this blouse, it belongs to Suzy. I just borrowed it." "It belongs to *Suzy*," Sarah snarled. "Who cares who it belongs to, it's a nice blouse. These Americans!" Her anger was incomprehensible to me. Even then I sensed that an appropriated blouse is not just any blouse, it leaves traces of its original owner. It's like watching 3-D without your 3-D glasses, those wobbly lines of energy bleeding from objects. I wonder how things would have gone down if it had been Kathy who was wearing Suzy's blouse. Would she have attributed it or not? Would it even matter? Kathy had such élan, everything she touched was somehow made grander. Everything she touched she owned. Kevin Killian: *She could be convincing, bending her body from the waist right into your face, turning those enormous eyes on you, making you feel—not listened to, exactly—but talked at in a most extraordinarily personal way, as though by being her audience of one you were fulfilling an important destiny you hadn't even, until this moment, known was yours.*

Possession is nine tenths of the wardrobe.

Sunday morning, we're sitting on Matias' stark orange sofa. Kathy ate tons of soymilk and tofu, Matias tells me, and that's what gave her breast cancer. "Kathy was a victim of soy." He says that after Kathy's death he could feel her clinging to life. "I'd say to her, 'Kathy, let go.'" But now he no longer feels her. "She's gone." I've known Matias since the '80s. He's someone I've always felt rather shy and formal around, but this visit my heart opens to him. Disliking the same people helps. I tell him about running across an email I received shortly after the 2002 NYU Acker conference: *Matias was very odd. He seemed to have no self. He was like the fag valet of the great diva who only lives for her. It was so old fashioned.* I don't have the email with me, so I paraphrase, "It said it was like you had no ego—as if that were a bad thing." He says, that's right, he didn't want to have an ego at the Kathy conference. "There were so many EGOS walking around that weekend, they didn't need mine added to the mix." I chuckle heartily. Kathy wreaked havoc—wherever she went she left a trail of victims behind her. Since her death they've come back with a vengeance, plotting conferences, group readings, exhibitions, anthologies. Our conversation turns to *certain people's* attempts to control and police Kathy's image—and the silliness of anyone trying to own Kathy. "She was an anarchist!" Matias exclaims. Kathy, like her writing, was full of trapdoors—as soon as you think *I'm getting this* the floor drops out from beneath your feet. Hers is a world of basements within basements within sub-basements like Dario Argento's film *Inferno*—or Matias' house. Rumor has it that when Chris Kraus was working on Kathy's biography, she was asking too many questions about Kathy's sex life, and people were told not to talk to her. Which is hilarious, because Kathy would tell anybody who would listen about her sex life. "He didn't want to use my toys, he wanted to use his own toys," she shouted at me in a restaurant. "He is the worst top I've ever met." Matias tells me it doesn't matter whether or not he agrees with what somebody writes about Kathy. The important thing is to keep Kathy's name alive—and to keep her books in print. "Matias, you're so right, but I have to leave for the airport in like 3 hours and I still don't have that jewelry." "Okay, honey, we'll look for it."

He goes upstairs to the abandoned office and several minutes later returns with a cosmetic bag. "The jewelry's not up there, but here's her keys, would you like a key?" I look in the bag and there's a dozen or more key rings loaded with keys. "Why'd she have so many keys?" "Most of them are motorcycle keys," Matias says, as if that were an explanation. In the bag I spy a small silver ring shaped like a pharaoh's head, with two naked women on either side, kneeling in supplication, and a silver charm of a spider on a web, holding a human skull in its rear legs. I remove the pharaoh ring from Kathy's key ring and slip it on mine. The spider charm's kind of gruesome, but I pocket it along with the keys it's attached to. I also take a set of keys with a red plastic tag that reads "Golden Gate Cycles of San Francisco." Matias says, "The only other place the jewelry might be is in with her clothes." So we go down to the garage and—surprise—behind the back wall of the garage there's a storage room I didn't know about.

On a shelf above our heads are stacked four large packing boxes. The bottom one is labeled in black marker "Acker's Clothes" in Kathy's own handwriting. The boxes were packed by professional movers on the eve of her return from London in fall 1997. When she arrived in San Francisco she checked into the Travelodge near me. Friends found her lying on the floor, buckled over in pain, so thin and weak she couldn't make it to the toilet. Matias says a couple of boxes are missing, that originally there were twelve, but he "edited them down" to six. "Andy must have put the rest of them in his storage locker." Once we get the boxes on the floor, we start to rummage through them. Matias pulls out a black mass of fabric. "This one's my favorite—I'll never get rid of it—because nobody has been able to figure out how you're supposed to wear it." It's a dress, but it only has one sleeve and a sort of diagonal band stretching from where the missing armpit would be. I pull out another black wad and jostle it and hold it in various directions until we agree it's a little pouffe skirt. Lots of flaps of fabric held together with buckles and straps. We examine piece after piece and ponder what part of the body it was meant to cover. "No, no, it's not a dress, look at the way it wraps around here, I'm sure it's a pair of pants." Matias says Kathy didn't take good care of her clothes, there's food stains on them, for instance. Lots of Gaultier, Vivienne Westwood, Comme des Garcons, with a spattering of Betsey Johnson and Yohji Yamamoto. Matias holds up a Ralph Lauren bathrobe. "This can't be Kathy's," he says, "Kathy would never wear Ralph Lauren." I pull out a black Gaultier dress with some sort of velvety text embossed on the back. "Can I have this one?" "Sure."

Memory: Kathy entering a room in a silver bodysuit that looked like a prop from David Bowie's Ziggy Stardust tour, a tiny spacesuit that would fit a doll's body. Everyone around her looking normal, in this diminished washed out way. Stuffed haphazardly in packing boxes, Kathy's clothes feel devoid of will, abandoned, subverting sentimentality by their strangeness, their creepiness. Deconstructed '80s and '90s glitz. Since no regular person would wear them, could one say these clothes ever were in fashion? Memory: Kathy holding court in a femmy short plaid dress, empire style, tight around her bust then flaring out. Some kind of frou frou at the shoulders. She looked like a clown, but a totally confident, powerful clown. Thurston Moore: *I knew Kathy A a little bit through the years, was attracted by her wildness but was always a bit conflicted by what I saw as maybe corny. Not corny like "painting in the '80s" or "madonna" but close, a true vibe of recklessness tempered the corn, not unlike Basquiat vibe. In retrospect, much like Basquiat, I see her, and her work, as wonderful.* The gap between our intentions and the effects we create is what Diane Arbus ruthlessly bought into her photographs—a gap, that whenever I recognize it, opens a pang of love in me. Kathy managed to create exactly the effect she intended, but her clownishness, her bald construction of a persona also opened that gap. Aggressive trendiness slips into masochistic vulnerability. Again I think of 3-D glasses—whenever I watched Kathy it was like the red and blues didn't quite line up. She moves through space, not singular, but a chord of being.

Acker: *I was wild because I was protected—I could do anything— who was going to touch me—really touch me like those others, like those poor people in the world—are touched?*

I dream I'm teaching a class at an art school and it's going terribly, I'm unprepared and the students are listless, so I decide to give them a midterm—due in two weeks. I grab a piece of chalk and write, but nothing appears because the chalk is the same khaki green as the blackboard. Art historian Pamela Lee on camouflage: *The will to blend into one's surroundings, to be absorbed into space by reversing one's distinction from it.* The students complain they can't read their assignment, so I find a white piece of chalk. It's still difficult to write, but I finally manage to scratch out: "Write about a box—or build a box—that represents the otherness of death." Acker: *Let one of art criticism's languages be silence so that we can hear the sounds of the body: winds and voices from far-off shores, the sounds of the unknown.* Pamela Lee: *The subject loses its borders—its figure—in succumbing to "the lure of space."* Acker: *Over and over again, in our false acts of absolute judgment and criticism, we deny the realm of death.*

Memory: Kathy's ashes sit on a low table in the middle of Bob Glück's living room, sealed in a gold-colored box. Matias Viegener: *In San Francisco we transferred her ashes from the anodized tin to a nineteenth-century French brass urn, something between Art Nouveau and Beaux Arts in style. Several of her friends gathered together to acknowledge her death, and then we spooned them from one receptacle to the other with a silver serving spoon. Everyone was crying.* I didn't touch the ashes. I didn't want to, and I knew she wouldn't have wanted me to. It's not that Kathy wasn't nice to me. She was. She gave me writerly advice, such as when you go out of town for a reading, if they put you up in a hotel find out where the hotel is or you might end up in a seedy neighborhood in a dump. But ours was a distanced relationship—we both knew that if we came too close it would have been Godzilla meets Mothra, screeches and roars, scales and feathers flying. As everybody else is scooping, Matias and Connie Samaras, who were with Kathy when she died, tell how they removed Kathy's piercings before she was sent to the crematorium. "The one in her labia was Kathy's favorite piercing." These intimacies are revealed with a tone of reverence and a disarming matter-of-factness. Matias and Connie poking around in a dead woman's genitals with no acknowledgement of the strangeness of the image—this is *so* Kathy.

Acker: *One of my students had a piercing through her labia. And she told me about how when you ride on a motorcycle, the little bead on the ring acts like a vibrator. Her story turned me on so I did it. I got two. It was very cool.*

Back to LA: I open the bathroom door and glimpse Matias in the guest room, perched on one foot, pulling on his jeans. The sweetness of his love for Kathy. When I get back home he emails I'm easy to live with, except I take too long in the bathroom. I write back that everything that deals with my body takes a long time, but I pee really quickly. Another email is from Kathy's French publisher who says she's interested in looking at *The Letters of Mina Harker*. Then I get food poisoning and vomit my guts out. I'm reminded of the section in *Mina* where I get sick after licking a drop of blood from Kevin's finger, how newly-turned vampires hang over the toilet once the transformation starts kicking in. Then my car gets broken into and my dry cleaning is stolen from the trunk. It's been in there for three weeks, and never made it to the cleaners. What kind of pervert would steal a mess of funky clothes. Flashes of weird masturbatory rituals, like the guy who broke into Maureen's house and jerked off over some of her underwear. Don't be such a drama queen I tell myself, you'll probably see them on 16th Street, on the sidewalk next to mildewed books and mismatched dinnerware, the tops all in a row, folded neatly as Kathy's Gaultier dress that now sits atop my dresser. A tiny stretchy dress that must have pulled tightly across her body, a body sloughing skin, oozing perspiration. Her body. Will Kathy's stuff change me, will it work some spell on my life? I walk through my days vigilant for evidence.

Other things start to go missing. My travel mug; the front of my car's CD player; my reading glasses; my fountain pen; my kitten Sylvia's toy, a 36-inch plastic rod with two six-inch neon yellow feathers. Then I remember that even before I left LA, I lost the back of my diamond earring. It fell into the gray carpet to the right of my bed. I saw where it landed, but it's like it vaporized. For the rest of the weekend Kevin and I kept getting down on our hands and knees and inching across the floor, but we never found it. The earrings were a gift from my mother. She hit a royal flush on the poker machine and bought herself a pair of new, bigger diamonds. I got the old pair, one third carat total. They're the only earrings I wear, not because I like diamonds, but because they belonged to her.

I find my glasses in my bathrobe pocket, go to the car and the front of my CD player is in the side pocket of the door (where I looked before) and my fountain pen is lying dead center in the middle of the driver's seat, perfectly parallel with the seat back, as if placed ritualistically. I drive to the post office to mail a copy of *Mina* to the French publisher. The line is long, so as I wait I fill out the customs declaration form, it takes like a minute, but this British guy standing behind me says, "Excuse me, but the way it works is that you fill out your form *before* you get in line. That's what I did—it's common courtesy." With his close cropped head and erect posture, he looks like the singer from Simple Minds, but with better teeth. I roll my eyes and say everybody fills out their forms in line, and then he drops another disdainful "common courtesy," and we bicker some more, and then I point to the guy in front of me who is messily wrapping a package, and I say, "What about him, why aren't you complaining about him, or is it only *women* you harass in line," and the Brit spits back "common courtesy" and I find myself screaming, "Stop talking to me—you're a looney tunes!" I can't believe I used that expression—looney tunes—before this snooty Brit I've become this wailing mass of American vulgarity. Acker: *I am a child of the forests and the wilds; I am all that is American.* When I get home, missing: my cherished Kate Spade sunglasses, I paid $50 for them at Nordstrom Rack. I find a similar pair on eBay and order them.

I'm distracted and forgetful and can't seem to get anything done, I feel stuck, as if my life were a web and I've blindly gotten myself all bumbled up in it. Missing: my wedding band and the iolite ring Lissa Wolsak made me. The next day Kevin finds them at the bottom of the wastepaper basket in the living room.

When I show the pharaoh ring to Amanda Davidson, she recoils, says that Kathy's writing so destabilizes her, she couldn't imagine taking on that energy. Amanda's been watching a lot of *Buffy* lately, she knows how energy clings to things. I've been reading about voodoo—it all started with my fingernail that was hanging by a thread, it was so painful, snagging on a blanket or piece of clothing, sharp jabs melting to raw and tender, so I gave it a yank and threw it in the trash. And then I got to thinking how a voodoo practitioner would never be so sloppy, how the piece has the same energy as the whole, how somebody could steal that nail and do some real harm. On the internet I find that to inflict pain on Dodie, all you need is:

  2 black candles
  A voodoo doll

Nail clippings or hair follicles or any item belonging to Dodie
Pins or another sharp object

Light the two black candles on the altar, take the voodoo doll and visualize with intensity it is Dodie before you, if you have a photo of Dodie put her face on the doll along with her nail clippings and hair follicles or the small item belonging to Dodie, this will make the connection more powerful. Once you have worked up the negative energy needed and drawn your anger near its boiling point slam the doll onto the altar and stab at it once in the place where you wish to afflict pain, take more pins and stab the doll again, each time you do this visualize the doll being Dodie. Dodie could be thousands of miles away, it doesn't matter.

I remember the bottle I found on the same shelving as Kathy's clothes. It was a small rectangular bottle filled with brightly colored liquid, green or blue. I picked it up and moved it closer to my glasses. Floating in it were herbs, tiny Christmas lights, plastic toys, other unrecognizable stringy things. I decided it must be some kind of mojo bottle, it had to be, and a pang of dread and revulsion shot through me, similar to when peeling back the husk of organic corn I find a furry green worm writhing. I dropped the bottle onto the shelf. "That was Kathy's," said Matias. But I already knew that—all the psychic healers and witch doctors she went to those last couple of years. "Would you like it?" asks Matias. Shaking my hand to remove contamination, I said, "No way." Acker: *To walk away from conventional medicine is to walk away from normal society.* Mojo for luck: one piece of Sampson Snake Root and a piece of Devil's Shoe Strings wrapped in a piece of Black Cloth folded always toward the maker and sewed with White Thread and then encased in a Red Flannel Bag, thoroughly wet with Whiskey or camphorated oil. Acker: *When I walked out of the surgeon's office and didn't know where to go, I asked myself what I could know.* Mojo for the return of an estranged lover: a black cat bone wrapped in cotton wool, fixed in a red flannel bag and dressed with Follow Me Boy Oil or Reconciliation Oil. Acker: *I am a person who wants to live, I live to want to live, I sing with it, I am a creature meant for wildness transformed into joy.* I got my black cat bone, all pure and dry/ I got a four-leaf clover, all hangin' high./ Got my hoodoo ashes all around your bed/ Got my black snake roots underneath your head. Acker: *My body has gone crazy. Shit lies over everything, the counterspace, the windowsill. Dripping down.* Mojo to remove a jinx: a broken length of chain, a broken ring, a rat bone or toy plastic rat, a catseye shell, a miniature metal skull, a pinch of five finger grass, and a miniature dagger, fixed in a red flannel bag and dressed with Stop Evil Condition Oil, Jinx Removing Oil, or Uncrossing Oil. Acker: *Inside my house, I started to scream. I couldn't stop. Mucus poured out of my nose and mouth. I had been coughing convulsively for days. My body is a scream.* I got a gypsy woman givin' me advice/ I got some red hot tips I got to keep on ice./ I got a rabbit foot, I know it's workin' right/ I got a strand of hair I'm keepin' day and night. Acker: *Our father who beginneth all things I will not collude with you I will not die.* Mojo for a wish to come true: seven wishing beans, a rabbit foot, and a piece of parchment upon which the wish has been written in Dragon's Blood ink, fixed in a red flannel bag and anointed with Van Van Oil. Acker: *I want to live, I really really want to live and more than that I want to be in wonder to dwell there I have tasted delight and once you've tasted delight you never want anything else.*

On a closed-circuit television, the nurses in the Tijuana hospital watched Kathy die. Connie Samaras watched with them. As Matias holds Kathy in his arms, their arrangement reminds Connie of a Renaissance painting, her head tilting back over his shoulder. A painting on a black and white TV monitor, as Kathy dissolves to image she is so lovely she glows in the dark. Connie Samaras: *Gently, I begin to touch you everywhere. I start by kissing your hand, letting my hair drift across your cunt. I look up. Delicately, I see you kissing the air.* I ask Bob Glück if he thinks Kathy had a transformation at the end. "What I believe," he says, his voice tense with held back emotion, "was that she was living in a magical world."

Acker: *The only religions are scatology and intensity.*

When I return to LA the following June I visit Kaucyila Brooke's studio in Koreatown. Kaucyila has photographed over 150 of Kathy's oufits—a project that has been well received in Europe, but has never been shown in the States. As we look through stacks of work prints that cover a large table, our imaginations are sparked by Kathy's weird designer garb. "That one looks like a gas mask," I say. "And that one looks like a straitjacket." Kaucyila holds up a print of an amorphous black blob, "At first I thought this one looked like a Rorschach blot, but now I think it's a ballet slipper." She points to the U-shape at the bottom, and I'm all, "You're right, it's totally a ballet slipper!" I've just met Kaucyila, so I'm nervous, but fantasizing about the pictures is like playing with dolls, and I soon find myself relaxing. Kaucyila says Kathy had a bit of Liberace about her. Imitating Liberace, Kaucyila twirls around and exclaims, "How do you like my outfit?" Once when Kaucyila saw Kathy read, she twirled as well. Kaucyila twirls with her and says, "How do you like my tattoos?" Kaucyila and I agree to a trade—an artist's proof of one of the photos in exchange for a catalogue essay to be written when needed. I choose # 9, Kaucyila's favorite, a simple stretchy black dress that she stuffed so it's awkward and misshapen. Kaucyila says it reminds her of her attempts as a child to draw a dress. I find the photo sweet and a bit pathetic. Perfect. When I take it in to be framed, Kelly, the framing girl tells me she went to the San Francisco Art Institute when Kathy taught there. Kelly, who's wearing layers of retro-punk black, thick black eyeliner with shadow so dark she looks like she's been punched in the eye, extravagant deep magenta lips lined with black, says, "She sure had some crazy outfits."

With her big red lips, her short blonde hair cut in spirals like a crop circle, her gym-taut body, tattoos, tight little dresses, eyes as round and bright as a spaniel's, Kathy exuded a potent femaleness. Matias said she was a shopaholic, if she found something she liked, she'd buy one in every color. When Bob Glück went sofa shopping with Kathy, she spotted a sofa with winged armrests, pointed at it from across the room, and shouted, "I want that one." In the '80s she spent $100 a month on face care products she mail-ordered from Canada. Kathy was always commending her hairdresser, her masseuse, her trainer, her psychic, her mechanic. I imagined a line of support staff trailing after her, their arms draped with steaming white towels. Despite her virulent consumerism, she critiqued capitalism—often and grandly. Everything Kathy did was grand, was instantly transformed to myth. In the early '90s, before the internet was ubiquitous, when it still had a William Gibsonesque radical hip cachet, Kathy announced in that deathly serious way of hers, "I spend four hours—each day—online." The clothes are superfluous to Kathy's writing, her real legacy—or are they? Could there have been a Kathy Acker without the clothes? Kathy understood image, its fluidity, its hypnotic power. A smokescreen, a puff of smoke—and out steps Kathy, a Gaultier-clad Houdini amazing the crowd.

I go to Sephora to try on NARS Orgasm, the most popular of all blush colors. On the sidewalk outside the cosmetic superstore a teenaged girl with short spiky blonde hair sits begging. She's holding a cream colored Teddy bear in her lap. Her smile says aren't I cute and vulnerable and young and aren't you just dying to take care of me—as if the sidewalk were her bedroom of suburban dreams. I think of Kathy's habit of chaining a stuffed animal to her exercise bike at Gold's Gym—as if to announce, I'm hardening my body, but I have a soft corny heart. Inside Sephora women in all directions stand in front of round mirrors smearing on makeup. I find the NARS Orgasm and get a wedge of foam. As I swipe the foam across the blush I think *I'm dipping into a pot of female contagion.* I rub it on, but the light's terrible and it's hard to see what I'm doing. I also try the matching Orgasm lip gloss. It's sticky and unbearable, like having your lips smeared with cum that will never dry, never wash off. I leave the store with dark peachy clownish cheeks, a streak of mascara smeared across my left cheek and ear. White rapper a block up Powell Street: *cracking up, cracking up, the world in bits and pieces.*

As I reach into my bag Kathy's pharaoh slips himself around my pinkie. Kathy's keys unlock the pharaoh's tomb/a foot-thick door made out of desert concrete swings open/stale air rushes out/the angry dead spirit has been waiting 3,000 years for an unwitting fool like me to spill a drop of blood on her sarcophagus. When I got back to San Francisco I ran over to Bed and Bath and bought the same electric sharpener that Matias has. WARNING reads the instruction manual KNIVES WILL BE SHARPER THAN YOU EXPECT. I core an apple and slice into the pad of my right thumb, dead center across my fingerprint. The bleeding is extravagant, bright red—drip, drip.

A copy of Kathy's *Hannibal Lecter, My Father* appears on my bedroom floor. A note tucked inside reminds me the book was a farewell gift from Laurie, a student who graduated a couple of years ago. Kathy would tell her students at the Art Institute,

"Don't let anybody tell you how to write"—a warning I gave to Laurie as well, to no avail. Kathy apparently didn't criticize student work, she just gave them permission. A typical Kathy assignment: write a piece in which you have sex with the most disgusting person in your family. Lynn Breedlove told me Kathy advised them to write while masturbating. Acker: *One thing I do is stick a vibrator up my cunt and start writing—writing from the point of orgasm and losing control of the language and seeing what that's like. Vanity Scare.* The Art Institute was too sterile for her methods, so she held her classes at a bar—the appropriately Gothic Edinburgh Castle. Bob Glück theorizes that students didn't learn from Kathy, they absorbed her. Kathy's ghoulish white face looms out at me from the back of *Hannibal Lecter.* All other details are obscured except a half-zipped leather jacket. The jacket splits open with the curvaceous grace of a calla lily, Kathy's head is its pistil, her right ear dripping with gewgaws, a studded choker about her neck, her short bangs dipping into a V, her puffy lips hinting at a pout. Beside her head, a quote from her "Diaries of Laure": *This writing is all fake (copied from other writing) so you should go away and not read any of it.* She looks like Billy Idol in his "White Wedding" video. *Hey little sister, shot gun.* Inside the book on the title page in the top right corner, written in black ballpoint: *Love, Acker.* Kathy's round childlike printing is unmistakable. I write in my journal: *Kathy's leaving me bread-crumbs—she's the witch at the end of the trail, stoking the fires of her big cunt oven.* I crack open *Hannibal Lecter* at random and read: *The desperate needs I feel are now burning.*

Kathy's unwashed Gaultier dress sits on my dresser, exuding flakes of energy. I keep trying to figure out a way to talk about it. I compare the dress to a doll, I sexualize it, I have sex and think about it. I write: *Kathy's Gaultier dress sits on my dresser, me on my bed writhing and grunting. It's as if the dress has consciousness, is waiting for something, as I come I hear something coming from the dresser, something faint, a rustle, a breath.* I write: *Kathy's dress sits atop my dresser, a dress that would fit a really small woman or a really big doll, we all want to turn the dead into dolls who do our bidding.* I write: *Kathy's dress sits atop my dresser and I want to turn this dress into a doll, it would resonate with voodoo, would resonate with Kathy's stolen doll fucking passage, but the dress refuses to budge in that direction—the dress has presence, an aura, it sits there haughty as a popular girl who refuses to talk to me— stubbornly inanimate.* Then I find my notes from Alicia Cohen's talk on orphic poetry at Small Press Traffic. My journal is dated March 24, in green ink. Beneath that is written: *Levinas—the philosopher never attempts to reveal/penetrate/grasp otherness.* Then more fragments about how orphic poetry implies an openness to listening, to what speaks through you. The point is to greet rather than capture and contain the self. I write in the margin in black: *This sounds so Kathy.* At this point everything's starting to sound like Kathy. How stupid of me to try to push Kathy's dress into some clever "meaning" rather than allowing it to speak on its own terms. To enter the dream beneath the seeming concreteness of reality, one must be vigilant. It's like watching digital TV and waiting for those places where the image suddenly pixilates, disrupting the predictable narrative flow. You never know when it will happen.

I remove Kathy's dress from my dresser, determined to listen to it. The dress has a wool skirt and high neck, the sleeves and back are sheer black mesh. Embossed on the back is a round shield made of black flock, a consecration cross with 69 in the center, a leaf pattern is wedged between the blades of the cross, and two lightning bolts snake down from either side. Arching above the cross are words in a stylized Goth font that are all but unreadable.

In LA, Kevin, Matias and I spent half an hour trying to make sense of them. Kevin came up with "Too Fab To," but then we gave up. I get a couple sheets of typing paper and slip them inside the dress, so that the Goth text now lies on a white background. It is only then that I realize there are words arching beneath the cross as well. Too fab to—too fab to what? Looking closely, there's an extra letter, so it can't be fab—it's too *fast* to—but the final word remains indecipherable, it begins with what looks like a down arrow followed by an arrow with points at both ends. I turn to the bottom, and within minutes I've come up with TOO YOUNG TO DIE, which fills me with the creepiness of messages that came through my high school Ouija board. The top I finally figure out, reads TOO FAST TO LIVE. Too fast to live, too young to die—a punk anthem, a line from that horrible James Dean song by the Eagles, the name of Vivienne Westwood's boutique before she changed it to Sex.

Digging through my nightstand for my glasses or my fountain pen, I find the Buddhist book on ghosts I brought back from San Diego last summer. When I saw *A Discussion of Ghosts* lying beside my bed in Eileen Myles' guest room, I was tempted to steal it. Instead I hinted for it, and when that didn't work, I whined, "Can I have this Eileen. Please." Eileen said she'd bought it for someone else, but she'd "lend" it to me. Of course I hope to never give it back to her. I open it, ravenous with possession. Here's what Venerable Master Hsing Yun has to tell me. Ghosts are more afraid of people than we are of them, ghosts move about in the dead of the night to avoid dangerous humans. If you hold a red rose out to a ghost then drop it, the ghost will ravenously jump on it and the rose will turn into the bone of a corpse. Happy ghosts live pleasant lives full of good food and beautiful clothes. They have vehicles to take them wherever they want to go. Many ghosts feel shame and embarrassment and envy. It is common for them to be confused, to ask, "How did I get this way?" Acker: *I want to live, I really really want to live.* There are ghosts who know wealth and prominence, there are ugly ghosts with runny noses and sores all over their bodies, greedy lustful cheating ghosts, ghosts who have a lot of fun, dirt poor ghosts, beautiful ghosts, temple ghosts, city ghosts and country ghosts. There are ghosts with long disheveled hair who wander about homeless, ghosts with dignity, ghosts without it, regal ghosts who live in fine castles, ghosts who are seven miles tall with skinny little necks, ghosts as small as newborns—but all ghosts, no matter what they look like or what they own, are hungry. If you care for your ghosts you leave them offerings of food. This essay is food for Kathy. Acker: *Pain exists because it means; the world is meaning. When you scream, it is love. Cry, darling; the earth has been parched for a long time. You will be cooled down.* Things come/ things return/ things open up their attributes. The dead are uncontainable, all we can do is greet them, allow them their otherness. Hello, Kathy, I humble myself before your otherness, an otherness I will never comprehend. I promise I won't even try.

I didn't like Kathy. I did at first, but then she set her sights on this guy I was having an affair with. She'd seen Ron around for ages, but the week I started sleeping with him, she looked at him across the room and said to Bob Glück, "I feel hunger," and started barraging Ron with "Let's have coffee," "Let's get together some time and talk." She was relentless. "I don't know why Dodie's so cold to me," she said to Kevin, all innocent. My boyfriend wasn't the only boyfriend Kathy, who never stopped subverting bourgeois notions of ownership, tried to sleep with. Thus I wrote in "Delinquent," my essay about Kathy:

> Feminism failed because women are thieves. Never having owned anything, not even their selves, they filch texts ... souls

... dreams ... space. The text has no power over its own violation, thus its name is WOMAN.

In an earlier version I had "boyfriends" included in the list of things women filch, but Kevin convinced me to remove it. I didn't scoop up Kathy's ashes because I didn't want to violate her. I imagine the fury of Sylvia Plath's spirit when home-wrecker Assia Gutman rummaged through her papers and declared that someday she might be Plath's biographer.

My fingernail grows back gnarled as a mutant claw that thrusts out of the shadows to scare children and rape beautiful dark-tressed women. Even I can't love it. It reminds me of stillborns in the teratology journal I looked at while temping at the UCSF med school, specimens so scrambled my brain stuttered trying to make sense out of them. Do the jumbled clothes of a cult writer nine years after her death, stacked in storage boxes in a room at the back of a garage mean anything? The clothes shift and twist—no logic in their contortions beyond the dumb fact of their being uninhabited. Sometimes I get all left brain and I tell myself to stop being so superstitious, so woo woo mystical about all of this. "These effects of Kathy's," my left brain says to me, "these trinkets of wool and silver, are just objects, mere dumb objects." But no matter how I try to rationalize them, they will not stop pointing beyond their thingness *listen to me listen to me*. Acker: *To live was to stay alive and not be reduced to materiality.* So here's how I read them:

> Gaultier dress = brevity of human existence
> Spider charm = NO BULLSHIT when the death spider's legs forcep
>   themselves about your skull
> Pharaoh ring = eternal life/the afterlife

Kevin wants to watch *The Skeleton Key*. "What's it about?" "It's scary and it stars Kate Hudson." "Okay." Kate is a caretaker for the dying. To an old black man who's lying in a hospital bed, she reads a passage from *Treasure Island* that's been edited to the edge of incomprehensibility:

> I lost no time, of course, in telling my mother all that I knew, and we saw ourselves at once in a difficult and dangerous position. Something must speedily be resolved upon, and it occurred to us at last to go forth together and seek help in the neighbouring hamlet. No sooner said than done. Bare-headed as we were, we ran out at once in the gathering evening and the frosty fog. The hamlet lay not many hundred yards away, though out of view, on the other side of the next cove; and what greatly encouraged me, it was in an opposite direction from that whence the blind man had made his appearance. [Close-up to the old man's glazed-over eyes.] And I shall never forget how much I was cheered to see the yellow shine in doors and windows; but that, as it proved, was the best of the help we were likely to get in that quarter. For—you would have thought men would have been ashamed of themselves—no soul would consent to return with us to the …

When the old man's eyes stare off into nothingness and close, Kate takes his pulse and says, "Sorry, Mr. Talcott's gone." Kate's supervisor tells her to throw away Mr. Talcott's stuff, but inside the dumpster are several file boxes full of other dead people's stuff, so Kate opens Mr. Talcott's box and takes a key ring shaped like a guitar that reads LIVE FAST DIE YOUNG. She puts her keys on it then drives to her new job as a private nurse in the New Orleans swamps. The swamps are dreamlike and frightening, and in the attic of her new house, Kate unlocks a hoodoo room full of bottles with all sorts of squirmy herbs and organs floating inside them. Kate's new employer Gena Rowlands is secretly an ancient hoodoo mistress. Gena steals a lock of Kate's hair in order to perform a soul switching ceremony so she can appropriate Kate's young dewy body as her own. We know Kate is really Gena when she lights up one of Gena's long brown cigarettes. New text, old soul. After viewing the movie, the abridged version of *Treasure Island*, vague as a fortune teller's warning, perfectly foreshadows Kate's plight. We turn off *The Skeleton Key* and land on *Bride of Chucky*. Jennifer Tilly, trashier than ever, stitches the smashed killer doll back together, places him in the center of a yellow pentagram that's positioned in the center of a circle, and reads out loud from *Voodoo for Dummies*. With her deep Kewpie doll voice and with her big breasts about to tumble out of her corset, Jennifer invokes Chucky back to life. Then Chucky sticks Jennifer's soul into a bride doll and the rest of the film involves Jennifer and Chucky's attempts to perform a soul switching ceremony so they can appropriate the young dewy bodies of a pair of high school lovers as their own. Two hoodoo soul-switching plots back to back, what are the odds? I'm tired and it's late and it frightens me how *Bride of Chucky* rhymes with *The Skeleton Key* which rhymes with so much about my experience with Kathy—Kathy's rewriting of *Treasure Island* in *Pussy King of the Pirates*, hoodoo bottles, digging through boxes of a dead person's stuff, taking a charm. How LIVE FAST DIE YOUNG on Mr. Talcott's guitar eerily echoes TOO FAST TO LIVE, TOO YOUNG TO DIE on Kathy's Gaultier dress.

Burroughs said that cut-ups predict the future. But it's not just cut-ups. Intense writing creates a vortex and the world opens to be read. It's not about meaning, it's about accident, pattern, connection. That night I dream of Kathy's writing. When I wake up all that remains is "words are like flames" and I think of the room full of candles in both hoodoo conjurings. Also in

my head is, "words are like sand," and I think of the brick dust
Kate Hudson sprinkles along a doorway to keep out those who
would harm her.

> Acker: *Are your books in any way methods for altering perception?*
> William Burroughs: *As far as they can be.*
> Acker: *How far do you think literature can work in that area?*
> Burroughs: *Any pain and consequence, you can read. In other words,*
> *there's a story in it—not a message. Not a message, but a story.*

More of the dream comes back to me. Kevin and I are at our
20th anniversary party and we're running through a parking lot
dressed as a bride and groom. I got my dress at the Goodwill for
$20—or at least I think I did for in the dream I can't quite
remember—and there's a car in the parking lot full of the band
who was just playing elsewhere in the restaurant and they're
going to their next gig, at a tacky chain restaurant and they're
rationalizing it's a quality chain, but I know it's Chucky Cheese.
Acker: *Come and make love to me. One kiss from your lips and all
the animals will again appear.* I google "Kathy Acker flames sand,"
and the first hit is an article I wrote for the NYFA *Quarterly*—the
section where we're transferring Kathy's ashes. Bellamy: *FLAMES
crackled in the fireplace, throwing shadows across the walls and
ceiling, and across the tense faces of the 17 of us present.* Bellamy:
*Afterwards, I kept thinking about Kathy's ashes, their gritty mate-
riality, the way they fell out of our hands and into the urn, how ashes
both fill up and conform to the surround. I connected this with
Acker's writing. Having no center, her writing could infiltrate other
avatars, other texts—from Charlotte Brontë to Rimbaud to George
Bush Senior to scenes from the soaps she sometimes watched while
working on her novels. Like SANDs through the hourglass, so are the
days of our lives.* My thumb slips on the keyboard and iTunes
begins playing "Frederick." Patti Smith: *all of the power that burns*

in the flame. In her essay "Painful Bodies: Kathy Acker's Last Texts," Nicole Cooley describes a reading Kathy gave in March 1997, just six months before she died: *Her performance was nothing short of riveting. On stage, in the dark, dressed in white, Acker read from "Eurydice in the Underworld." Her voice was low, her body completely still, the audience enthralled.* As so often, Kathy's outfit seems intrinsic to the experience. A slash of white in the darkness, she becomes an angel, Eurydice the death angel, her completely still body bleached in the darkness like a marble figure perched atop a tomb. When we transferred her ashes to the urn, ashy dust poofed into the air. All of us must have breathed it in. Video clip of Kathy from the '80s. She's sitting in a chair, swimming in an oversized black leather jacket with thick white stripes on the biceps. A black leather bandana is wrapped about her head, and her cropped hair has been dyed the same reddish brown as her leopard spotted pants. She plays with a huge rectangular earring as she says: *We have to be allowed to talk about things. We have to talk about things as they are.* If I wrapped a swatch of the dress, the pharaoh ring, the spider charm in bag of red flannel and dressed it with virgin olive oil, what would my mojo bring to me? From what would it protect me?

11

JULY 4, 2011

for Pamela Lu

In the background fireworks boom and crackle, but tonight I'm housebound with a cold, searching for videos of the Casey Anthony trial. The judge cancelled today's holiday, and the jury is now deliberating on whether or not Casey murdered her almost-3-year-old daughter, Caylee. I spent the morning watching the prosecution's closing rebuttal, all two hours' worth. A talking head says the Anthony trial is the biggest national crime event since OJ Simpson. The number one news app for smart phones is "Casey Anthony Trial with LIVE STREAM, News, Videos, Audio, Documents and more," downloadable for ninety-nine cents. On this day of barbecues and sparklers, millions are hooked in, waiting for the verdict. Killing an innocent little girl is bad. It is murder. Killing murderers is not bad. It is justice. Killing the enemy is not bad. It saves our country. US Armed Forces planes and tanks and ships swoop in and blast the shit out of the space alien/nuclear waste-crazed monster/Nazis, and normalcy is restored. This is how I was raised. This is how all Americans were raised, except communists. Communists were bad. They collaborated with the enemy, they deserved the electric chair. I associate the 4th of July with the Revolutionary War or maybe the War of Independence. Are they the same thing? That war was good *no taxation without representation* even though it was fought over money. Is the 4th of July the day the war ended? I look it up online. It was the day the Declaration of Independence was signed. Maybe. *Historians have long disputed whether Congress actually signed the Declaration of Independence on July 4, even though Thomas Jefferson, John Adams, and Benjamin Franklin all later wrote that they had signed it on that day. Most historians have concluded that the Declaration was signed nearly a month after its adoption, on August 2, 1776, and not on July 4 as is commonly believed.* I wash my hair with Earth, one of the revolving five elements shampoos I use (the fifth element is Chi), Earth is brown, doesn't lather, and contains clay, it's like washing my hair with the mud Caylee was buried in. Earth smells spicy-fruity, not a fruit I recognize, a fruit from another world. Whether Casey Anthony is found innocent or guilty, we may never know what really happened. If crime weren't a mystery, who would watch it? Who would commit it? During Vietnam I learned to distrust the American government, I learned there were covert reasons for war that usually involved money, I learned that war could be bad. Did the Declaration of Independence signal the beginning or the end of the Revolutionary War? Answer: It marked the beginning. When war was declared in Iraq, I had my leg in a cast and hardly ever left my apartment, due to my ineptitude on crutches, utter lack of upper body strength, the three flights of stairs with only partial railings, and ensuing depression. On my birthday when I tried to hop up from the sidewalk to the front landing, I fell over backwards and just missed cracking my head open on a post. To fix lunch I sat on a desk chair and wheeled myself across the kitchen floor. Overhead the incessant roar of helicopters as protesting poet-friends were arrested at Civic Center, a few blocks from my apartment. I felt like a cripple in a warzone. Minus the danger. A rightwing neo-Confederate declares that the Civil War wasn't about slavery, it was about property rights. Of course the big between-the-liner is that slaves were property, asshole. Everybody knows the war in Iraq is fucked—right? The Oil War, etc. But the war feels so remote, like an abstraction theory-heads debate, thanks to government policy that bans media images of Iraq bloodshed. Media images of war casualties are now bad, no gruesome Vietnam-era photos of mangled corpses, no body bags lumpy with dead GIs, no Vietcong's face whooshed to the side with a bullet's impact. Our craving for visuals remains, grows intense, we search the back pages of Google Images, eager to consume. Caylee Anthony's duct-taped skull pokes from swampy ground, bones gnawed by animals, her filthy matted hair on a muslin-colored cloth, beside it a white gloved hand holds a vivid sky blue ruler of some sort. This afternoon, in a book by my Buddhist ex, I read that his uncle was killed in a head-on collision. He told me the same story, except it was his mother, not his uncle, who died in a car crash. Where does the truth in violence lie? Perhaps the truth in violence is always a lie. My daughter is not dumped in a swamp, my daughter is at Disney World with a nanny named Zanny, having the time of her life. The Declaration of Independence originally contained an anti-slavery clause ... *cruel War against human Nature itself, violating its most Sacred Right of Life & Liberty in the Persons of a distant People who never offended him, captivating & carrying them into Slavery in another Hemisphere, or to incur miserable death in their Transportation thither ... this execrable Commerce, determining to keep open a market where* MEN *should be bought & sold ...* but this clause was deleted before the document was presented to Congress. The language of the Declaration of Independence is less Pleasant and more Active than everyday English, a fact which may be explained by the document's revolutionary purposes, and by its contents. The Declaration of Independence is more abstract than everyday English (lower in concrete Imagery), probably as a result of its inclusion of statements of abstract principle. Knowing that "independence" didn't include them, thousands of African slaves escaped from Southern states and fought with the British against the colonists. Through a densely wooded area littered with fragments of beer bottles and signs for an old day care, a path leads to the child's remains, barely discernible through the flowering vegetation. Near a rotting log, they've been there so long that vines are entwined with the bone. The skull is embedded in debris up to the level of the eye sockets. In my sore-throated feverish state the horror of these images doesn't penetrate, it scatters like beads of perspiration along the surface of my skin. But back in October, 2001, a month after the attack on the World Trade Center, when the Blue Angels came to San Francisco, I cowered in terror at the sound of jets zooming overhead. <u>9/11 made me realize that images could take up residence in my neighborhood, that images could get me.</u> On WikiLeaks I watch a 2007 video shot from a US Apache helicopter gunship in Iraq as the soldiers mistake Reuters Wire Service reporters and their cameras for terrorists brandishing AK-47s. A cross hatch hovers over the men on the ground, a line of ever-changing digital numbers at the top of the screen. The cross hatch glides over the tops of buildings, circles around until all eight men on the ground are unprotected, and the gunships open fire. Rat-tat-tat—delay—then dust balls explode on the ground, men crouch run collapse are buried in dust. On the soundtrack we hear, "Keep shooting, keep shooting." When the dust clears we hear, "Look at those dead bastards." "Nice." "Good shooting." This is the glee of boys playing a videogame, and it is hard even for me, sitting up in bed, having read about the incident beforehand, to see these scampering figures as flesh and blood men, their limbs and guts exploding in the grainy distance. One man survives and is crawling along the ground. A soldier shouts into the helicopter's mike, "Pick up a gun, pick up a gun," so he can shoot him again. Two more civilians arrive in a van and pick up the wounded man. The helicopter gunman begs, "Let us shoot, let us shoot." Permission is granted rat-tat-tat I cough and blow my nose they all die. When he hears there are two little girls in the van who are seriously wounded, one helicopter gunner quips, "Well, it's their fault for bringing their kids into a battle," and the gunner in the other ship quickly replies, "That's right." On YouTube, 11,622,780 people have watched this clip and been appalled by the GIs' callousness. *that fucking jock dick amercan pilot probably thinks he's a hero, the sick-fuck is actually the exact steroeotypical triger happy death loving american guy i thought didnt really exist that much.* Dust and sun and boxy buildings—Iraq is so stark compared to the lushness of Vietnam, orange clouds of napalm rising from opulent greenery. Nick Ut's Pulitzer Prize winning photograph of a 9-year-old girl burned by a napalm bomb, running naked down the street, arms stretched out at her sides like wings, her mouth a huge hole of screams, armed Americans walking behind her. Ut took the girl to the hospital before turning in the film. My Vietnam vet boyfriend wasn't drafted like all the other guys I knew who were sent there. He joined. "I felt great," he said. "In the Army I was in the best shape ever in my life." He frequented Vietnamese whorehouses, where he said women were truly treated as objects. One time somebody's legs got blown off—I seem to remember it was a woman, but maybe not—and the helicopter pilot didn't want to take "her" to the hospital because he didn't want to get the helicopter dirty, and my boyfriend pointed his M-16 at the guy and forced him to fly. When he got out of the Army, my boyfriend threw his purple heart in a bonfire at an anti-Vietnam protest. Movies about Iraq are not profitable, and thus I assume Iraq vets are not as sexy as Vietnam vets *Jon Voight Christopher Walken.* My Vietnam vet boyfriend was very sexy, and he fucked with an abandon I have not experienced before or since, I was addicted to fucking him, would have done anything to get more of it, so in a way I relate to party-crazed Casey Anthony. I killed my unborn baby so it would not interfere with my lifestyle. Casey Anthony, age 25, is the most hated woman in America. My Vietnam vet boyfriend smoked grass, dropped acid, snorted coke, drank like a fish, and was predictably messed up. Even though I hadn't done drugs in years, I did drugs with him. In comparison to everyday English, the Declaration of Independence is a linguistically complex document because it includes a rather high proportion of rare words (15% in comparison to the norm of 10%), relatively long words (closer to 5 rather than the norm of 4 letters long), and extremely long sentences (40 words long as compared to adult everyday English norms of 15–20 words long). In my grad fiction workshop two Iraq vets sit beside each other, a man and a woman. The woman is writing about her sex life in the Army, beginning with the recruiter who helped her lose the weight necessary to be inducted. He was a liar, all recruiters are liars she jokes with the male vet. They call the government "Uncle Sam," just like my World War II vet father did. Uncle Sam—as if the US military-industrial complex were a grumpy family member that maybe drinks too much at holidays and embarrasses everybody, but you gotta love him nevertheless. The vets point out that I've scheduled class on Veterans Day, a school holiday. I'm flabbergasted, as I checked the academic calendar and don't know how I missed that, and now I'll have to revise an already too-tight syllabus. I try to make a joke of it. "Oh, Veterans Day," I say, "it's one of those holidays that nobody knows what it's for." The vets look shocked, and the female vet says sternly, "That's insulting." The thought of her in Iraq, of any woman in Iraq, makes me cringe, all that softness in such a hard place, like an egg yolk rolling through a field of blades. "I'm sorry," I say. "That came out wrong." But the vets glare at me. Guilty Dodie. My Vietnam vet boyfriend kept a plastic toy M-16 leaning against the wall beside his bed. He liked to rat-tat-tat it when he was drunk. One night he hit me in the face so hard I learned it's not just a cartoon thing—you really do see stars. Afterwards he said I deserved it. On YouTube Marvin Gaye sings "The Star Spangled Banner" at the 1983 NBA All Star Game. Stripping the song of bombast, he delivers it with the sweetness and intimacy of a love song, drawing out each velvet syllable as if he has all the time in the world. But this is his final public performance, in a little over a year he will be shot to death by his father. Accompanied by a drum machine, in gray suit and tie, he stands very still. Occasionally he rolls his head, licks his lips, clenches his fists or opens his hands, his gestures so minimal, we cling to every understated twitch. For "land of the free" he bends his knees, arches his back slightly, raises his fists, broadens his smile, getting across all the nuances of a black man up there singing about freedom—a mixture of pride and what a joke. Stars bursting off his aviator sunglasses, Marvin Gaye has made the "National Anthem" sexy and cool. The sensuality of his rendition is perverse, it's like he's fucking with rah-rah patriotism big time, like he's laying bare the libidinal pleasures of group consciousness. The crowd claps and cheers. By the end I find my fuzzy-brained sweaty self ridiculously smiling, feel giggly, stoned. I slurp the Thai coconut soup Kevin picked up for me, and click replay again and again. The front of the skull has duct tape on it. Around it is an off white canvas bag, black plastic bags, a red Disney bag and a white blanket so worn it looks like a towel. Forensic experts testify that Casey's car trunk stank of human decomposition. But my 11-inch MacBook Air emits no little girl stench. On the far side of its aluminum glass and plastic unibody, the real is remote as from a cockpit. There is no discernible difference between fiction and reality on a flatscreen—some movies even mimic the roughness of live video feed to amp up the aura of the real—and I often find fiction more satisfying because I get to see more—not all these frustrating gaps and contradictions. On Turner Classic Movies, Groucho Marx snarls, "I'm sick of messages from the front. Don't we ever get messages from the side?" A giant missile slowly sails through an open window, across the room, and out through a wall, creating a giant irregular hole. The Marx Brothers are soldiers ogling a woman whose house is being bombed. From scene to scene Groucho's uniform changes, from WWI to Confederate to Union Civil War to Davy Crockett's coonskin cap to Boy Scout Scoutmaster, as if he were the spirit of militarism past and present. In a long shot the roof is blasted to pieces, and there's a constant assault of bullets, but the Marx Brothers are impervious, except for their hats. Groucho's 18-inch tall British Palace Guard bearskin cap gets blown off, and Harpo's Napoleonic bicorn spins on his head like those twirly foil flowers on sticks I blew on as a child imagining myself a puffy-cheeked wind goddess. A guilty verdict will give us something to chew over for a day or two. But with not guilty there is no recourse—and therefore, grievance, anguish and recriminations will never end. After we broke up, my Vietnam vet boyfriend became a staff photographer for *Guns & Ammo*. I stand at my kitchen window searching for dandelion-head bursts of fireworks over distant rooftops, I've seen them in previous years, but no visual appears over the boom boom boom audio track of tonight's moment. When the enemy storms the house, Zeppo lifts up the helmet of each one, and Harpo conks him on the head with a brick. They trap the enemy commander's head in the door and hurl fruit at him until he begs to surrender. The ogled woman shouts, "Victory is ours!" and in a high cloying voice sings "Hail, hail Freedonia." The Marx Brothers pummel her with the remaining fruit. Even though he refused to apologize for knocking me across the room, my Vietnam vet boyfriend wanted to continue as friends. I said no. But, had the opportunity arisen, I probably would have fucked him again. Kevin says, "You *do* know someone who went to Iraq— Brendan, my nephew, which makes him your nephew too,

Dodie." Brendan was a troubled teen, and all the family agrees that the Marines and the Gulf turned him into a responsible man, got his life back on track, just like the recruiters promise. I worried the insulted vets in my fiction workshop would complain to the chair about me, but apparently they didn't. In the 1990s, *Spy* magazine convinced several members of Congress to issue statements condemning the "ethnic cleansing in Freedonia," without their realizing that Freedonia was a fictional country. On his website my Vietnam vet boyfriend writes, "Please don't ask me what war is like. I can't tell you. If I could truly relate the experience I would be the greatest artist of all time. I know of no one who has done it. If they had, there would be no war." Because of its linguistic complexity, the average reader would find the Declaration of Independence more difficult to read than a novel or newspaper report.

12

THE BEATING OF OUR HEARTS

1

The 2012 pro-Obama "Wake the Fuck Up" video opens with a long shot of a cozy hamlet with all the lights turned out. In voiceover Samuel L. Jackson informs us that though the villagers are currently "snuggled up in their sheets ... four years before they were out in the streets." The only one who knows what's at stake is little Susie, who's sitting up too worried to sleep. Romney's platform scares her to death. She can't figure out why her family is so passive when in the previous election they all worked together for Obama. "We canvassed and phone-banked with passion and pluck." She goes into the living room where her parents are collapsed on the couch, zonked out before the TV. When Susie reminds them that the election is coming up, her dad replies, "We're tired right now, hun, go back to your room." Samuel Jackson beams into the living room, blocking the TV, and intones, "An out of touch millionaire has just declared war on schools, the environment, unions, fair pay." When Susie's brother says he has no time for campaigning, and besides, "all politicians are the same," Samuel Jackson twirls him around in his desk chair and screeches, "They're all the same? Big brother, please!" Jackson reminds him of all the good stuff Obama did that

Romney would eradicate (including student loan overhaul), and urges him to Wake the Fuck Up. Next we find Susie's sister and her friend excitedly playing on Facebook. As Susie confiscates their laptop, Jackson reminisces about how for the last election the girls held bake sales for Obama. Jackson brings up threats to planned parenthood and shouts at them through a megaphone with such force their hair blows backwards, "Get out there and sell some cakes and cookies—now!" On to the grandparents, who are engaged in enthusiastic sex. Jackson, lying in bed beside them, hidden by grandpa's huge belly, pops up and warns them about threats to Medicare. "You can sleep when you're dead," he says. "Right now, wake the fuck up." Finally, Susie sticks her head out the window and shrieks "wake the fuck up," and all the lights in the sleeping homes turn on, blink blink blink, until the hamlet is blazing.

Though "Wake the Fuck Up" trumpets threats imposed by Romney's agenda, it suggests that the real enemy is our own complacency, that bourgeois blankness that immobilizes us. It's not that we're incapable of movement; it's that we've lost the will to move. In a crisis—a fire, a deadline, an accident, an attack— we not only shoot up off our asses, we shove autos over our heads. Rightwing "I don't care what those heathen evolutionists say—according to my pastor's interpretation of Genesis, the world is no older than 6,000 years and dinosaurs are fake— they're dragon bones buried by the Jews to fool us" conspiracy theorists are plenty motivated, toiling for their cause with the single-minded determination of zombies. The aim of Jackson's video, like all protest media, is to fire up our synapses, our juices, to slap indolent liberals into awareness of the state of emergency that's not down the road or in the future, but right now, right here. DANGER! DANGER!

Susie's shouting out the window reminds me of Susan Birchenough's poem, "Pussy Love":

> there's a saying
> in my village
> when a pussy screams
> the world wakes up

I found "Pussy Love" in the recent poetry anthology *Catechism* (2012). *Catechism*, a collection of (mostly) UK poets, is a tribute to the members of the Russian feminist punk-rock collective Pussy Riot who were sentenced to two years in prison after performing "Punk Prayer—Mother of God, Chase Putin Away!" in a Moscow cathedral. Wearing contrasting candy-colored tights, sleeveless shifts, and balaclavas, the young women bounce up and down shouting, "Shit, shit, shit, the Lord's shit." Behind them the church's gilded sanctuary gleams, as if in competition with Pussy Riot's gaudy rage. In the forward to *Catechism*, editors Mark Burnhope, Sarah Crewe, and Sophie Mayer describe the project as "an offertory for three women whose actions have woken up the need for change, in not just their own authoritarian state, but also in how we address gender politics and all forms of oppression in our own society." Mayer emailed me, "*Catechism* has been such an incredible and exciting project: we couldn't believe it when potential contributors started tweeting from all over the country naming themselves feminist poets. Unheard of in the UK for decades." I love the inclusivity here—one is a feminist when one claims the title—the resultant wide rainbow of styles and aesthetics is inspiring.

In addition to the print and eBook editions, dozens of videos of contributing poets reading their work pop up on YouTube. Poetry will never compete with action stars—Jackson's video received over a million views; Birchenough's received ten. The commitment is what matters. As poet George Szirtes reminds us in his introduction to *Catechism*, "An anthology of poems dedicated to a political purpose is not so much an anthology of poems as a political act in poetic form." Of course this argument has been made before, but it's taken me a long time to believe it—it's like I've had a vision, and I see so clearly: all art is political. You either reinscribe dominant cultural values or you resist them. There's no escaping that. The commitment to resistance is beautiful. In their videos the *Catechism* poets exude a vibrancy that most poor suckers would kill for.

For her clip, Francesca Lisette reads a collaboration she wrote with poet Connie Scozzaro, racking up nearly 115 views. The Lisette/Scozzaro piece collages together material from numerous sources, including semi-illiterate YouTube comments on Pussy Riot's cathedral performance, American congressman Todd Akin's statement about "legitimate rape," and a passage from Lea Vergine's *Body Art and Performance*. In a deep gruff tone, Lisette begins, "Feminism … so stupid. What did they think? Poutine or not, this is not how you do to make change. Being half naked outside and thinking this is freedom … Feminism made women in occident objects. That's what they are. Stupid objects. Act with you brain, not your body." Lisette then switches to a flat American accent and reads a Oulipian spoof of Akin's comments. Here's what Akin actually said: "First of all, from what I understand from doctors, that's really rare. If it's a legitimate rape, the female body has ways to try to shut that whole thing down." Here's what Lisette reads: "It seems to me, from what I understand from doctorates, that's really rare. If it's a legitimate rapid, the feminist bodyguard has wayfarers to send that whole thingamabob down-and-out." Later on, Akin's comments get perverted even further. "It seems to me, from what I understand from documentaries, that's really rare. If it's a legitimate rapid, the ferment boiler has weans to try to sickbed that whole thistle dowse." The Lisette/Scozzaro parody of Akin's idiocy is witty as hell, but the anger behind it bristles.

I don't know if it will stick, but recent rightwing attacks on reproductive rights have reinvigorated feminist impulses in the States. Feminism has been out of fashion with many younger women, who consider themselves strong, sexually in charge, competitive. For them, feminism is archaic, the provenance of their grandmothers. But when birth control, let alone abortion, is under attack, the struggles of second wave feminists suddenly have resonance. Any time a woman grows up to feel powerful it's a marvelous thing—but no matter how powerful a woman may be, she cannot survive by self determination alone. Autonomy is a seductive myth. In Wayne Burrows' contribution to *Catechism*, "Ne (No)," a poem based on a 1969 protest song by banned Czech singer Marta Kubišová, the speaker imagines building "a house on the deepest ocean's floor" or a castle in the clouds, but she realizes there is no escaping the long arm of the State:

> But I'd find the sea lanes are guarded by warships,
> carrying tons and kilos of bullets and bombs.
> If I went under, deeper, submarines would plunge
> and soon find my home in the water-caves.
> In the sky are airplanes and satellites, as you know—
> is there anywhere, then, where I might go?

The poem is heartbreaking. Like the speaker of "Ne (No)," like little Susie's family, we all long for a safe harbor where we can snuggle up, all insular and snoozy. But, whether we accept it or not, we're all part of a larger collective; we're all battered about by big, scary forces, be it massive storms caused by global warming, or biologically-challenged misogynists. During this past election, the internet was flooded with campaign videos by female celebrities aimed at inciting women to vote for progressive candidates. Scarlett Johansson: "If you think this election won't affect you and your life, think again." Eva Longoria: "Trying to force women to undergo invasive ultrasounds." Cher: "We need you to come together, to protect women's rights." Kathy Griffin: "This is Cher, bitches, do what she says." Lena Dunham: "You don't want to do it with a guy who says, 'Oh hey I'm at the library studying,' when really he's out not signing the Lilly Ledbetter Act, who thinks gay people should never have beautiful complicated weddings like the kind we see on Bravo or TLC all the time." Sarah Silverman: "Lawmakers are trying to fuck you in your assholes." Lesley Gore: "You don't own me." No longer can we take anything—even a no-brainer like birth control—for granted. In such a precarious atmosphere, women are reconsidering: maybe, just maybe, there's more to feminist activism besides frumpy losers whining about their injustices. When the pussy screams, the world wakes up.

The protest poster—and in this internet age, I include viral media such as memes and videos—is an intimate gesture. GIRLS ARE POWERFUL—BLACK WOMEN WILL NOT BE INTIMIDATED—THE STATE & SEXIST ADVERTISING CAUSE ILLNESS DON'T LET THESE MEN INVADE YOUR HOMES. The political poster reaches beyond our intellectual understanding, our sophistication, and sidles up to our vulnerability: people are hurting, bad things are being done. DON'T LET RACISM DIVIDE US—SO LONG AS WOMEN ARE NOT FREE PEOPLE ARE NOT FREE—SOLIDARITY WITH WOMENS STRUGGLES ALLOVER THE WORLD—SAVE THE CHILDREN. Will a poster proclaiming SAVE THE CHILDREN actually save anybody? The pessimist in me says probably not. The realist says it doesn't matter. CAPITALISM ALSO DEPENDS ON DOMESTIC LABOUR—A WOMAN'S

WORK IS NEVER DONE—EQUAL PAY NOW—ALONE WE ARE POWER-
LESS … TOGETHER WE ARE STRONG. The protest poster shames
us out of our comfortable narcissism. We should know better.
The protest poster is a call to awaken, to expand awareness, to
get informed, engaged, stand up, resist, fight, refuse, strike.
DON'T LET THEM KEEP US BOTTLED UP—DON'T BREAK DOWN/
BREAK OUT—WOMEN HOLD UP HALF THE SKY—UNDERNEATH
EVERY WOMAN'S 'CURVE' LIES A MUSCLE! In the urgency of a
protest poster there's no room for pretence or subtlety. Out of
the darkness, the poster flashes a moment of clarity. WE DEMAND
WE DEMAND WE DEMAND WE DEMAND.

We good liberals didn't believe that Reagan could get elected. But
he did. We didn't believe that George Bush could get elected. But
he did. In fact, two of them did. The popularity of Romney's
extremism scared the shit out of us, but the idiocy of his campaign
fertilized all kinds of parody. The Romney-related memes that
raged across Facebook and Twitter made the unbearable—not
bearable, but a teeny bit less unbearable. Take Eastwooding. At
the Republican National Convention, iconic sharpshooter Clint
Eastwood pointed to an empty chair and pretended an invisible
Obama was sitting in it. "And I think it's that time," he told the
chair. "And I think if you just step aside and Mr. Romney can
kind of take over. You can maybe still use a plane. Though maybe
a smaller one. Not that big gas guzzler you are going around to
colleges and talking about student loans and stuff like that."
Instantly the term "Eastwooding" was born, and the internet was
flooded with images of celebrities, pets, ordinary people, children,
disembodied hands, and toy figures pointing to empty chairs.
There was even an image of a Van Gogh chair labeled "Eastwooding in Art History." I looked at dozens of Eastwooding
images, and when I ran out of images I googled for more and
more, my giggles swelling into belly laughs, and as my throat

opened and these uncontrollable cackles burst forth, I experienced a wonderful release. No longer did I feel alone in my fear, for the inventiveness and generosity of the human spirit comforted me, our urge to create for the sheer pleasure of it.

2

In July, 2012, I read with Francesca Lisette at Woolsey, a series curated by Paul Ebenkamp and Andrew Kenower at their apartment on Woolsey Street in Berkeley. With the plummeting of arts funding and the general disappearance of public space, salon-style events ("house readings") are taken very seriously in the Bay Area; performing at one can garner more kudos than at a public venue. House readings frequently take place on the weekend and are just as devoted to partying as to poetizing. Though all ages are welcome, most who attend are in their 20s or 30s. When the reading begins the party slams to a halt and attention is rapt. The atmosphere may be casual—those not lucky enough to snag a seat on a couch are crammed together on the floor, some are sprawled across a mattress that somebody—who knows who—actually sleeps on, but this audience knows poetry, and they listen with razorlike precision. At house events I love to share fresh work, writing I have frantically edited until an hour beforehand, for it is at such a reading that my work feels most vital, leaping off the page and into these others who "get" me. At such readings, whether I'm performer or audience, I feel like a beat in a larger matrix of communal creativity. And I, who am *so* not a group person, enjoy this. At Woolsey, Francesca read a range of her writing, beginning with a Cambridge-inflected, intellectually rigorous, ironic style. These poems were solidly constructed, impressive—but the later work, which Francesca felt understandably insecure about, was full of risks, in both form and content—it turned angry and vulgar and outrageous, heckling distressing political inanities. It was a writing bursting its seams, and she blew the room away. When the applause ended, the party picked up again, full swing.

Many of the regulars at the party are dedicated participants in the Occupy Oakland movement. These folks have been battered and tear-gassed and locked up. In a sister demonstration at UC Berkeley, police thugs clubbed former US poet laureate Robert Hass, after throwing his wife, poet Brenda Hillman, to the ground. "Particularly shocking to me," wrote Hass in *The New York Times*, "was that they assaulted both the young men and the young women with the same indiscriminate force. If the students turned away, they pounded their ribs. If they turned further away to escape, they hit them on their spines." In their riot gear the cops, like so many Darth Vaders, dragged a Wordsworth scholar across the grass by her hair. Despite escalating police brutality, the Occupy poets kept going back, day after day. They're hero poets. The Occupy movement has had a profound effect on San Francisco Bay Area experimental writing, fostering an activism that leaves behind panel discussions and moves out into the streets, and an aesthetics that assumes, in the words of Juliana Spahr and Joshua Clover, "that poetry has a role to play in the larger political and intellectual sphere of contemporary culture, and that any poetry which subtracts itself from such engagements is no longer of interest."

In his poem "We Do the Polis in Different Voices," Oakland poet David Buuck explores how political engagement has engendered new forms of community and writing:

The improbable
trembles

in each arched
body

what are
the forms

we'd like
to live in

From I to
we is an other

zoned outside
coterie comforts

the forms
drop away

and new ones
rise up

In blurring the distinction between polis and poetry, Buuck is
suggesting that shifts in social relations catalyze shifts in literary
form, that activism could become lived poetry.

Some East Bay poets work for Food Not Bombs, an organization
that "recovers and shares free vegan or vegetarian food with the
public without restriction in over 1,000 cities around the world
to protest war, poverty and the destruction of the environment."
Food Not Bombs, among other things, salvages food that
restaurants would normally discard and redistributes it to poor
people. They also helped feed the Occupy Oakland demonstra-
tions. In the darkened house on Woolsey Street, after Francesca
and I finished reading, this Food Not Bombs guy came walking
in with a huge stack of pizzas rescued from Cheese Board Bakery

of Berkeley's "Gourmet Ghetto." East Bayers love Cheese Board pizza. Here's an excerpt from the flood of rave Yelp reviews: "If Cheeseboard was a man, he would be quality, unique, dynamic, generous, warm, loving, healthy, creative, vegetarian, and make you feel like you were the queen of the world." The pizzas ranged from first quality to scorched. While I carefully chose the most pristine piece I could find, the woman standing beside—one of the more hardcore of the Occupy Oakland poets, those who call one another "comrade"—grabbed a slice with the crust burnt totally black, and chomped into it. As I cringed, she took another big healthy bite, and I thought—this must be an affirmation of her comrade-ness. A true comrade is not bourgeois picky about what she eats; when she dumpster dives she doesn't waste activist energy critiquing the bounty.

Suddenly the Tommy James & the Shondell's 1967 hit "I Think We're Alone Now" blasted through the superb sound system—on vinyl, of course, the original 45. In response, a group of poets hurled selves across the living room and began a spontaneous freeform dance, writhing and flailing together in a frenzy. Lindsey Boldt, Sara Wintz, David Brazil, Steve Orth, Sara Larsen, among others, aped dramatic Modern Dance moves, confronting and spinning one another in Bob Fosse meets apache meets punk maneuvers that were at once stagy, awkward, and sexy. All conversation stopped. Those of us who weren't dancing, witnessed. Even though the song is only two minutes and thirteen seconds long, the performance seemed to go on forever. When you step into a moment like this, its energy so dense it ricochets off the walls, time buckles and nothing exists but the present. Poet dancers and poet audience fuse like blobby masses seen beneath a microscope, whose cell walls open and they spit their squishy guts into one another. Tommy James sings, "The beating of our hearts is the only sound," and the momentarily isolated base line, like a heart beating, activates the lush materiality of the "now." If only things were still that simple. In our transition from analogue to digital, psychological fragmentation has sky-rocketed. Slaves to our media delivery devices, we are ever available to this vague, demanding elsewhere, and our ability to experience the "now" is dissolving. People are desperate to get it back, to experience this exotic thing, the present moment. Kinky sex, amusement parks, $$$ weekends with Pema Chodron, extreme sports, being thwacked in the ribs with a billy club all invite us to step away from the anemic glow of our monitors and into sunlight and disco balls. Even though I can't get myself to dance with the Occupy poets, just watching them I feel profoundly alive. As the song fades, David and Steve throw themselves on the ground and convulse. Applause. I look over at Francesca standing in the doorway, glass of wine in hand, lips pursed, eyes locked on the dancers, absorbing.

Throughout "We Do the Polis in Different Voices," David Buuck observes how the intensity of political intervention alters the participants' experience of time:

> Of space-time
> compressing
>
> momentum
> without target
>
> running not
> yet amok
>
> inside the tent-
> ative present

And later in the poem:

the play-
ing field

opens ops
for now-time

Though Buuck's language is abstract and flat here—surprisingly
so, compared to the libidinal excess of other recent work—the
poem vividly evokes the tense readiness of public action, its power
to pull participants out of rambling, distracted individuality into
focused collective purpose. Buuck's short lines hug the left hand
margin, burrowing a tunnel down the page. Attention is so
focused on what's directly in front of it, multi-syllabic words
such as tent-ative and play-ing cannot be contained in a single
line, but need to be broken into smaller components. The "tent"
of tentative holds both bodies and awareness. I imagine an
observer who longs to get so close to the outside, he won't be
satisfied until he licks his eyeball against it like a tongue.

Circled by cops in riot gear, the "tent" of both sentience and
encampment is endangered. This sense of endangerment is
everywhere in "I Think We're Alone Now." Throughout the
song, the insularity the "we" longs for remains conditional, never
progressing from I *think* we're alone to we *are* alone. With the
ubiquity of surveillance systems—way back in 2007 Fox News
reported that in England there was one security camera for every
14 people, and that the average big city resident in the States was
photographed 75 times a day—none of us can ever be sure of
being alone. It's poignant that this song in particular would
inspire the Occupy Poets for these writers, committed as they are
to collective action, know that aloneness is a dream, a fragile
dream that wavers between anarchist fantasy and capitalist nightmare. The We of "I Think We're Alone Now" is so ambiguous, it

could be anybody on the run. Because of the youth of the band and the pop song's intended teen audience, we assume the We is a couple of young lovers hiding from parental eyes—and it is the hormonal frenzy of disenfranchised youth that the Oakland poets were parodying in their wink-wink PoMo tarantella. But what do we really know about the song's We? They're called children and told to behave by an unidentified Authoritarian Eye. Because the We is misunderstood, they're running fast, trying to get away, to find cover under darkness. They hold hands, one of them puts their arms around the other, and they fall to the ground. Their hearts are audibly beating. They're hiding because something bad would happen if the Authoritarian Eye discovered something about them. With the slightest shift in angle, the We could be despairing victims from the world of "Ne (No)," fleeing an oppressive regime. Off the dance floor, of course, the Occupy poets do not flee. Through direct political action they dig in their heels and shout, "No more!"

"I Think We're Alone Now" could easily be reclaimed as an anthem for revolutionaries on the run. This interpretation is realized in the video *Nazi Zombies: I Think We're Alone Now*, a fan-made short based on the *Call of Duty: Zombies* video game. Shot in stark black and white, the video opens with close-ups of overgrown nature. On the soundtrack a heart beats loudly. As a booted foot splashes into a pond, the heart melts away and "I Think We're Alone" begins, sung a capella in German, slowly and sweetly, like a ballad. The camera pulls back to reveal a motley crew of soldiers running through a woods. A mob of Nazi zombies appears and chases them. As our heroes fight the zombies, machine gun blasts and the boom of a grenade threaten to drown out the singing. All of this is in slow motion, and the soldiers' smiles are broad and manic, as if they were savoring every nuance of the battle. When the last zombie is killed, the soundtrack returns to the beating heart. Glorious aloneness—for the moment—has been restored. The beauty of zombie flicks is that there's no question who the enemy is—and who our community is. Our newly formed tribal bonds are unshakeable. The alive feel *really* alive— pure hearts pumping paramilitary blood—and those pussies who lobbied for gun control lie splayed and dead on the killing floor.

The commitment to radicalism, like a religious conversion, is not arrived at logically. It is caught—through a gesture, an image that strikes us to our core. The Occupy poets are so sexy. Who wouldn't want to join them? In high school, as media images of the civil rights movement were pumped into my rightwing, racist, Rust Belt living room, I swooned before the hotness of the protestors. So marvelously intense they were in their horn-rimmed glasses, suits, and sheath skirts. As they lifted their ALL MEN ARE CREATED EQUAL signs I gasped before the sweat circles under the armpits of their button-down shirts. Whenever I could seize control of the family television, I watched liberal talk shows, and late into the night I listened to a folk music radio station that introduced me to Pete Seeger and Bob Dylan. One of my friends' older brothers was in SDS. Around her neck, Vicky wore an IUD hanging from a chain. She sometimes accompanied her brother to protests in Chicago, and even though he stumbled with cerebral palsy, the police still beat him up. I was familiar with reasoned calls for social justice, but it was my lust for the protestors, imagining myself marching and sweating among them, IUD necklace bouncing against my breasts, that convinced me that all my parents stood for was bullshit.

3

Months later, at Kevin's Christmas Eve birthday party, I stand in a doorway with Andrew Kenower. Andrew's read an earlier version of this essay, and he says to me, "It wasn't Tommy James & the Shondells we danced to at Woolsey. It was Tiffany played at the wrong speed." "Tiffany!" I exclaim. "Yes, Tiffany. Tiffany slowed down sounds like a man." "Tiffany of the mall tour?" I ask all innocent, even though, being an over-researcher, I know all about Tiffany's *The Beautiful You: Celebrating The Good Life Shopping Mall Tour '87*. Andrew hangs his head and flashes an embarrassed smirk. "I know, it's terrible, but she was everywhere in the '80s when we were kids." Tiffany was only 15 when she recorded "I Think We're Alone Now." Before the mall tour, her debut album, *Tiffany*, wasn't going anywhere. While no singer had previously been marketed via malls, various corporations— Campbell Soup, Clairol, General Foods—had staged successful promotions in which they gave away free samples. During summer break from her Christian high school, Tiffany toured 10 malls across the US, doing three 20-minute sets a day, signing autographs at each show. Accompanied by backing tapes, wearing sparkled tennis shoes, oversized shoulder-padded jeans jacket, huge hoop earrings, giggling and pouting like a chipmunky Madonna, she sang to increasingly large and enthusiastic crowds of shoppers. Teenagers, wild over their free samples of Tiffany, called in requests for her songs to their local radio stations, and in a few weeks Tiffany flipped from pop flop to pop idol. Her album sold four million copies, and by September "I Think We're Alone Now" supplanted Michael Jackson's "Bad" as the number one single in the USA. In the music video for the song, Tiffany prances and lip-synchs before a crush of fans at Utah's Ogden City Mall. Escaping the shopping center, she finds Larry Clark's America waiting for her. She bops around beside a moving freight train, or ambles down a seedy street, people bumping into her. The camera lingers on the darkly shadowed riverbank beneath a wooden bridge then pans upward to reveal Tiffany crossing the bridge. Later she sits on a sandbank in the middle of the river waving her arms over her head. We get a flash of her in the side view mirror of a car she's hanging out of. She gyrates beside a small private airplane, dejectedly walks towards a black car parked at the side of a rural road, its doors open as if waiting to swallow her. If we look closely there's a shadowy guy slumped in the front seat, perhaps the same guy earlier in the video she sits beside, a hunky guy in a wife beater. Tiffany twirls her hair and peeks at him, her gaze sweeping the length of bulging arm, and a shock of desire crosses her face—the one instance in all four minutes and twenty-seven seconds that hints an interiority, an agency beyond her giddily consumerist packaging. The video suggests a disturbing double life, the chipper mall performer and this vulnerable, clueless nymphet for whom all roads lead to abduction. She sweeps her hand through her long teased shag and sings lyrics not in the original song, "Let me touch your heart beat, I can change your heart beat."

Standing in the doorway, Andrew says, "You and Buuck are so right about time." He tells me that during an encampment life is so intense, so condensed, what he went through in six hours while Occupying *love despair horror hope community and on and on,* would take six months to experience in regular life. The next day on YouTube he uploads "Tiffany—I Think We're Alone Now | Slowed and Throwed." In the notes section he writes, "Tiffany's producer found some old luudes in the break room. 45 go 33.3." It's still upbeat, but the bass is boomy, with sloppy reverb like a bouncing Slinky. This is a music of impulse and slippage, its tempo thick, as if the band were hopping through viscous air. Tiffany's pitch plummets and slurs; from her nubile lungs emerges a sluggish man, a drunk, a liar. She claims to be running fast, but nobody wading through this wall of jello is going very fast. I'm amazed that when I watched the poets dancing to this, I didn't notice anything strange going on. David Brazil: "Music played at the wrong speed," pausing to smile and savor, "is essential Woolsey." All the good comrades at Woolsey have experienced the altered temporality of Occupy … bending and folding to this fucked up version of "I Think We're Alone Now" they cast themselves into time warp … *six months' worth in six hours* … the *Nazi Zombies* video is also filmed in slo-mo … *the play-/ ing field // opens ops/ for now-time* … whether we fight zombies or capitalism, in the full height of our passion chronos caresses us, stretches out until it's ready to snap … *the beat-ing of our harrrrrtz* … Tiffany flips gender, she's all body, all perverse desire in a wife beater, the kind of guy who would throw open a car door for a confused teen idol.

I check out the other 45 videos Andrew has posted to YouTube, an eclectic mix of Occupy Oakland footage, poetry readings, and music—much of which has been "slowed and throwed." *This is what a baton to a video camera looks like (ultra slow)* is "a clip of an officer hitting my camera during the eviction of the Occupy-Cal encampment." The action is so decelerated the police fade in and out of readability. Beautiful abstract smears—yellow, magenta, lime green, Francis Bacon pink—morph poetically and then there's a spotlight of tense faces in riot gear, the crisp edge of a baton. Our vision is both blurred and forensic as shards of bodies leap into focus. But this is no Muybridge demystification, where frame by frame the horse's trot is stopped and caught, and the horse is going forward, forward. Here, legibility is always on the verge, within reach but never quite there, like the orgasm you've spent your entire life grunting for. Things change but chronology is so obscured it might as well not exist. Each time I play the video different images emerge. A smudged white figure with arms outstretched moves down the frame on the diagonal. Streaks of white, red, maroon, misty blue shift in the darkness then a shock of guns, batons, head gear. Surrounded by a vagueness of unarmed others the adrenalized cops are the ones who look scared. There's something on the white figure's head. Maybe a helmet. Maybe a blond pompadour. Maybe it's holding something. A gun? Sounds glide one into another, merge into a hollow roar. There's no melody but I hear music, like when recordings of disembodied spirits are cleaned up. If you record and play back the static on radio signals, CB Radio transmissions, or wireless baby monitors, ghostly voices speak, and when that static is erased, music emerges between the ghost's words. Not everyone believes in ghost language or music. Thomas Edison did, but killjoy scientists label it "auditory pareidolia," the brain's tendency to interpret random patterns as being familiar patterns. The human brain evolved to recognize patterns, and find patterns it will. In the notes section of *This is what a baton to a video camera looks like (ultra slow)*, Andrew writes, "I believe a type of truth resides in ghosted fragments, in the stretching of sound beyond reference." Shifting images lend a rhythm to the sounds. I hear endless ocean waves. I hear the reverberant inside of a primitive drum. I hear snores of a sleeping beast. I hear a reaching backwards, the white noise of times past, the sound that exists between sounds, the humming of substance itself … so many vectors of accessibility … a building a woman wearing a lime green scarf magenta hat a man holding something—a gun? The hat scarf gun? melt into kaleidoscopic swirls. Devoid of context we enter the realm of WOW, recapture that childhood on our backs on the grass, faces skyward, cloud-morphing delight … *not a picture but an event* … we shift from object to the struggle itself … the white figure with arms held above head is maybe holding something, maybe a grenade. Towards the end, in a final flash of clarity, nestled between cops I see a corpulent blob who looks exactly like Alfred Hitchcock wearing headphones. The white figure elongates into a rodent, the mouse I saw on its back cut open in the genetics lab in Berkeley, the pink-nosed rat I trained in "Rat Lab," my undergrad Skinnerian psychology class. What truth resides in these fragments? *This is what a baton to a video camera looks like (ultra slow)*—even the title is indeterminate. Is the video camera the object of the baton? *This is what a baton hitting a video camera looks like.* Or is the video camera the observer? *This is what a baton looks like to a video camera.* Either interpretation might apply. Who is subject? Who is object? Whose or what's point of view are we seeing this through? And the terror—for ultimately the subject of this video is terror—who's doling it out, who's receiving it? Based on the cops' clenched faces, the baton is a weak talisman against terror. The baton conducts the whole display. It's not on anybody's side.

In January I attend Norman Fischer's dharma seminar. From the Tiburon exit, I follow three miles of winding rural road to the top of an unlit hill. When I turn off the car, the night is unrelenting, a darkness so total the church's parking lot and my body are absorbed into it, and the sky is so crowded with stars, I fear it will lose its grip and the stars will come tumbling down. In the dimmed meeting room, Norman sits on the floor in front of a crackling fire. The rest of us face him, on zafus and in chairs. On the mantel above him is a nativity scene comprised of abstract cut metal figures. Before class a woman remarked playfully, "Everyone has their backs turned to the Baby Jesus!" and she rearranged the pieces so Baby Jesus was in the center of the animals' and wise men's gaze. Norman strikes a singing bowl, signaling the beginning of meditation. He suggests that instead of focusing on the breath or our bodies, we place our attention on awareness itself. So I'm sitting here … and sitting here … wondering how the fuck do I approach awareness … sitting here … throat gets itchy … need to cough … this totally silent group most of whom have been practicing since they were in diapers will hear me cough … sure they don't care if I cough … don't want to cough ... decide to wait ... see if the itch passes ... sitting here ... it does ... now my eyes are tearing ... wonder if it's from not coughing or the smoke, suddenly from out of the fire shoot brilliant rays of yellow light, an excess of FX worthy of *Poltergeist* or Charlton Heston on the mountain in *The Ten Commandments*—or the light show in *This is what a baton to a video camera looks like (ultra slow)*. Norman cross-legged on the floor still as a brick in his dark robes, these golden beams of light shooting out from behind him—I wonder, maybe this is it, the nature of awareness, unveiled in all its glory, the figurative and the abstract overlaid, this simultaneity. I think of my friend Anna, who since her stroke can only live in the present moment. No longer can she access the things she used to obsess and fret about. I said to her over breakfast in her kitchen in Napa, "Just think about all those people who spend thousands of dollars on meditation retreats to find what you already have." Without missing a beat, she quipped, "When all you need is a few minutes of lack of oxygen to the brain." What type of truth do these ghosts reveal? No matter how banal, how dreary, if we observe anything through the right lens, the right speed, it offers itself up to us. Slowed down, Tiffany is no longer tacky. Slowed down, belligerent cops fill us with awe. Slowed down, a fire seen through watery eyes can blow our minds. The truth is, connection hails us when least unexpected. Christmas Eve, chatting in a doorway with an acquaintance, a 30-something guy, blonde and lanky, oversized glasses, he says *six months in six hours*, and I am so stunned by his humanity, time shifts. Lang-or-ous-ly he beats before me ... frame ... by ... frame ... it's like I'm staring through a tunnel and at the very end of it, there he bursts, a golden flame. The rest of the world, the party, swirls by, outside the tunnel, and I can feel it, I too have slowed. I too am flame-ing. I say, "I think I'm going to get some more wine," and Andrew says, "Yeah. I'm going outside for a smoke."

13

I MUST NOT FORGET WHAT

I ALREADY KNOW

I continued my tearful journey here on Earth, learning about emotions unknown to me such as fear, anger, and aggression. As we walked through the living room toward the stairs she said worriedly, I just don't know what I'm going to do with you. Movie stars. Don't you know anything about them? Well, I don't know. I don't know. I don't know, I said. It just looks funny to me. Well, I don't know. I suppose there are such menacing creatures as the blob on the lower Astral Plane, but I don't know of any on the Physical Plane. I already knew what she was trying to teach me, but I surely couldn't let her know. I don't know, he said. This disturbed me. You don't know? I also know what ten take away five is, I said. How did you know that? he asked. Part of my quietness came from not knowing what to do and being afraid of saying or doing something wrong. Asking questions embarrassed me because it attracted attention to something I didn't know. Feeling very grown up, off by myself, and wearing red lipstick, what I didn't know was that my life had been very protected during these first Earth years. I wished I had known. Why he had such a terrible temper I didn't know. We spent our days slashing and stamping around in a huge foot tub in the living room, squishing the grapes, bananas, oranges, and who knows what else with our bare feet. Yes I said. I feel it. I know I must succeed. He took my small hand in his weathered hand. I am known by many names. One is Chief Nawa Laki. I really did not know what queer meant. Well, if I would have known, I really wouldn't have come. Knowing how peaceful and wonderful my life on Venus had been, made a rotten life here even worse. You know, you don't have a chance. We know he's dangerous. We know something is wrong. If I would have known what he did, I would have taken a pistol and blown his brains out. The psychiatrist just looked at me, didn't know what to think, didn't know what to say. I didn't know whether to be happy or sad. Something about him bothered me, but I did not know what it was. I felt we had known and loved each other in past lifetimes. He knows I am not a virgin anymore. I'm engaged to be married and I just don't know what to do. Many people say that a woman cannot be raped in the first place. But the fact is that I know differently. I did not know much about nutrition, and I was not aware of the poisonous preservatives in food at that time. You know, I'd love to take some pictures of you 'cause I do photography for Vogue. Well, honey, how do you know this? No woman had ever told him when her baby would be born. Should I tell him that I was communicating with the child? Nobody would believe me. So I said: I just know. I didn't know what to do. I didn't know the kind of person he was. I really did not much know about him. I did not know exactly how to do it. It seems everyone except myself knows, I thought. The Martian laughed: Perhaps they do. I have been told that my Venusian name is to be used only after I start my spiritual work by those who know where I come from. With his words came a feeling within me of wanting to cry and bury my face in his warmth and strength of his being, but also the feeling of joy to know I was not suffering for nothing. In the future I would make myself known by writing a book; this had been foreseen. The spiritual Master was someone I had known very well in past lives, and whom I had seen as a child. My uncle predicted that very soon I would find the spiritual teachings I had known on Venus as a child. The Brotherhood of the Planets had tried in many ways to make their existence known, little by little. My uncle did not know the name under which they would appear. I know I'm being selfish, but I crave affection and understanding. I know that your life will change. I do know many things that have happened to you, even though you cannot see or hear me. I will let you know, somehow, if your father translates. I had never seen hippies before and I did not know what they were. I did not know about the Vietnamese war, or LSD, or any of these things. I said yes, thank you knowing I had never drank tea except in Tibet! I did not know what to do. I did not know whether to run, or to act like I hadn't seen anything, or what. I know that this sounds strange, to tell a stranger all of this. I wanted him to know all about me. I was talking, not knowing what else to do. One night, Stanley asked if I would like some pot. I did not know what that was, I told him. I don't know how it happened, and neither one of us can remember how we ended up on our knees in the bathroom, facing each other. Do you know what's happening? I don't know. How could you know? I don't know how to explain this to you. I know that you are a smart young woman. I didn't know how you would accept it. Yes, I know what you mean. I know what you're talking about. Stanley had tried several new ways, but for me they all lacked the truth of the teachings I had known on Venus. I know that on Earth there have to be many different teachings because of the many levels of consciousness. I didn't know what to think when he smiled and asked me to sit. I know who you really are, he said. I do not know how Stan slept unless it was wine and pot. Ink was known to be a natural disinfectant. Apparently it was not yet the right time to make my mission known all over the world. This is Muhammad Ali! Don't you know him? I know you are an old Soul and one that I know.

Some people explained that snow did not make a sound. I said: Well, how do we know? Don't be stupid, God knows who you are! I don't know whether to be insulted or impressed. It was now to be known who I was. It later became part of my mission here on Earth to tell unknown truths about this great Soul. Now it is up to you to let people know about their true heritage and that the truth has been hidden from them. My only purpose in this life is to help you remember the things that you already know. I can't remember what I have forgotten, but I must not forget what I already know. He asked, How do we know that you are 220 or even 41? She did not know why but when she read my name she felt a sense of urgency and importance to meet me. I agreed even though I did not know what I would teach at the workshops. When I asked Uncle Odin and the Masters they simply replied: You share with them your knowledge, perspective, and under-standing. I enjoy every moment of my life with the certainty that I am always guided the right way and that I head into my future feeling positive and knowing it shall be an adventure of inspiration.

14

IN THE SHADOW OF TWITTER TOWERS

"San Francisco was no longer very safe."
— Fritz Leiber, *Our Lady of Darkness*

1

I park my car in the cul-de-sac on Natoma. Many alleys in my South of Market neighborhood bear women's names—Natoma, Clementina, Clara, Jessie, Isis—in homage, it is said, to San Francisco's famous 19th Century madams. Minna, the street I live on, was named during the Gold Rush after a Minna Quilfelt. As I approach Lafayette Street, a thin woman maybe in her early 20s passes me. She'd be attractive if it weren't for the sores on her face and the way she confronts me with too much eye contact and a sort of glazed smile. She's wearing a short white dress and one brown lace-up boot. Her other foot is bare.

Her presence doesn't surprise me. Since 2012, when Twitter established its headquarters two blocks away, there's been an ongoing battle to transform "Mid-Market" from sketchy skid row to up-and-coming "New Market," as boosters and realtors have named it, or even the hip truncation, NEMA. Many of the displaced have moved West, to my micro-neighborhood. One guy regularly sits on the corner of my alley, shouting in different voices. His range is remarkable. Kevin and I lean over the outdoor landing of our rent-controlled Victorian and snoop. Rocking and wailing with his arms wrapped around his knees, the guy looks tiny. He doesn't seem to be saying words so much as painfully expelling them. At times he sounds just like Regan in *The Exorcist* and I'm convinced he's possessed, even though I don't really believe in possession. Stupidly I call the cops and say, "There's a guy on my corner who needs help." The same migration happened when the City cleaned up Civic Center; it has been happening over and over ever since I moved to South of Market in 1990. In San Francisco when neighborhood associations or other vectors of power complain loud enough, police herd undesirables to the next neighborhood over, until that neighborhood generates enough political clout, and then they're herded elsewhere. I learned this during the crack years. The crack years were scary, but fascinating to watch from my bedroom window and as I walked down 11th Street between Market and Mission. Vans distributed to bicycles that distributed to individuals. Person to person sales reminded me of gay cruising, the way transactions happen in plain sight. Two people approach one another, and without making eye contact, one stuffs something into the hand of another. The one receiving the good then heads to the closest alley, my alley, to smoke it. I used to joke I knew so much about crack sale and distribution I could go into business myself.

The one-booted woman loses interest in me and walks down Natoma towards 11th, weaving in the middle of the street with an indifference that could be described either as saunter or stagger. She seems weightless. Her otherworldliness and that one boot—it's as if *Bess*—the title character of Daphne Gottlieb's 2013 Spolia chapbook—has materialized before my eyes. Bess too wears only one shoe: "What I haven't done a good enough job of telling you yet: How gone Bess is. She is the a-Bess. She is covered in menstrual blood, a Carrie in pink long johns wearing one shoe."

The story of a drug-addicted young woman lost to psychosis, Bess is a Gothic horror novel distilled to 3100 words. The drug/prostitution maze of the single resident occupancy hotel (SRO) has entrapped Bess and endangers all who enter, including her case workers. Of it the female case worker ponders, "Can a place itself be bad? Is the ground under Auschwitz—the land itself—the brown earth that smells just like dirt—is the land itself evil? Is the land under Ted Bundy's house cursed? Was there blood spilled under the labyrinth that made it hungry for more? Is there a reason people get swallowed up or snuffed out or trapped in a labyrinth?" Stephen King would answer, yes, the SRO has become a Bad Place. From *Danse Macabre*: "When we go home and shoot the bolt on the door, we like to think we're locking trouble out. The good horror story about the Bad Place whispers that we are not locking the world out; we are locking ourselves in … with them." In Bess it's difficult to locate where corruption lies. We have the behemoth of social services, designed to assist, but which threatens to dehumanize all involved. We have the two case workers trying their damnedest to be the good guys in a system that invites failure. "This is what I do: I take lost people and I give them beds in places with big rooms with many beds." And then we have Bess, who remains remote, manipulative, un-exorcize-able. "[O]ne Frye-boot on, still makes with the vacant, absent look. Nothing much matters to her, I think. Nothing is getting through. She's gone away someplace." In her schizophrenic haze, Bess is unable to take care of herself, and thus legally absorbable by the social services system. "She is the graybrown of the walls. Her pinpick eyes glare right through the curtain of hair. Her mouth is an asterisk. She nods that she will come with us because she has no choice."

Bess will not leave me. Fragments of her presence are everywhere. Third Street on the walkway beside Moscone Center—above the concrete expanse slopes manicured leafy green stuff, and sitting on the ledge is a white woman beside a tall black guy who's standing with his back to me. He's going through a bag—a backpack—something's black, the guy's clothes or the bag or both—this all happens very quickly—walking past I don't register them until I see the woman's eyes. A stare that is way beyond vacant—as if the external world had ceased to exist—like she's looking at an invisible screen and her eyes have been pinned open. Her lips are pursed and her cheeks hollow. Head droops slightly from neck—so still, the stillness of one who has utterly given up, like a mistreated dog waiting. Sharp contrast to the quick determined movements of the guy. She has a skin tone I've seen in other homeless women, a streaky gray that looks like it's been painted on by an incompetent mortician. Her hair is chopped short, poking erratically in all directions. But it is her eyes that stop me. It's impossible to tell if she's seeing nothing or an endless loop of horror. *Bess:* "She has met the police before. They responded to noise complaints at a hotel to find her chained to the bed wearing a dog's shock collar. She was for sale. She's broken." I remember having dinner with Lorian when she was still doing social work, and I asked her what life was like for homeless women in San Francisco. We were at the Pacific Cafe, a cozy seafood restaurant that hasn't changed since the '70s— dark booths and Shrimp Louie, free wine for our long wait. "Is it true that homeless women only sleep three hours a night?" I asked. Lorian told me of a client who'd been gang raped then locked in a car trunk and the men set the car on fire. I remember fifteen men, but I tell myself my memory is wrong.

I leave behind Moscone Center and enter Yerba Buena Gardens, where there's security guards to make us feel safe. Beside the waterfall a photographer clicks away at a guy in a suit and a woman in a tight full-skirted magenta dress. Assistants hold reflective cards that modify the light. When I get to Samovar Tea Lounge, I choose a corner table and order a $10 pot of tea. Sitting at the next table is a tech-geek couple—sallow-skinned San Francisco clichés, but friendly. When the waiter tells me that all the table tops are sticky, not just mine, the couple confirms that theirs too is sticky. Both are in their early 20s. He's sort of blond and she's sporting a chin-length colorless bob. He says, "The only thing you're forcing is the RAM." I tune out and write in my journal. The next time I come up for air, the woman is talking about the 11th dimension, but the context eludes me. They're clearly on a date, leaning against one another. I sip my bright green, perfectly brewed ryokucha. The woman says, "If she's ten years old and knows how to program stuff, she's way ahead of the game!" She laughs with a high-pitched machine gun giggle. She's working with a client to create a "super child," and she advocates teaching programming through dance choreography in order to get more girls excited about programming. I continue jotting down notes about the woman sitting next to Moscone Center. "She is not quite anorexic, but her skull is prominent beneath her dusty skin." Then they're on their iPhones, researching traffic patterns for their three-hour drive. When they stand up to leave, I'm impressed how thin they are. The woman's like three feet shorter than the guy. She's wearing a tight gray mini-dress without looking anyway sexy. Training bra breasts. "Hope you enjoyed your birthday meal," she exclaims, letting out a cheery rat-tat-tat. "I'm paying next time," he says. "Fair enough," she chirps, wrapping herself around his arm. They're so in synch I imagine they have good sex. In the bathroom I stumble upon the fashion-shoot model. She's switched from magenta dress to slouchy black top, black jeans—comfort clothes. Standing in front of the mirror she uses a contouring brush to slather on more make up over her already slathered face. For her the photo shoot must never end.

I misplace my copy of *Bess* so I order another. The day it arrives I take it to CCA and scan the entire chapbook, cover included, email it to myself, download it on my iMac, rotate it 90° on rotatepdf.com, upload it to Dropbox, download it onto my iPad Mini. Bess is no longer subject to loss and decay. Her spirit has entered the Cloud, where we can access her from all our devices.

In the Marina on a chilly, overcast afternoon, I approach a woman who looks "normal"—jeans and tan anorak, a white woman in her early thirties, shoulder-length bob cut. And then I see her skin up close, its coarseness—and the glazed desperation in her eyes. It's obvious she's homeless. Her eyes bespeak horror— not a singular trauma, but a series of traumas, a long series. *Bess*: "The girl needs help. She is a buttercup picked and left on the pavement for two days." As the homeless woman stares off, I touch the gold-trimmed abalone shell hanging from my neck, finger its sleek white iridescence. She's not a buttercup, she's an unshelled abalone, plucked and tossed on the street, a mound of creamy muscle quivering. I read that wild abalones will be extinct within 200 years due to anthropogenic carbon dioxide acidifying the oceans and eroding their shells. Also known as sea ears, their shells are smoothed from repeated tumbles in the sand, and thus abalones remind us that no matter how circumstance may toss and turn us, in the end our true beauty shines. The homeless woman turns a corner or crosses the street, impervious to me. Clinging for dear life in the depths, the sea ears listen. I call out—"Woo hoo! Woo hoo!" They resonate with my heart chakra, clearing it. Some day we'll all live in a gleaming white tower—me, the abalones and the homeless woman—she and I will hold hands and jig together, two late-blooming Rapunzels with soft wild hair.

In the "Experimental Writing" seminar I'm teaching at San Francisco State, the students loved *Bess*. They each had to go online, order the $8 chapbook directly from the publisher, and checkout with PayPal—there is no other way to get it. Rather than complaining, the students discussed how the difficulty in acquiring the text enhances the marginality of its subject matter. Then Philip said that *Bess* exemplified the point of all our readings this semester, that experimental writing allows you to address experiences that wouldn't be possible in conventional writing, and I wanted to hug him. Class ends at 7:00, I'm hungry and don't feel like cooking, so I zoom over to the super-trendy Bi-Rite Market. When I get to the Mission, driving turns rush-hour slow due to the towering Google buses, the white 2-decker Wi-Fi enabled shuttles hauling tech workers back from Silicon Valley. They glide through the streets like snakes—no, worms—no, slugs with dark eyeless windows—giant white slugs of capitalism clogging traffic with their slime. It's not just Google—it's Facebook, Yahoo, Apple, and Genentech—but all the buses are called Google buses. In her 2013 "Diary" piece in *The London Review of Books*, Rebecca Solnit suggests that this latest wave of tech invasion, the one that these Google buses have come to symbolize, has turned San Francisco into a boomtown. "Boomtowns also drive out people who perform essential services for relatively modest salaries, the teachers, firefighters, mechanics and carpenters, along with people who might have time for civic engagement. I look in wonder at the store clerks and dishwashers, wondering how they hang on or how long their commute is. Sometimes the tech workers on their buses seem like bees who belong to a great hive, but the hive isn't civil society or a city; it's a corporation." At 18th Street the bus in front of me unloads a mass of sneakered twenty-somethings carrying Rickshaw messenger bags, dozens of them walking towards Valencia. I'm reminded of when my grade school let out and 173rd Street would be packed with children trudging towards freedom. Maybe that's where the phrase school of fish comes from—a communal mass flowing towards a destination. Since the buses arrived, San Francisco rents have risen astronomically and no-fault evictions have gone through the roof. On Dolores, across the street from where my friend Wayne lives, they evicted a woman in her 80s with cancer who'd lived in her apartment for like 500 years. I hear these stories constantly, and my rent-controlled funky railroad flat is feeling awfully precarious.

South of Market is the kind of neighborhood in which when you approach or exit your car you need to scan the pavement for human shit. Twenty-five years ago when we moved in, the neighborhood still held traces of the old bohemia—the punk era, the hippie era, and even before that, the Beats, the proletarian writers of the '30s—in fact eighty or a hundred years of old San Francisco were still on the grid. In the '70s, artists associated with poet Jack Spicer lived in our building—we did not know this when we moved in, and since Kevin is an editor and biographer of Spicer, an eerie coincidence. Video artist Cecilia Dougherty, who at the time lived on California Street in the same building as Spicer when he wrote *Homage to Creeley* and *The Holy Grail*, told us about the apartment. We own a water color painted by Bill McNeill of Potrero Hill as seen from the bedroom window of the apartment next door. Before the onslaught of the condos, we too could see all the way to Potrero Hill. Samuel Delany and Marilyn Hacker lived a few blocks away; Delaney wrote a fantastical version of the local leather scene in his novels. In 1990 our neighborhood was a cozy enclave of artists, Filipino families, and warehouses. Down the street from us lived artists Rex Ray and Michael Brown, and journalist John Karr, who still lives here.

There was also a stable community of homeless men who were treated as neighbors by the housed, though crack changed that. There was a sweatshop on Lafayette, a large garage with a wide roll-up door, the inside packed with rows of sewing machines and bright overhead lights. I'd see CP Shades trucks outside, so I assume that's what they made. The clothes wheeled to the trucks were all a creamy white, skirts and knit tops and sacky dresses that looked naked and prototypical, like they were waiting to be programmed with color. Middle-aged Chinese seamstresses did Qi Gong on the sidewalk, their slo-mo movements so dreamlike I have a hard time accepting I'm not making this up.

The gay bathhouses had only been closed for a few years, and alleys were still used for hook-ups. Gay guys and an occasional prostitute still had sex against the dumpster in the vacant lot across the street. We watched them through the bedroom window, feeling edgy. I witnessed scores of men pissing, but only a handful of women. I remember the first one—she was crouching between two cars, bright turquoise panties around her ankles. On another weekday afternoon, while I was waiting for the light on the corner of Van Ness and Mission with a handful of others, this one woman bent over at the waist, her body forming an L-shape. Her faded blue jeans, as if of their own accord, slid down, revealing a pale untoned ass. Slowly from it a long smooth turd emerged, light brown. She seemed to hardly register what was going on. The light changed, she pulled up her pants, crossed the street. And now I'm remembering the night I heard a woman shrieking. I peek from behind the shades at a nude woman beneath the streetlight, her skin so pasty she kind of glows. She's thin with perky little breasts, and she's screaming at two black guys who beg her to put her clothes back on. She runs in circles and yells, "Is this what you want?" The guys shove clothes at her. Eventually she dresses and they all walk off together. I've always been struck by how thin the social veneer really is, a bird shell covering vast animal being. It is profound and oddly affirming to see street nudity and sex, like we'd all be better off if we dropped the pretense and went around sniffing one another's asses. But then one night I came home from teaching, and as I climbed the open-air stairs to my apartment I glanced over at the monstrous pink condo complex that replaced the vacant lot. On the couch in front of her two-floor high wall of windows, the owner is having sex with some guy. She's nude, and he's clothed, fucking her from behind, doggy-style. Remember, this is an alley, a street so narrow there is only one-sided parking. I dug out my iPhone, leaned over the balcony, and snapped a picture. After they finished, she sat on a stool next to an open window, still naked, legs casually crossed, and smoked a cigarette. People fucking on the street feels necessary, urgent—but witnessing this woman fuck in her million dollar jewel box pissed me off. I was feeling the rage of the French peasantry when Marie Antoinette played shepherdess at the Petit Trianon. My photo "Condo Trash" was a big hit on Facebook. Both times I posted it. Her condo is a legacy of the original dot-com invasion, when Mayor Willie Brown turned a blind eye to developers who exploited live/work loopholes meant for the construction of affordable housing for artists—and used them instead to make a killing on luxury lofts. With all the City fees and building codes—such as accessibility requirements— that could be evaded, in the '90s lofts spread South of Market like acne.

When I was deciding whether to move into our super-cheap apartment, I called Southern Station and asked a cop if my street was safe. He said, "It's an alley. People do there what people do in alleys. I wouldn't let my daughter move there." I told the landlord no, but he practically begged us to take the place. "All the walls are painted black." "I'll paint them white." "We have cats."

"I'll put the cats in the lease." "The refrigerator's too small." "I'll get you a bigger one." Our next door neighbor (who played Kevin's daughter in one of Cecilia Dougherty's videos) said, "One thing you need to know is that the people in this building do drugs." The day we moved in the evicted junkies on the first floor were finally vacating. There had been so many ODs in that apartment and on the landing, residents knew the names of the ambulance crews. Once an artist from LA visited, and when she saw where we lived she burst out laughing. "That's where I used to pick up my heroin! When I was an undergrad at the San Francisco Art Institute, from this dumpster that used to be right there out front." My neighbors also made indie movies, jewelry, art, and music. They watered one another's plants, cat-sat, gifted unwanted furniture and homemade ice cream, traded me a necklace for help on a writing project. One guy filmed a death scene from a horror film in our kitchen. He worked at a porn video store in the Tenderloin, which he said was killing his sex drive. One guy from Brian Jonestown Massacre regularly crashed in the apartment beneath us. He would play music so loud the walls shook. I remember steeling up my nerve and knocking on the door, and him answering totally naked and too stoned to notice. One night after somebody called the cops, he threw a rock through a neighbor's window and sped away on a bicycle. But then when the camera panned to him playing guitar in the rock documentary *Dig!*, Kevin and I pointed at the TV and exclaimed, "There he is!"

As I write this, a block away cabbies circle past Uber honking nonstop in protest, and I shout, "Worker solidarity!" After an hour the honking's giving me a headache, it's unendurable, but San Francisco won't stop screeching as if its heart were being ripped out. A bad place doesn't spring up on its own. Something creates it. Atrocity births ghosts; soulless gentrification herds the desperate into ghettos away from moneyed eyes of tourists. Bruce, who lives in the Castro down the hill from Facebook founder Mark Zuckerberg, tells Kevin that a friend of his—a black man who owns a business on Castro Street—happened to walk past Zuckerberg's home, and private security guards stopped and queried him. "For walking while black," says Kevin. I say hi to a young guy at a bus stop and he turns his head away. I share a table in a cafe with a woman and she stares at her phone the entire meal, never acknowledging my presence. All these clean, clean people—I stare at them trying to crack the mystery of how they do it, walk down the street impeccable as a doll wrapped in plastic. Person after person bumps into me without saying sorry. I begin to feel like a surplus byte in a video game. Shady usage of the Ellis Act—which allows landlords who want to go out of the rental business to evict tenants—has decimated San Francisco's bohemia. Ousted from rent-controlled apartments, writers flee to Oakland to Brooklyn to back home with Mom and Dad, artists flee to Los Angeles. Places like Detroit are sounding better and better. But even Cincinnati, a friend tells me, has caught the gentrification bug.

It's not just the fear of losing housing and having nowhere to go, it's this sense of having one's habitat destroyed around you, a sort of soul-level extinction. Since I read *Bess*, I've been following Daphne Gottlieb's Facebook feed, and this is how Daphne put it:

> Hey, did anyone on here live on the Lower East Side between the '80s and the '90s? A little more recently, Hell's Kitchen or Williamsburg? Or were you in another city, state, place, neighborhood that changed drastically because of a seizure by people with money? What did you do? Where did you go? I was just thinking that I haven't been evicted (yet), but my culture has.

I have been in San Francisco 24 years. San Francisco raised me. I don't know if I could survive in the wild. Where do I go? What do I do?

Your here has become an elsewhere. Around every corner extermination waits, ready to pounce. December 2014, at the Center for Sex and Culture, one block over from Twitter, porn star Jiz Lee reads a shit-eating scene from *120 Days of Sodom*. Kevin and I sit near the front of the hall, in a sea of stackable chairs. To our right are floor to ceiling shelves of sex books, VHS tapes, DVDs. To our left, erotic art lines the wall. When she finishes reading, Jiz Lee pulls down her pants, bends over, and holds a chocolate-covered almond in front of her asshole. "Anybody want this?" she asks. "Come and get it with your mouth." The Center's lease is up in 18 months. Its rent will triple, and they don't know if they'll be able to stay in the City. Carol Queen, the Center's founder, half-jokes/half-laments that she and her friends have spent their adult lives developing careers that make them unfit to live anywhere else.

I get up in the middle of the night to use the bathroom. In the hallway my geriatric cat has left a pile of shit, which I step in and track through the kitchen, through my office, and into the bathroom. When I finally realize it, I remove the encrusted clog but leave on the other. I flush the toilet and retrace my path, lopsided hips jerking up and down. Step-thud. Step-thud. Shit is everywhere. Too much—step-thud—shit. Life has too much. Shit. My drowsy mind is one step-thud away from crawling back into stupor and leaving the stench. I bend over with a kleenex and swipe up a turd, my brain porous as menses on a pair of pink sweatpants, feathering out. The sweatpants say *each process of becoming is also a process of unbecoming.* From the kitchen window fog has descended to street level, flattening perception. The neighborhood looks soft and speckled, punctuated by blurred orbs of streetlight—so quiet and intimate. I write in my journal, "As I walked down Market Street, it's as if Death were following behind me, rolling up the sidewalk."

Circle Community Acupuncture on Harrison at Dore Alley. Treatments are $15 a pop. Patients stretch back on barcaloungers covered with twin sheets, which the staff changes often but not after every patient (in order to conserve water). The man to my right has purple welts on his calves, elongated and irregular like islands. The guy to my left is unconscious, mouth drooping open. Melissa is teeny and elf-like, inserting the needles with a series of quick taps. Painless. "How are you doing?" she whispers. "Fine." "If you have any problems, just give me that wide-eyed look." She covers me with a blanket and I close my eyes, sink into my chair, absorbing the molecules of previous occupants. A few minutes later she returns. "Are you okay? If you need anything, just give me that look." Behind me is a painting of a red haired man and woman, a montage of several erotic encounters melding into one another, human body parts melding into white birds and fish, their focal point the woman's left nipple, rust-red and big as a quarter, which the man is tweaking. I love it here. I wonder how long their lease is for—they've been here forever but how much longer. To my left hangs a poster of two giant ears. In the left ear is a skeletal arm and hand and a backwards-bending spine in the shape of a C. Skull at the bottom of the spine, two bone legs and feet floating about it. It looks like the skeleton of a human fish, a missing link. The ear on the right is full of fleshy bits in various shades of pink: stomach, kidneys, heart, lungs, spleen. The brain is white with pink squiggles, and something shaped like an upside down dolphin is orange. Reflex points. Afterwards as I walk across the scarred sidewalk, I think of each step, each crack, each human encounter as a reflex point. The ear is the homunculus of the human body, San Francisco is the homunculus of the world. What happens here is happening, on some scale, everywhere. I read that the West is becoming more East and the East is becoming more West, that Tehran will eventually turn into a sort of hybrid of Beirut and Brooklyn, and that Africa will rapidly grow in wealth. Eventually the Earth will be one sprawling corporately-managed mall.

Realizing that I'm not sure what the initials "SRO" stand for exactly, I look it up and find that it means Single Room Occupancy or Single Resident Occupancy, referring to hotels that provide permanent housing to low-income tenants. In San Francisco, many of these properties are managed by nonprofits dedicated to finding permanent housing for the homeless. The hotel in which Louis lives in the film *Interview with the Vampire* is now an SRO (the San Cristina), as is 811 Geary, the building in which both Fritz Leiber and his protagonist in *Our Lady of Darkness*, Franz Western, resided (Hotel Union). I continue googling and end up reading James Hosking's and Jeremy Lybarger's "Life Inside SF's Vanishing Single Resident Occupancies," which profiles six residents of San Francisco's SROs. The "vanishing" in the title refers to the slew of SRO units that have been demolished or turned into condos (15,000 from 1970 to 2000)—a trend that isn't slowing down. When I get to Cynthia, who lives at the Mission Hotel, I yell out to Kevin, "Mission Hotel—isn't that where Danielle Steel's son OD'ed?" Kevin doesn't know, so I look it up and find that Steel's son, Nicholas Traina, did OD in 1997, but it was at his home in Pleasant Hill. The following year Danielle Steel began helping the homeless. "After Nicky died, I went to church and prayed for a way to help. Nicky was always very kind to homeless people, buying them a sandwich or a pack of smokes. And 'helping the homeless' is what kept returning to my mind." Steel and her staff drove vans around the city in the middle of the night, handing out long johns, tarps, ponchos, food, toiletries, sleeping bags, and teddy bears. After they encountered some scary situations, police officers volunteered their time to keep them safe. Eventually I find that it was Boz Scaggs' son, Oscar, who OD'ed in an SRO—in 1999—but it was a different one, the Royan Hotel on Valencia. So, Cynthia moved to San Francisco because she's a Deadhead. On the wall beside her bed is a world map on which she's written the names of movies she plans to check out of the library. "Dallas Buyers Club." "The Spectacular Now." "About Time." "All Is Lost." "Gimme Shelter." "The Worlds End." Tacked to her ceiling is a blanket printed with Van Gogh's *Starry Night*. She found it, she tells the journalist, in Golden Gate Park.

Circle Community Acupuncture. This time, after 45 minutes when I open my eyes everything seems to be vibrating. To my left, the faintest of shadows—so faint I wonder if I'm hallucinating them—move across the wall. Beneath them a big round clock says 2:30. Walking over here I kept encountering groups of twenty-somethings ambling, I assume back to their tech jobs after lunch break. Some wore business casual, others jeans and sweaters shaped like hoodies, an occasional real hoodie, gray. Their neutral-toned sneakers were flawless. I heard snippets of conversation *I'm working on this project ... my team*. Women in skirts carried small white Chinese take-out boxes. I can't remember any particular walker, so bland were they, bland as the aliens in *The World's End*, which I watched last night. Twenty years after graduating, high school buddies return to their hometown with the sole purpose of repeating their youthful bar-hopping itinerary. But—big surprise—the bars have lost their quirky individuality, all now sporting the same layout, same look, as if a mall architect plugged in a CAD block labeled "English Pub." All the mates the buddies used to love and hate are strangely affectless, raising pints of beer to mouths in unison. The populace *looks* human, but when you smash an arm or pull a head off, they bleed bright blue blood. You stand beside one of them at a bus stop or check-out line and attempt chitchat, and the humanoid beside you stares straight ahead or at its device, gives no acknowledgement of your existence, it's like they've erected a force field that renders you invisible. I have an urge to slap them, but their shield is so intractable I imagine my hand bouncing right off or, worse, tasered and spasming helplessly as the 22 Fillmore arrives and the humanoid glides aboard, guiltlessly claims one of the reserved-for-the-disabled seats at the front. In *The World's End* the blue-blooded "blanks" and all the tech innovations of the past decades were created by the Network in order to prepare Earth to join a larger space alien community. When eyes mouth hands ears incessantly input and receive, glands squirt out cortisol and adrenaline, and everybody everywhere is wired. White-lined ideograms of cell phones and computers float through the air. The drunken buddies shout at the Network, "Leave us to our own devices, you intergalactic asshole!" (Great pun on "devices," I think.) Frustrated, the Network withdraws, civilization is destroyed, and roughing it around campfires in a post-apocalyptic world, our heroes recover their authentic selves. If progress equals conformity, salvation can only be found by winding backwards. David, the acupuncturist, is hunched over, removing needles from the patient lying in the chair beside me. He has shoulder-length wavy hair and a beard, and exudes a gentleness that's rare. His T-shirt reads "Acupunk." Up by the ceiling the shadows bend forward, each stalk flickers one after the other like an apparition running through grass. Walking over here, on 10th Street I passed a guy who was talking on a cell phone, cigarette dangling from mouth. He had thick geometric tattoos over his arms neck and face. *Him* I remember.

In 2007 residents near Corona Heights, a steep hillside perched over the Castro, complained about homeless squatters hiding in the thickets. "They've built campsites up there," said one home-owner, "and no wonder. They've got a $4 million view." The homeless built fires, left behind dangerous paraphernalia, cohabitated with Northern and Southern alligator lizards, garter snakes, butterflies, red-tailed hawks, ravens, Western scrub jays, mourning doves, downy woodpeckers, chestnut-backed chickadees, pygmy nuthatches, towhees, bushtits, white-crowned sparrows, dark-eyed juncos, robins, and American goldfinches. The pitch of the slope is extremely steep—to make an arrest, cops would have to scramble over tree branches, loose gravel and poison oak. There's always been something creepy about the area. Thirty years earlier, horror novelist Fritz Leiber opened *Our Lady of Darkness* there: "The solitary, steep hill called Corona Heights was black as pitch and very silent, like the heart of the unknown. It looked steadily downward and northeast away at the nervous, bright lights of downtown San Francisco as if it were a great predatory beast of night surveying its territory in patient search of prey." Since reaching the encampments was so treacherous, a herd of goats was brought in to eat the brush. The goats ate native plant communities protected under the natural areas program as well as non-local plants. The goats wiped out all hiding space, and the homeless moved on. When I wake up, my mind is racing with grazing goats, their slow steady nondiscriminating erasure—nightmarish as drones—no refuge, no cover. I stress-google like crazy and discover that high-powered hoses are used to clear the homeless from Mid-Market near Twitter. City workers blast the sidewalk at 4:30 a.m. and then again at 6:00 a.m. Hoses are not supposed to be aimed at people but witnesses report homeless screaming while being sprayed. No cover. I think of that moment when you know it's all over, that you're about to lose your job your lover your husband best friend biggest fan—that pause of

calm so devastatingly clear you want to remain there forever—
that instant during sex when anatomy crystallizes and you don't
have to strive any more you're going to come—that beat of
freefall before the inevitable explodes. I wonder if pre-death feels
like this too. The hoses wash away urine feces needles garbage
people. *Our Lady of Darkness*: "Perhaps some wilder and more
secret animal that had never submitted to man's rule, yet lived
almost unglimpsed amongst him." I remember from my childhood
the shock of opening *Life* magazine in spring of 1963 and seeing
images of protesting black students blasted by a high-pressure
water jet. These pictures showed like nothing else the insane cruelty
of the police, of the state itself. The hoses are like goats, they keep
coming and coming, no matter how tight you curl yourself, how
small you become, squeezing yourself behind a dumpster, in a
doorway, under an overpass, in a park, on a steep incline, behind
some bushes, they will find you, glimpsed or unglimpsed, they
will beat you kill you rape you root you out. For you there no
longer is a personal. You are public refuse 24/7. Brett McLeod,
39, ousted from Corona Heights, says, "What do they want us to
do? Float in the air? Everybody's got to be somewhere."

Hungry and lazy after teaching, I exit the subway at Van Ness
and approach the gourmet food court on the ground floor of
1355 Market. Built in 1936, a block-long Art Deco wonder with
an ornamental terra cotta facade, the former Western Merchandise
Mart is now the world headquarters for Twitter. The food court's
only been open a couple of months. So far I've had salad, asparagus
bisque, fava risotto, and tacos—all of them excellent, especially
the tacos. In the common eating area amid a sea of Macbook Airs
and jeans with fancy washes, my fellow diners have been friendly,
as techies go. When I've plopped down beside them they've
nodded, and the one guy I asked if they had Wi-Fi answered me.
At 10th Street I wait for the light in front of NEMA, the 37-story

luxury apartment building—black glass and sharp angles—built soon after Twitter's arrival. Studios in NEMA cost over three times as much as what we pay for our one-bedroom with an enclosed back porch we use as an office. "We used to leave here late, and there was nobody on the street," said Barbara Guacos of Mercy Housing, a low-income housing provider at 10th and Mission. "Now, people at night are walking their dogs. Dogs wearing booties, with manicures. The most perfect dogs you've ever seen." Since NEMA's just across the street from Twitter, people call it Twitter Towers. Sometimes the Twitter building itself is called Twitter Towers though its eleven stories offer more of a squat, sprawling profile—a beige ranch house crouched beside NEMA's shiny black spires. A number of high rise apartments are being constructed around 9th and 10th, spreading Westward towards Van Ness. The Goodwill a half a block from where I live will soon be gone, as will Tower Car Wash and the Honda dealership on South Van Ness, and the donut shop and parking lot across the street on Market. But NEMA receives the brunt of locals' rage. In addition to Twitter Towers, people call it ENEMA. The first time I walked past it, with Aaron and Katy, Katy shouted, "Fuck you ENEMA!"

A long white vertical sign, like a banner, runs down one corner of Twitter HQ. Printed on it sideways in gold: @twitter. At the top and right-side up, the blue Twitter bird. "Twitter is the bird, the bird is Twitter," former creative director, Doug Bowman, announced in 2012. The Twitter bird was created from three sets of overlapping circles, representing the interaction of interests, events and people on Twitter. The bird is always blue or white; never black or other colors. Speech bubbles must never emerge from the bird; the bird must never rotate or change directions; the bird must not be animated, anthropomorphized, flocked with other birds or creatures, subjected to special effects. The bird's beak and body point towards the sky, a gesture which Bowman theorizes as "the ultimate representation of freedom, hope and limitless possibility." When I open the tall glass door of the Twitter building, my muscles tense up, for the first time I was here the security guard followed me through the artisanal cheeses to the salad bar. Now he ignores me, which makes me feel accepted.

I used to belong to the neighborhood association's listserv, but it was clear I wasn't in synch with their agenda. When a condo-dweller grabbed a tagger's paint canister and sprayed the tagger, people praised him with a footnote warning him to watch out because taggers tend to travel in pairs. I said, hey, this is assault, crimes against persons are worse than crimes against property. When another condo-dweller posted a photo of cops arresting two black teen boys he reported for climbing up a building and walking across a roof, people on the listserv treated him as a hero. "Way to go!" "Yay, got 'em!" My internet-rage took over and I wrote that the arrest of teenagers was not a cause for celebration, that the neighborhood had gone to hell since the condoites moved in, that it was better when the crackheads were here. I signed off the list in a huff, and this guy who lives in the condo across the street started sending me backchannel emails.

Dodie,

I felt the need to reply to your assertion that you miss the crackheads now that the "condoites" are here. For as long as I have lived here I have not seen you do ONE thing to improve this neighborhood. You don't pick up in front of your building, you don't help with the plants, you don't help paint over the graffiti, you don't hose down the human waste when peeple [sic] shit in front of your building. Basically you do nothing yet enjoy the results of others labor then you have the audacity to complain about them. What a joke. If you own your place then we have helped increase your property value. However I'm assuming you are living in a rent controlled building so you feel no desire to help. You are getting over so why bother. As for "leaving the group," if someone who never did anything to help chose to leave would anyone miss her? I'm going with no.

Trey

Trey is obsessed with garbage. He's out most afternoons with a plastic bucket and one of those pinchers-on-a-stick trash picker-uppers, wearing his special garbage-eradication outfit—white overalls and cap, pale blue long-sleeve shirt. He used to only do our alley, but now he does the cross streets as well. Once the pavement is free of large debris, he pulls out an insanely long hose and sprays everything down. Then he paints over the ever-accruing graffiti. He has paint to match the exteriors of each of the local businesses, which he acquired from the owners. When he's finished for the day, all signs of recent life have been eradicated, and the streets have that eerie precision of a soundstage. Featureless, like Trey's face. Once when a woman got out of her car, a tissue dropped on the ground, and Trey yelled at her, "Pick that up!" She said, "Excuse me?" and he said, "I said pick that up!" She said no, and a shouting match ensued.

Trey: "I take notice of people who do absolutely nothing yet take upon themselves to ridicule others for making the neighborhood better. 20 years, Dodie, and you haven't done a damn thing to help this neighborhood. You should be very proud of yourself. I guess together you and your mate have done 40 years of nothing. Quite an accomplishment."

Trey hangs out his condo window and yells at some guy across the street who's climbing down the fire escape, "What the fuck are you doing?" The guy says he's retrieving a necklace. Trey yells "fucking dangerous," "hit somebody on the fucking head," and then he calls the guy a "stupid renter."

Trey's Yelp review of Public Storage: "The neighborhood adjacent to this Public Storage has been trying, for many years to get them to maintain their property. It seems it takes almost an act of god to get them to do anything. We have had to invoke DWP, the district supervisor, the mayor's office to even agree to meet with the neighborhood to discuss the maintenance issues. So next time you go there or are thinking about it, ask them if they respect their neighbors? Ask them if they believe they have a civic duty to maintain their property. If they look at you like you landed from Mars, then walk out!" Trey has given negative reviews to five other neighborhood businesses who leave too many flyers on doorknobs, double-park delivery trucks, don't turn on enough outside lights at night, or don't pick up trash quickly enough. All the reviews begin: "Can ya give less than one star?" "Can I give less than one star??" "Can you give less than a Star???"

Trey: "No worries we will still pick up in front of your building regardless of how lazy you are. We will still paint over the graffiti on the buildings next to you regardless of how lazy you are. We will still hose down the feces on our street regardless of how lazy you are."

Driving down Folsom Street—pot hole ka-chunks compress and expand my spine as I zone out on the pale gray boulevard stained with grit and oil, ornate in its decrepitude, its tar-dripped crop circles, rusty smears. I pass a cheery municipal sign that reads "Welcome to the Future Home of Smooth Pavement," and I feel gentrification fever rising. No more scarred undulations of roadway no more gravely patchwork of blacktop asphalt crushed stones concrete no more bumps and dips cracks and history no more shifting textures gravely fissures tracing the City's life-line/loveline no more pockmarks of weather tonnage slapdash repair no more fuck ups and dreams—the future glides beneath our wheels like a bituminous conveyor belt, a path so smooth we feel weightless, like we're not moving at all. Sometimes when I exit my car I'll covertly drop a crumple of paper and feel a little thrill. Trey: "Oh and no I don't call big brother but even if I did I bet you would be too lazy to get off your butt to answer the door."

To the left of my desk is a picture window that looks out on the clock tower of the Goodwill, and above it Bank of America office buildings, and then Twitter Towers, black glass blades scraping. The other day I went out to dinner with a neighbor who visited Twitter Towers. Google commissioned an artist friend of his to paint a mural, and they put him up in one of the apartments they rent in the building. The apartment was tiny, high tech and sterile, with unfinished concrete floors, like a dwelling from the future, where a drawer would open from the wall bearing your food pills for dinner. There's a common area on each floor and a swimming pool on the roof. He said it didn't feel like a home; it felt like a dorm.

Advertising on the side of Twitter Towers:

EFFICIENT,

ENGAGED,

AND FULLY

WIRED.

INNOVATE
DON'T IMITATE.

COOL ON
ON THE OUTSIDE,
WARM ON
THE INSIDE.

AMENITIES,
NO ENEMIES.
TECH SAVVY,
NOT SHABBY.

Yelpers respond to the building: The windows are filthy, pop 40 music is blasted in the courtyard until 10 in the evening, one side of the building is brutally hot, the other side is cold, the concrete floors are unbearable and stain when touched, the two-burner stoves are useless, you have to wait 10 minutes to get your car from the garage and the valet parkers keep losing and crashing vehicles, noisy, noisy, noisy, the high-tech security which tracks you down to which floors you stop the elevator at is more Orwellian than comforting, the walls are thin, the futuristic design will be dated in two years, the water in the rooftop pool is cold, Market Street is scary, hallways are dirty and always smell like weed, other tenants don't have respect for the building, tenant partying in common areas are not mellow get togethers but fireball shots and yelling, you can smell cigarette smoke from neighboring units, homeless go through the garbage bin at the entrance to the garage and leave a mess, no air conditioning, the garbage chute is rarely operating, the laundry room has been broken for three weeks, the free coffee is broken, the wind on the 11th floor deck is so severe that it can blow out the gas grills even with the lid closed, garbage trucks arrive EVERY WEEK DAY beginning at 3 a.m., bright lights in the courtyard penetrate the shades, when the courtyard lights are turned off others can see directly into units through the shades like a one-way mirror, dogs are urinating just outside the front door of the building and outside the parking garage and in the elevators, the urine smell is so awful in the elevators lobby common area and parking garage some tenants literally have to put scarves over their noses. Most people are spending between $4000 to $6500 a month to live here. Fabergé on the outside, rotten on the inside.

FIRST,
NOT LAST.
TORTOISE,
NOT HARE.

For eight years Rebeca worked as a prop person in Los Angeles. We sit in her Project Artaud studio sipping tea that smells like potpourri and looking at images from prop rental websites. Especially the rocks—flat rocks, round rocks, big rocks on wheels. Before the internet streamlined things, a studio assistant would tell Rebeca what kind of rock the director wanted, then Rebeca would visit prop houses and photograph likely rocks, then she'd give the photos to the assistant who would pass the photos to another assistant and so on until they reached the director who would approve the rocks or not. If approved, Rebeca would go back and rent the rocks. She shows me a Southwestern set with rocks scattered all over the place. "Every one of those rocks," she says, "was chosen by somebody." The time Rebeca spent in prop houses taught her to abstract narrative and fuck with perspective. She tells me about two young women standing in front of the beautiful old building across the street. One says to the other, "San Francisco's historic preservation policy is ridiculous." *Our Lady of Darkness*: there came a faint, breathy buzzing, as if Time were clearing her throat.

Historical preservation has been replaced with the ahistoricism of repurposing. The reception desk at Twitter is partially comprised of wood reclaimed from bowling alley lanes. From its previous headquarters, Twitter brought along two life-size neon-green deer. Tree branches stretch across the walls, keeping the deer company. *Business Insider*: "Stepping off the elevator, you get a nature theme. You feel like you're stepping into a huge bird house." To create a lounge space in the employee cafeteria, Twitter purchased two weather-beaten 1870s cabins, which they disassembled and shipped from the Montana plains to HQ. The cleaned wood from the two 20 x 20-foot buildings was conjoined when reassembled. The interior of the hybrid cabin features built-in corner tables, booth seating, and TV monitors for entertainment. Alan Farnham via *Good Morning America*: "20-somethings can talk bits and bytes where the pioneers shivered." In its common area, Twitter also boasts a 225 square foot living wall, comprised of 1,008 potted plants. By bringing nature in from the outside, the wall creates a peaceful and healing retreat. The plants consume CO_2 and release O_2, which gives Twitter employees more energy-rich oxygen to breathe easier. This reduces stress and improves their mental well-being, and in turn enhances their creativity and productivity. Hanging on the living wall is a large Twitter bird that looks like it might be redwood. Twitter requested the wall be a uniform green in order to make the iconic bird logo the focal point. The living wall reflects Twitter's guiding principles— simplicity, constraint, and craftsmanship.

All detail blasted away, all color, all complexity lost in some bleached-out nothing realm. In our pristine post-Twitter cityscape, no longer will rank heaps of feces ferment on the street and sidewalks. Soundstage homeless will shit tasty piles of chocolate-covered almonds. I walk past ENEMA and a 20-something guy exits the building with a dog on a leash—he's wearing flip-flops and plaid flannel pajama bottoms as if Market Street were an extension of his bedroom, and I think meanly *put on some fucking clothes*—I think of the guy earlier in the week who was standing across the street when I got into my car—three blocks away from ENEMA—a tall black guy also wearing flannel pajama bottoms, his were red print—he's shaking out a gray blanket, I figure to make a bed for himself. I lock the car door and sit and watch. He holds the blanket in front of him and kicks it. To remove dirt, I assume. Then he points to someone in the street, someone invisible to me—and starts shouting at them. Now he's moved to the street, kicking the blanket in a very focused way, as if attacking a foe. I start my car, hoping he gets back on the sidewalk so I can pull away. Even though the condos have dramatically increased the population in my neighborhood, the streets are still empty at night; unless they have a dog on a leash, the condoites don't walk around; they slide into parking garages in vehicles with blinding halogen headlights. It's not the flannelled guy who frightens me so much as the bleakness of an alley at night—it makes me feel like Alice in Jacques Tourneur's *Cat People*, the click of her heels against the soundstage sidewalk quickening as the unseen pursues.

In an email, Daphne Gottlieb shares some of her challenges in writing *Bess*: "[A]s someone who works with the homeless, I am dealing with confidential information as well as a power differential, working with stories that are not mine. How do you depict a culture that isn't yours? What is the responsible way to depict severe mental illness? Without me and my middle age white lady privilege, they will die. When does [one] cross the line into explication?" Gottlieb is a professional. I am an amateur. When I step out my front door, I see all these distressed people yet I know zilch about their whys and wherefores, so I start googling homelessness. I find so many statistics my eyes twirl. I read that homelessness is caused by shitty public policy. I read that Ronald Reagan created homelessness as we know it in the early '80s by cutting $65 billion from federal housing subsidies that helped provide permanent housing for the poor, and replacing that with $880 million in shelter funding, which offered temporary housing. He also gouged unemployment, disability, food stamps, and family welfare programs. The way people remember where they were when Kennedy was shot or the World Trade Center collapsed, I remember where I was when Reagan was elected. I was sharing a flat in the Mission with Christine, a politically progressive resident in psychiatry at San Francisco General. We were standing in the kitchen, our mouths gaping. *This cannot be happening* we voiced back and forth to one another, as if by saying it enough we could make it not be true. And then overnight it seemed the Mission District went from a handful of drunks and pan-handling hippies who always had a place to crash—Christine herself did a stint of dumpster diving before she went to med school—it seemed as if overnight all these desperate people emerged, this subclass that was increasingly reviled. I read that in San Francisco the treatment of the homeless has changed with each mayor, the focus shifting from temporary to permanent housing, from harassing to not harassing to reharassing, and always there's cutbacks cutbacks cutbacks. I read that the more marketable the name of a policy—Care Not Cash, the Matrix program—the more it fucks the homeless. Voters don't want to help the homeless—they want to eradicate them, but stupidly vote for policies that ensure even more people will end up on the streets. For a politician to appear too helpful is career suicide. I read how San Francisco has become the most expensive city in the US, how the income disparity between ordinary folk and Twitter and its 1600 new millionaires and their like is growing, while affordable housing is dwindling, and so many people have no place to go. Thank you Mayor Lee and the Board of Supervisors. I read that not all homeless are drug addicts who move here for the good weather, that homeless are children, vets, women, queer, mentally ill, seniors, disabled, living with HIV and other chronic illnesses. A disproportionate number of them are Hispanic, black, and LGBT teens. I read that the frequency of murder, suicide, and harassment (police and otherwise) for transgender homeless is insanely high. The rates of assault for cis women are also outlandish. I read that hate crimes against the homeless jumped 24% in 2013 and that more hate crimes are committed against the homeless than all other hate crimes in the US combined, with California and Florida together accounting for nearly half of those crimes. When determining hate crime statistics the FBI does not recognize homelessness as a protected class. I read how the shelters are horrible—bugs, violence, claustrophobia, stench, theft—and, depending on who's counting and how, there's beds for a quarter (or a third or a sixth) of the seven to ten thousand individuals who need them. The rest of the homeless sleep in parks, cars, jail, or sobering centers; on sidewalks, BART or buses. Sleeping on buses can be risky because if you don't get a nice driver, you have to get off every hour or two and you may find yourself on the street alone at three in the morning. People at risk sleep during the day to avoid assaults. Not allowed to lie on the floor, they sit in plastic chairs in drop in centers. The lucky ones get a chair by the wall to rest their heads against. Others let their heads hang. I read that bowing to the pressure of luxury housing developers, San Francisco has closed several recycling centers, denying income to impoverished San Franciscans who redeem cans and bottles for hard-earned cash. As a result, the City now has a severe lack of recycling centers and isn't reaching its zero waste goals.

The Twitter Towers folder on my hard drive contains dozens of pdfs analyzing homelessness and gentrification, and thirty pages of notes—so many data bits, I feel buried in a heap of left-brain rubbish. Just when I try to unsnarl one fact, another tumbles on top of me and I lose track of the first. How much do I have to read in order to have a right to write about these people? Doesn't my research just move me closer to armchair Marxists with their *I know this subject therefore I own it* smugness? Or to those bourgies who rub their faces with coffee grounds and go on urban retreats with their spiritual group? They panhandle, eat in soup kitchens, meditate in parks together, sneak leftovers from restaurants, sleep on cardboard. As if otherness were a costume one could don for a weekend. A student who has written about being homeless tells me that folks in recovery jokingly refer to him as an "outdoorsman" because he was only on the streets for six weeks and either camped out in safe places or stayed in detox centers. A few years ago another student was working on a novel about a teen girl who slept in Golden Gate Park. Class comments consistently praised the text for its authenticity. What I remember most is the incredible alienness of "straight" people—e.g., me—and a girl whose sense of self is lower than low—and a scene where she steels deodorant from a Walgreens in the Haight. The following semester, when we worked one on one, the student confided that her story was autobiographical, that she was a famous missing teen, her picture on the news and telephone poles.

Throughout *Bess* Daphne Gottlieb, a prize-winning poet, renders experience in bald language that ranges from clinical to desperate. As a sort of emotional echo chamber, Gottlieb overlays the characters' everyday hell with the myth of Theseus and the Minotaur. But Bess and her social worker are never recast as artsy-fartsy mythic heroes. Rather, fragments of the myth resonate with the clinician's psyche as she encounters the nightmare of her client's plight—the labyrinthine corridors of the SRO—the terror of being lost—the longing for an escape route—the desire to destroy evil, to locate it in a single source, the Minotaur, rather than a systemic crisis that's unstoppable, like a perpetual entropy machine. Narrative used to go like this: order is disrupted, and the trajectory of the plot brings things to a new state of order. But what's happening in San Francisco is escalating disorder with no restoration in sight. When Bess is sent to a mental institution, it's not satisfying, but it creates a sense of closure. For her. For the book. For now. But the labyrinthine systems that trapped her spiral on and on and on. All of this in language that is so plain it's practically transparent.

How do I look at someone who cannot refuse my gaze and not patronize them? For now, it seems, all I can do is hold this impossible gulf and blunder on. On 11th Street I see the woman whose cart was blocking my way last night when I was driving to Bi-Rite. Get your fucking cart out of the street I said to myself, all snooty pants. She'd left the cart double-parked as she foraged through recycling bins left on the sidewalk for the night. As soon as she saw me approach, she moved the cart and I zoomed towards my weekly dose of premium-priced deli food. Now she's pushing her cart on the sidewalk, bent over as if she has to put all her weight into the effort. She's short, maybe five feet. Middle-aged with chin-length faded reddish hair held in place with a wide headband. Brown plaid jacket, baggy pants. She turns around and asks me if I have a dime. I say it's hard to get to my money, but I'll give her some. I lean my computer-heavy back-pack against another shopping cart that's been turned on its side beside the trash can at Firestone Tires, and dig through my bag until I find a couple of dollars. "God bless you," she says, then gestures to her cart and asks me if I want some flowers. I wonder if she's the woman who Kevin found living in his station wagon. He went to move it, and she had covered the hood, the roof, every available surface with hundreds of artificial flowers. She said, "This is my car now. Two black guys sold it to me." From the glove compartment she pulled out a pink piece of paper that had the words PINK SLIP written on it in ballpoint, and she said, "This is my pink slip." As we wait at the light on Mission Street, I look down at her feet. The left one is wearing a plain brown shoe. Her right shoe is more jaunty, gray with a pink neon Nike swoosh on the side. I'm reminded of a mnemonic illustration that demonstrates the difference between the left and right halves of the brain. An L in bold san serif demonstrates the practical, rational side, contrasted with an R gussied up in a curlicue script to represent the intuitive. The woman's bright foot moves across Mission Street, catching the sun like a pink wing.

The TV series *Looking* has taken over the Jessica McClintock warehouse across the street from the CCA writers studio, where I teach a creative nonfiction workshop. Huge trucks and trailers line the streets taking up primo parking spaces. Students say there's a soundstage inside the warehouse, but security won't let anybody get close enough to really know. Kevin saw one of the stars ride up on a bicycle. He plays the aging gay guy on the show, but in real life Kevin says he looks young—like they do something to make him look old on camera. Once there was a group of casually dressed people—backpacks, etc.—gathered outside the building, and as I passed them it became clear they were extras waiting to be shuttled somewhere to play normal people. Another day I saw a homeless guy standing on the corner, and I couldn't tell if he was real homeless or pretend homeless. I doubt that human perception is capable of nonfiction. On *The Walking Dead* when a character dies, the cast holds a death dinner, with a death cake, and they all get drunk and cry. We know it's fiction but our mourning is real. Our hearts spill fresh blood onto the soundstage, vivifying the vampire, the zombie, the "old" guy on *Loving*, the virtual avatar. From Gawker's predictions for

2015: *Twitter is a money pit, a company that costs more to run than it can generate in revenues ... they are spending a dollar fifty to make a dollar ... Facebook is trading at 72 times earnings, and Twitter has a $20 billion market cap even though it is losing huge amounts of money, and Salesforce.com has a $37 billion market cap even though it doesn't have any earnings either ... and ohmygod a fucking food delivery startup just raised $220 million at a valuation of $2 billion and Snapchat just raised money at a $20 billion valuation even though they have no revenues and the company is burning cash like crazy and now I'm starting to get that feeling where I know it's not an actual heart attack but I still think that maybe it is a heart attack and I should probably go to the emergency room just in case.*

Our Lady of Darkness: I live firmly in the world of art, where reality and fantasy are one.

I sit in the Trader Joe's parking lot at 9th and Bryant, eating a veggie taco and photographing a one-legged pigeon that's hopping about pecking at scraps. My former neighbor, Mary, appears and watches the pigeon too. She pushes up her pinky purple glasses and says that pigeons are a type of dove. Rock doves. She says a neighborhood coalition fought against the construction of NEMA, arguing it was too tall, but lost. Mary heads over to the Nordstrom Rack and I think back to the late '70s when I decided to move to San Francisco, and friends in Chicago called it the land of the fruits and nuts, said there were no jobs, warned of women-hating gay hairdressers who would give me a bad cut on purpose. For twelve years I made corporate slide shows—speaker support and big-budget motivational modules with smiling employee heads flashing to the beat of pop songs reworded to reflect company values. To work I wore jeans with a rip in the ass and made more money than any of my friends. Some slide houses provided free cocaine. Then corporations started downsizing and personal computers allowed secretaries to make the simple stuff and videos became sexier than slides. When the bubble burst I found myself reduced to temp secretarial work. The bubble always bursts. In the first dot-com explosion my neighborhood lost our corner store—run by a Filipino family for 18 years—and our Brazilian pizza parlor. Then there was the dot-bomb and suddenly SOMA was full of vacant commercial spaces, and the destruction of these long-standing small businesses seemed like such a fucking waste. When this latest boom collapses, I imagine NEMA towers corroded and rat-infested, a fine layer of gray dust everywhere, ragged as downtown Atlanta on *The Walking Dead*. Pigeons perched on broken windows tweet-tweet-tweeting. Behind them squatters cook Mulligan stew over stoves made from wastepaper baskets topped with wire coat-hangers. Standing in front of the Twitter building a woman with one boot and a bird with one leg utter a succession of light chirping sounds, they chirrup, speak rapidly in a light tremulous manner. They giggle nervously, titter. They tremble with nervous agitation. They flutter as they talk excitedly, twit and reproach. They utter half-suppressed laughs or giggles. They are intermittent. They quiver and palpitate in a fright. They are shreds, fragments, gummy thready substances. They are of imitative origin, especially when they chatter of trivial matters. Suddenly they occur as audible events. They cheep, chirp, chirrup, whistle, trill, warble, and peep. They are always high-pitched when they gossip or rabbit on, when they babble, prattle, natter, jabber, blather, and prate. Here is the song they sing as they spin unevenly, bunching and twisting: "A twitcher with a twittish 'twixt-brain twitches twittle-twattle twixt a twitting twitlark and twitchy twite in Twittenham's twitten."

Driving with Kevin down Natoma—a guy slouches on the sidewalk with a cigarette dangling from his mouth, staring aggressively into the car. Bright blue blanket over his crotch and trailing to the left. Something round under the blanket bobbing up and down. "That guy's getting a blowjob!" I announce to Kevin. It's been years since I've seen a sidewalk blowjob. I say, "He looks like that actor, the one Dennis had Thanksgiving with, the one who loses all the weight for his parts." "Christian Bale?" "Yeah, him." One time there was this guy going through a dumpster beside my building, crazy and rambling, of course—but what was odd about him is that he was wearing matching tan linen pants and vest, with a dress shirt, impeccable, and he looked just like Robert Downey Junior. It was around the time Downey had the big breakdown/drug problem that landed him in prison, so it's not totally unreasonable to assume that it actually was Robert Downey Junior rummaging through the dumpster. We circle around the block and it seems clear that this guy is not Christian Bale.

On Market near 4th a man stands on the sidewalk, legs spread, arms straight out at sides, knit-hatted head drooping—a human scarecrow. He holds the pose for several minutes, then walks away, Reeboks flopping. At least two sizes too big. Somewhere a child is screaming, its pitch as high as a whistle. Life is not a movie. I can stop and stare, but I cannot pause, cannot rewind.

I wake up to phone call from Bank of America reporting suspicious activity on my account—two high ticket items from Office Depot and another from Best Buy. I imagine it's a start-up furnishing their headquarters on the cheap. There's a start-up in my building. One of them—or their guests—vomited on the ground floor landing next to the mailboxes and left it, this chunky orange blob studded with grains of white rice. They should chew their food better, I thought right before I noticed it smushed into the sole of my boot, its sharp stench. Their living room used to be lined with white desks where tall young white guys sat at monitors talking on headsets something about insurance. They never shut the front door, so every time I was on the stairs I had to confront them. I once heard them conducting a job interview on the sidewalk in front of the building. After a few months the desks and guys vanished and the door's been mostly closed. The one time I got a good look inside, the white carpeting was scattered with pizza boxes and other garbage. The focal point for the trash was a low coffee table, the only furniture. The shelf molding that runs along two walls was lined with empty wine bottles, dozens of them. It looked like a child's room, a child who drinks wine.

St. Mary's Cathedral installed sprinkler systems in its doorways to discourage the people from sleeping there. Such systems are common in the Financial District "as a safety and cleanliness measure." Starting before sunset, the sprinklers ran for about 75 seconds, about every half hour, soaking homeless sleepers and their belongings. Innovative homeless slept under umbrellas and waterproof gear. In March, 2015, following public outrage fueled by media reports, the church apologized and removed the sprinklers. A news broadcaster concludes with "There will be no more rains of not-so-holy water." Nighttime park and plaza closures, large vehicle parking bans, recycling center closures. Nature is reconstituted as parklets poking into gasoline-fumed streets, as living walls and neon deer. I sit at my computer trying to ignore the male voice outside who rants incessantly. I can't make out any words—it's like he's spewing the preverbal rage that's choking the rest of us—rage I see whenever I check the news or Facebook or Twitter—rage that's been compacted to slogan, a pressurized neutron of meaning. The man's vocals explode in the street, rattling the black glass of Twitter Towers. This piece has 117,002 characters. That's 836 tweets. Some students—even in graduate writing programs—make each sentence a new paragraph. It's like they don't know how to connect one thing to another. Perhaps these one sentence paragraphs best reflect our current reality—a series of discrete bits—better than my horse and buggy paragraphs that trot on for pages. In *Bess* each short paragraph is numbered. The numbers reflect bureaucracy's drive to catalogue incidents that will never add up, its determination to sanitize an impossibly vulnerable messiness. When I quoted *Bess* here, I removed the numbers, I don't know why—I guess I just I didn't want them.

Kevin and I visit Ed Roberson, UC Berkeley's current Holloway Poet. Ed gives us a copy of three poems he wrote performing the exercises he gave his class. The first, "de Chirico," is based on the ekphrastic assignment:

> Something   you can't see
>   on the other side
>   of a wall from this side
>
>   casts a shadow

The real enemy is always unseen, I think, the real enemy hides in systems too vast to fathom—capitalism, entitlement, dehumanization, greed. Over Sauvignon Blanc and cheese, I tell Ed and his friend Pat Sawzik about the changes happening in San Francisco, our fears of eviction. Pat smiles broadly and suggests I propose a writing workshop for Twitter employees. "You should ask for $100,000 a year!" she exclaims. "And that they buy for you the three-story Victorian you live in." She says I could be the bridge between the techies and reality, teach them how to reinhabit their bodies.

Dear Twitter,

I've taught Somatic Engagement to industrial designers and architects at California College of the Arts. One of my students—an interactive design major—was hired by Facebook before he graduated. He showed me how to use the search function on my iPhone. When I asked him what interactive designers do, he said they made technology more human. Students reported that I humanized their fields. One student exclaimed, "If there were no human bodies, buildings would not exist!"

Twitter is all about first personal narrative—my specialty. I can bring your employees to a new appreciation of the person. I can teach them how to connect tweets into longer narratives to counter the fragmentation inherent in the 140-character modality. As a long-time resident in your neighborhood, I can provide Twitter employees with an appreciation of our neighborhood's history, its rich cultural production and diversity.

Rampant technological expansion without heart is unsustainable. Reconnecting your employees to their bodies will counteract the fragmentation inherent in micro-content management, lengthening attention span, and thereby increasing worker productivity. As a representative of the SOMA/Mid-Market district, I would like to share its heart with Twitter.

For all this I'm only asking a mere $100,000 a year—and that you purchase for me the 3-story Victorian in which I now reside to serve as my residence and headquarters of the Tech Heart Institute. I will teach writing from the heart in the heart of tech gentrification—what I call techrification—our slogan would be "Techrification with Heart." The Tech Heart Institute will offer a historically preserved in situ learning environment, a visionary intersection of technology, arts, entertainment and culture. If Twitter can purchase two ancient log cabins, renovate and move them to its cafeteria as a lounge, purchasing a neighborhood Victorian for my institute is small potatoes. I guarantee you won't regret it.

We could advertise on the side of the luxurious NEMA Towers, which have so dramatically augmented the Mid-Market skyline:

WHEN HEART

WRITES,

FOCUS

REIGNITES.

Thank you in advance for your consideration. I eagerly await hearing from you.

Dodie Bellamy, M.S.

White guy with shaved head, pinkish against oversized white T-shirt, pacing on Natoma Street. As I park my car, he raises a hand blocking his face from me, and mutters, "It's not my fault. It's not my fault." A few days later on 11th Street I see a white guy with shaved head wearing an oversized white T-shirt who has his arms in the air and is shouting something I can't understand from across the street where I'm walking excruciatingly slow in order to not catch up with him, then he thrusts his crotch against the side of a trash can—BAM BAM BAM—then he turns around and races over to a building, arms still in air, humps the building, then struts down the street, arms raised, hands in fists. A woman passes without incident, then he turns around and yells at her, flailing his arms and hip-thrusting. When he gets to Howard Street, he takes off running between oncoming cars, in this mechanical zigzag pattern, like a killer robot. I'm on my way to pick up an order from Basil Canteen, there's only one more block to go but it feels endless and I'm wondering is my Choo Chee Salmon worth it. After I get the food and am walking back home, a guy approaches from behind on a bicycle. He's in the street, I'm on the sidewalk, he would barely register—except he's white with a shaved head, wearing an oversized white T-shirt.

Three of these guys, is this some weird ass coincidence, or are they the same person? Like the three-legged dogs I frequently see being walked on leashes. Is there an epidemic of three-legged dogs in my neighborhood or am I seeing the same one or two over and over? I vow to pay closer attention to the dogs. The guy on the bicycle takes a turn on Mission Street and pedals out of sight.

TECH ON
ON THE OUTSIDE,
HEART ON
THE INSIDE.

EMBRACEMENT,
NOT DISPLACEMENT.
DREAMER,
NOT ASS REAMER.

There is no narrative. There is daily life with Kevin and the cats and an outside that beams into my devices, and which I occasionally leave my microcosm and touch. I open the back door and step onto the porch. Two-thirty a.m., the longest night of the year. The sky is bursting with stars—shocking for the City— must be the darkness of the new moon. I bend my head back, mouth gaping at the vastness, unable to discern the stars' patterns, these crucial arrangements named after gods—or maybe they *were* gods, I don't know. I imagine myself a prehistoric nomad, trying to make sense of this amazing display, how mysterious it must have been, how mysterious it still is. Even in San Francisco the stars remind us the universe does not belong to us. Sound of generators and traffic—I look over at the Bank of America office building—a white slab that manages to look both tall and squat, entire floors lit 24/7—through the windows I see partitioned beige mazes. When armored money trucks pull up to the garage, blocking the sidewalk, I've found myself waiting impatiently as guards stick those reflective bomb mirrors under them, just like you see on TV. No one should live a half a block away from bomb mirrors. Someone asked me, "Aren't you afraid of living that close to Twitter? ISIS hates Twitter and say they're targeting it." When I googled "ISIS hates Twitter," all I found was "ISIS hates the West," "ISIS hates Obama," "ISIS *literally* hates kittens." But when I looked up "ISIS threatens Twitter" I found *#The_Concept_of_Lone_Wolf_Attacks: The time has arrived to respond to Twitter's management by directly attacking their employees and physically assassinating them!! Those who will carry this out are the sleepers cells of death.* I find *#The_Concept_of_Lone_Wolf_Attacks: Every Twitter employee in San Francisco in the United States should bear in mind and watch over himself because on his doorstep there might be a lone wolf assassin waiting.* Isis is the name of a street in the neighborhood—sympathetic magic that refuses to comfort since I know not whether it protects or summons. Behind BofA the black glass of Twitter Towers bleeds into the moonless night, single red light at the top, always visible—as if NEMA were beaming messages to outer space. I read that the dominant life form in the cosmos is probably nonorganic, some kind of super-intelligent robots, the kind of consciousness that could relate to the red light's alien Morse code nuggets, each 140 characters long. I think *architectural nightmares,* I think *offenses to nature.* In the late '70s when I moved to San Francisco someone told me that the construction of the Transamerica Pyramid was proof the inhabitants of San Francisco were reincarnated from Atlantis, doomed to again sink beneath the ocean. I scoffed back then, but I believe them now. The End of Days—we all can feel it, the Kali Yuga, when negativity soars and everything falls apart. *Our Lady of Darkness:* And the entire world was just as bad; it was perishing of pollution, drowning and suffocating in chemical and atomic poisons, detergents and insecticides, industrial effluvia, smog, the stench of sulfuric acid, the quantities of steel, cement, aluminum ever bright, eternal plastics, omnipresent paper, gas and electron floods—electro-mephitic city-stuff indeed! *#The_Concept_of_ Lone_Wolf_Attacks: Twitter management should know that if they do not stop their campaign in the virtual world, we will the bring the war to them in the real world on the ground.* The Doomsday Clock moves two minutes closer to doom. *Tick. Tick.* "It is now three minutes to midnight," says atomic scientist Kennette Benedict. "The probability of global catastrophe is very high. This is about the end of civilization as we know it." *Tick.* I soak up the stars a bit longer then sit cross-legged on the couch and pray to the vast solstice night to heal me and Kevin and the cats, to heal ISIS and Twitter and climate change and nuclear proliferation, to sprinkle its fairy dust on Daphne Gottlieb and Bess, on all those who kick their blankets and speak to the unseen, to tweet its twinkles down to the street where one-footed souls twitch and twirl.

2

I thought this piece was finished. I was wrong.

It's Sunday afternoon, 11th Street is empty as I walk past the block-long flagship Goodwill. I try to imagine the gray enameled two-story building zooming into the air another fifteen stories, as if it took a bite of the Hookah-Smoking Caterpillar's mushroom, a big bite. *"What can all that green stuff be?" said Alice. "And where have my shoulders got to? And oh, my poor hands, how is it I can't see you?" She was moving them about as she spoke, but no result seemed to follow, except a little shaking among the distant green leaves.* With a pang of dread I look down at the ground. Against the Goodwill's wall are stacked three piles of white garbage. Only white garbage. They look like snow drifts, each less than a foot high, each meticulously arranged with little shreds of this and that: paper, styrofoam, cotton. To express scale an artist will often insert a human figure. On 11th Street, I am that figure, looming over this loveliness that would be so easy to stomp past, stomp over with my mammoth booted feet. To fully appreciate the detail, I would need to kneel down on the urine—and who knows what else—soaked pavement, the filth of the street seeping into skin and clothing. In San Francisco, the housed are perpendicular. Only the homeless are horizontal, sitting or lying on the street, accruing $100 tickets for doing so. To counteract laws that discriminate against the homeless, Right to Rest legislation keeps being introduced in California and keeps going nowhere. Like clouds or sheep in mattress ads, these three white mounds beckon me to crawl towards them and lay my head against their impossible softness. I do bend over, tentatively, for I'm self-conscious about moving my body from upright to hunched. I feel unstable and vulnerable leaning towards these tiny white morsels so totally at the mercy of movement or wind. Nothing to hold them in place. Life at pavement level is precious because it's so contingent. I marvel at this miracle of evanescence and synchronicity, that I should be walking past this installation at its pinnacle before its bits poofed into the air like feathers in a pillow fight.

To my right a tree grows out of a square of dirt that's been cut from the sidewalk. The tree is young and leans over at a 45° angle, as if it too were tired of standing. Its scrawny trunk is supported by two wooden poles and some rope—a tree on crutches. Arranged over the dirt at its base are two concentric circles comprised of teeny bits of fruit—raspberries and some-thing orange—like cut up mango—or persimmon skin—and I wonder what kind of ritual, what kind of street witch presided here. I wish her magic were powerful enough to save the Goodwill.

I'm reminded of the woman who a couple of weeks ago was rummaging in the jade plants that grow at the base of the bottle brush tree in front of my building. I assumed she was looking for crack—I've seen many crackheads digging in planters—but then I saw she was picking up bits of something from the street and putting them into the dirt—*oh she's hiding crack*—I walk down the stairs to the second floor landing to get a better look—her movements are quick and focused and it's not crack but scraps of garbage she's placing in the dirt—one particle after another. I thought she was crazy, but now I suspect it was a spell.

Six weeks later, late afternoon on Wednesday, January 28, I park my car on Lafayette and bump into Suzanne, my downstairs neighbor. She's who cleaned up the dot-com neighbor's vomit. We stand in front of Pork Belly Burgers discussing the recent rise of scary people on the street. One time when Suzanne was waiting for the bus by Trader Joe's, she caught the eye of this guy who starting yelling things like "Who do you think you are!" and he hit her in the head with his backpack. Standing nearby were a group of people holding Trader Joe's bags. When Suzanne moved into the street to get away from her backpack-swinging attacker, not only did her fellow shoppers not help her, they tittered. Suzanne says, "If someone attacks you, no one will help you." I shake my head then I walk over to acupuncture and then Rainbow Grocery, and by time I return to Lafayette it's dark out and there are several cops on the street with flashlights, looking around. One cop emerges from the basement of a condo, and I ask him what's up. "Nothing," he says. "Just looking for something." On my block there are more cops with flashlights, one of them searching in the jade plants in front of my building, other cops racing around on 11th Street. I'm convinced that something bad has happened and they're looking for a weapon.

It wasn't until the next day I learned that someone had left a suitcase containing a human torso and leg on 11th Street, among the rest of the discards in front of the entrance to the Goodwill's As-If shop. Somebody called the cops because of the smell. The headline in USA *Today* read "Suitcase of body parts found near Twitter HQ." The article said the suitcase was discovered at 4:14 in the afternoon—the same time Suzanne and I had our chat. The article said the police scoured the area looking for more body parts—and I wondered what they hoped to find in my jade plants. A tooth? A finger? They should have looked deeper for in those plants the urban witch left so much meaning, so many pieces. I thought back to the three piles of white garbage heaped against the side of the Goodwill, the fruit bits arranged in concentric circles, and it felt like I had stumbled into a gateway. What kind of ritual had been enacted there? A blessing or a cure, or feng sui-type energy realignment? Their placement a few feet away from where the body parts were abandoned suggests a cleansing, a warning. Things broken down into bits and reorganized. Trash reconfigured as beauty reconfigured as horror. The superstitious part of my psyche flares wildly. I read online that scientists suspect the universe is a computer simulation. A new metaphor for what the ancients knew—that reality is fluid, that we live in a dream. And then the steady march towards capitalist myopia. Cabs circle Uber headquarters, cabs banging horns nonstop for all of us who are being phased out. When I google "Capitalism is the antichrist," I find "Capitalism is the Antichrist. Isn't it obvious? Jesus Christ didn't say, 'before I heal you, you need to pay me, and I need to see proof of insurance.'" Another site names capitalism one of the Four Horsemen of the Apocalypse, the black horse. Though mostly it's right-wingers railing against communists like Barack Obama. Violence rips the veil and the magical unconscious spills out.

BE A CON-
DUCTOR,
NOT A
FUCKER.

Police found another leg in the trashcan in front of Firestone Tires. Trey's Yelp review of Firestone: Firestone has been extremely supportive to the local SOMA community in providing paint for graffiti abatement, allowing us to dispose of trash in their garbage, etc. Support those businesses that support the community. Thanks!

Bess: Her eyes don't waver, staring at me. *So*, she says, savoring the words, *Have you been back to the hotel?* Her eyes transport me there, make me shudder. *You should go back there*, she says. The hair on my arms stands up, listening, or it's so cold. It might be evil. Can a place be evil? Can a person be abducted by evil?

Surveillance cameras show the guy wheeled the suitcase around the neighborhood for hours. I watch a video of him pulling it past Pork Belly Burgers—right where Suzanne and I were talking— a thin scraggly bearded guy. He's Mark Jeffrey Andrus, a small, quiet 54-year-old man who grew up in Missoula, Montana. Previous arrests include suspected drug possession, theft, burglary and bail jumping. On Friday Police receive an anonymous tip to his whereabouts. At 7:30 p.m. they arrive at 430 Turk Street, a flat gray public housing complex with bright turquoise security gates. They knock loudly on the apartment door of 55-year-old Mark Keever, startling Keever and Andrus, who are inside watching a movie on the *Syfy* channel. Keever and Andrus met three years ago while standing in line at the methadone clinic across the street from Keever's apartment. Andrus bummed a cigarette and the two hit it off. Keever: "I noticed he needed a place to stay and offered it up." Ever since then, Andrus will stop by to hang out, shower, eat, and sometimes spend the night. Neighbors call Andrus "the leprechaun" because he's short and doesn't speak much. Keever lets the police in. When they pat down and handcuff Andrus, Keever says, "Mark, don't fight." Andrus says, "Okay." The police put a white sheet over Andrus' head and take him downstairs to the squad car. He looks like a child with a really shitty Halloween ghost costume. They take Keever into custody as well. I'm piecing these bits together from dozens of sources. On a rogue news site I catch a glimpse of Keever hunched over and rushing to the squad car. He's tall, extremely thin, effeminate. Light-colored or graying hair, longish. Investigators scour the apartment, which has a hard linoleum floor, a small television and several ragged chairs near the meager cot Keever sleeps on. They take pictures inside Keever's closet, bathroom and kitchen. On Saturday Keever is released but Andrus is arrested on suspicion of murder and five outstanding traffic warrants. Seven days prior to the suitcase discovery, Andrus' former SRO roommate, 58-year-old Omar Shahwan, was reported missing. Andrus is in possession of Shahwan's state-issued ID card.

The guy pulled the suitcase around for hours, dousing the area with malevolence, like a truck trailing a fog of pesticide. The parts were so mangled, investigators didn't know at first if they were human or animal. What if I saw him—when I walked to my car on Wednesday—I keep having glints of a thin scraggly bearded guy rolling a suitcase. A flash then dissolve, a vision that won't quite materialize—as if I were in a Dario Argento film enacting his recurring plot of someone who has witnessed something important but can't remember what. I definitely did see a man pulling a large black suitcase—but was it that guy, that day—I don't remember—so many dicey guys so many days, so many lives wheeled in shopping carts and baby carriages and luggage—even I have wheeled a suitcase the four long blocks from Civic Center BART past the Hotel Whitcomb, past Twitter, past Square and Uber and the BofA bank machines, past the Goodwill As-If shop, across Mission, past the Firestone trash can, down my alley and through the front gate of my building.

Dear Twitter,

I saw a photo online of Jack Dorsey, your co-founder and chairman of the board, standing beside Alissa Anderson—my personal friend—in her eco-boutique Foggy Notion—Jack, who in March 2006 sent the first tweet ever—"just setting up my twttr"—see, I've done my homework. Alissa is a photographer, musician, designer—I regularly carry one of her shoulder bags. In the photo Jack's wearing gray high v-neck T, jeans, tattooed arm, and beard—a regular guy who clearly supports the arts, who appreciates larger temporalities than 140-word spasms, who longs for hand-crafted meticulous moments that build to a gloriously nuanced whole—Alissa can vouch for me, I can lead Twitter employees …

The following Tuesday, February 3, Andrus is released due to lack of evidence. Once he's lawyered up, Andrus looks squeaky clean in a brightly striped sweater, mostly red and blue, with black, yellow, white accents. On Friday he visits Keever to borrow a sleeping bag. Keever says, "Hi Mark, how you doing? Good to see you're out." Andrus says, "Yeah, I didn't do it, I don't know what the problem was." On Saturday Andrus admits himself to San Francisco General and dies of drug-related septic shock. San Francisco General will soon be renamed Pricilla and Mark Zuckerberg San Francisco General Hospital and Trauma Center due to the Zuckerbergs' $75 million donation. Kevin jokes that Facebook General would be a better name.

I take public transportation to SF State and back, and then later to Nob Hill, so repeatedly in one day I walk past where the suitcase was deposited, and each time I feel a frisson. Every sidewalk stain I imagine as blood. And then there's the trashcan of death in front of Firestone Tires. I keep thinking of *Bess*. Can a place be bad? This place where I live, is it bad? Or is this an uprising, the twitches and trembles of the discarded, all these men and women and children with no place to belong creating a massive tremor knocking us out of complacency. No one can remain buffered. No one can not look. The more I learn about the guy rolling the cut-up torso around, the more unreal life feels. *Our Lady of Darkness*: And now something seemed to stir in the massed darkness there. The parts never add up. SROs, evictions, tech money in the background. I'm outside both ends of the socio-economic ladder, for now. Due to rent hikes, the owner of a clothing boutique on Castro Street closed the business after 26 years and ended up living in his Chrysler Sebring convertible for eight months until the AIDS Housing Alliance was able to find a place for him. The owner of the Castro travel agency I used to go to—Now Voyager—facing eviction, jumped off the Golden Gate Bridge. I dream I'm separating lentils from rice. I'm told by a disembodied female voice that's what I have to do. She can read the state of a person by the coarseness of their grains/lentils. I feel an incredible urge to organize the muddle. Of course this is a reference to the tasks of Psyche. It's about discernment, about knowing where things belong. It's about patience, commitment, endurance. About fragmentation and order. Snow white heaps of trash followed by jumbled parts in suitcase and trash can. Altar of purity followed by altar of horror—that's the wrong order. Though I write with the graininess of surveillance footage, gathering these narrative flecks I too negotiate with the unseen.

MAKE AMENDS.

CHOCOLATE

ALMONDS.

On Wednesday, February 11, the San Francisco Medical Examiner's Office confirms it was Omar Shahwan's dismembered body in the suitcase and trashcan. Since his head and hands were never found, authorities swabbed Shahwan's father's cheek for a DNA sample to compare to the body. After living for decades in Jerusalem, 83-year-old Ali Shahwan moved to Vallejo to be closer to his son. In the Vallejo living room a giant reproduction of DaVinci's Birth of Venus looms over a pale gray sofa, which Ali brought with him from Jerusalem. He says that Omar was a gentle man—a nature enthusiast, an artist, an animal lover who had a special connection with the family pet, a 2-year-old German shepherd named Rocky. A painting by Omar fills the screen with the soft bleeds of a watercolor. It's the head and shoulders of a New York Yankee against a vivid blue mottled background—the sky? The Yankee's face is pale and bloated. He looks sad. Both his flesh and uniform are rendered in cream with gray shadows so that it's hard to tell where uniform begins and flesh ends. The blue stripes of his uniform, though more turquoise that the blue of the background, look as if the sky were running in rivulets over his shoulders. Channel 2 has run a royal blue banner across the bottom of the painting which reads in white: DISMEMBERED BODY CASE. Though Ali provided a room for him in his home, Omar would go into the City and stay with friends for days at a time. In 2010 Shahwan lived with Andrus at the Krupa Hotel, a SRO at 700 Jones Street in the Tenderloin. The two filed lawsuits in San Francisco Superior Court after the building's landlord tried to evict them. Ali Shahwan: "He was the greatest guy on Earth. He is my son. He is my love. He is my heart." Omar's obituary concludes with a Bible quote: "Tho they slay me—yet will I trust in thee dear God."

Krupa Hotel, one star review entitled "Steer clear!!!" We checked in and were told the room we had booked had a broken door, so if we could get it open we could stay there! I tried but to no avail, so we had to climb another 3 flights of stairs with our suitcases. When we entered the room we were shocked, there were stains on the wall which looked suspiciously like fecal matter and the room absolutely stank! My friend and I had to share a double bed, and we slept in hoodies and tracksuit bottoms on top of the duvet because the sheets were filthy. I hardly slept because I was bitten all over by bed bugs, literally from head to toe, it was disgusting! We got up the next morning and literally ran out of the place. I am deadly serious when I say avoid this dump at all costs it is a health hazard!!!!!

At 11th Street waiting for the light at Mission, I stand beside a young black guy, late teens/early 20s. He's quiet, self-contained, wearing white earbuds and an olive green backpack with "Eat more fruits and vegetables. Be Healthy." printed across it. As soon as he crosses Mission and steps onto the sidewalk beside the Goodwill he starts shouting and jerking. Even though I'm in a hurry to get to the optometrist I wait for the next light, so I can't make out what he's saying. There was no transition from guy I felt comfortable beside to these explosions of rage, as if the act of stepping onto that stretch of sidewalk flipped a switch and a new script was launched. It's as if some outside force has taken control, supercharging his musculature, his vocal chords. In *Our Lady of Darkness* the accumulation of what Fritz Leiber calls "city-stuff"—the weight of all that steel, electricity, and paper—calls forth paramentals, malicious elemental spirits. I look up at the Bank of America office buildings on both sides of the street, tall slabs of dense matter looming over a concrete corridor—soulless—the configuration creates a wind tunnel so intense that sometimes I have to bend over in order to walk through it. If any place could summon badness, it's here.

Waiting for the streetcar at the Van Ness underground station. A sad-eyed elderly man holds the leash of a small bright-eyed dog. The dog wears a studded leather collar; the man wears a black knit cap imprinted with a green marijuana leaf. The dog comes up to me wagging its tail, wanting connection. "Are you having a good morning?" I say as I pet him. The man smiles. We're having a moment, I think.

Urban Eyes, Market near Castro, where I've been going since the '90s, sitting in a teeny room packed with eye-testing equipment—I bring up gentrification and the optometrist has so much to say, it seems my eye exam will never begin. He tells me about a nearby small business whose rent was raised $5,000. The rent for most commercial spaces in the Castro is now $10,000 a month, and his lease is up and he's on a month to month basis, and frame sales are down because people buy online, and he doesn't know how long he can stay in business. He says the neighborhood is against chains, but only chains will be able to afford the rents.

After the optometrist I get Indian buffet a few doors down. Through the restaurant window on Market an old white guy with shoulder-length white hair and matching beard is trailing another guy waving his arms and doing the rage-shouting. He's wearing a filthy knee-length white coat, a lab coat perhaps. He looks like a mad scientist. The next time I look out the window, he's climbed up onto the wheelchair boarding platform at the streetcar stop. Standing there with his long hair and beard shouting at the traffic, he reminds me of Moses. I take the underground home. In the back of the car is a young fleshy Asian guy. In quick oblique glances I take in his black and bright blue windbreaker, the thick black frame of his glasses. He's just sitting there and looks totally normal, but something about him prompts me to move to the front of the car. I take the aisle seat beside a techy guy whose "you're not welcome" vibes are weaker than my "it's my right to sit here" vibes. As soon as we pull out of Church Street Station, the black and blue windbreaker guy starts pacing and shouting. The only word I can make out is FUCK. They all say FUCK. Woman after woman scurries to the front of the car near me. Amidst the cowering women a beefy heavily-tattooed guy in his 40s sits side-wise in the senior and disabled seats. "Mexican" is inked in script on his forearm as well as his neck. The way he scowls at the shouting makes us feel safe. When I exit the Van Ness station, I peer down 11th Street, feeling in my gut there's got to be another one. But all seems calm. I take a few steps and at the bus stop a woman begins howling. Long greasy brown hair, black short-shorts and a crop top that reveals a big pale belly. Tears stream down her face as her mouth stretches open and emits another wail.

A LOVING

THREAD,

NOT THE

LIVING DEAD.

I dream that as a fundraiser a homeless rights organization is selling scrub brushes in a rainbow of colors—purple, blue, pink, etc.—and when I wake up I have this compulsion to buy a dayglo yellow scrub brush—a round brush, its plastic handle shaped like a button mushroom. What I do buy is a small globe-shaped votive candle holder in vivid yellow glass. I burn a candle to change the energy of the dream, to release something, but I don't quite know what it is. Suffering, I suppose, to brighten the suffering of others, to make it flicker and rise and disappear.

The facts of the case sound fishy to everybody. Online theories abound. Andrus knew the cops would figure out Shahwan was in the suitcase so he committed suicide. Andrus became infected with bacteria while hacking up Shahwan's body and that's how he went septic. Both deaths were mob hits—though naysayers ask why would the mob bother with a couple of homeless guys. Some say whoever killed Shahwan gave Andrus bad drugs. Some suspect the landlord. "I am tellin' ya … look at the owner of the SRO the vic sued." Others play up the "hobosexual" angle, claim Andrus and Shahwan were lovers. Lots of mention in the media of male "friends" sleeping over. Mark Keever professes his "friend" Andrus' innocence over and over. "With all my heart and soul, it's not him, and that's the honest-to-God's truth." Ali Shahwan: Andrus killed his son because of a dispute over money. Someone else suspects the police let Andrus go because they knew he was dying. It's not a coincidence. Something smells fishy. "I guess it's true when they say everybody has baggage." Maybe it was Shahwan's dying wish to have his limbs strewn about the city. Andrus got a bunch of bad drugs. Andrus and Shahwan went on a bender. Shahwan OD'd, Andrus panicked and tried to get rid of the body because he was paranoid about the cops. "Andrus eventually succumbed to said bad gear/went on a massive bender with the same stash after being in jail for a few days." Andrus got sepsis from smoking meth, which destroys your teeth due to lack of saliva production and leads to tooth decay and eventual infection that gets into the blood stream. Andrus got sepsis from "skin popping." After years of shooting up an addict's veins get ruined, so out of desperation he injects himself under the skin of the abdomen or other fatty part of his body. When this is done, infection is imminent, regardless of the quality of the drugs. Ali Shahwan: "That's probably why he killed my son. Because my son wanted to get away from him." Leaving body parts around is sloppy "no matter how you look at it," but hiding the head and hands show the killer "went the extra yard." Sawing or chopping up a body is strenuous work. Most hatchets and simple chainsaws aren't effective. A hacksaw works best. Cutting up a body and draining the blood is so difficult and messy, even most hardened criminals can't handle it. To maintain the necessary level of determination a person must be psychotic or just plain evil. Public Defender Jeff Adachi: "During the short time I represented Mark, I found him to be a kind and engaging person." Mark Keever: "I have full-blown AIDS, and many times he would help me clean my house." Manager at the Krupa Hotel: Andrus helped her out by doing such things as taking out the garbage. Keever: "He's given me a lot of things—he even bought me cockroach spray for my apartment." Adachi: "From what I can tell, Mark was a good person." Keever: "He was a good little guy." Ali Shahwan: "I didn't like him. The man doesn't look to me that he's decent." Ali Shahwan's Vallejo neighbor: "There was something off about him." Ali Shahwan: "He got his death penalty from God."

Shahwan's missing upper limbs and head call to mind the dismemberment of Osiris. Osiris' cock was eaten by fish, so when Isis reassembled him she made him a gold cock instead. In the form of a giant falcon Isis breathed life into Osiris with her wings and fucked his golden cock, conceiving a son. In 2011 Mid-Market had a commercial vacancy rate of thirty percent, the highest in the city. Then San Francisco offered a payroll tax break to businesses in the area, and nineteen technology companies moved in. In 2013 alone, the companies reduced their payroll tax liability by $4.2 million. San Francisco fucks the golden cock again and again and again. Mayor Lee, the biggest fucker of all, was on my plane when I recently flew to Seattle. He was wearing a baseball cap, which he took off when getting his picture taken with a Virgin America stewardess. During boarding I walked right past him—he was standing in front of seat 12C, organizing his stuff. Without his security guards the mayor looked like any other passenger, short and bland. I wanted to blurt out, "Why are you destroying San Francisco?" Instead I trudged toward the back, muted by shyness. He didn't even notice me.

Big blonde guy, muscles so bulgy they look inflated, shouting fuck fuck fucking fuck you fuck fuck, with slight variations in a nonstop loop. Storming down 11th Street, determined and hyper-visceral as a mercenary assassin, he's heading directly toward me. Casually, as if I don't notice the onrush of fucking fuck fucks, I step into the street and cross to the other side. I continue to the BofA bank machines. On Market a male voice shouts something and before I have time to see him, panic shoots through my torso. When I do look, it's just some guy yelling at his friend to wait a minute. I've read that trauma is always in the present tense. The body marries the then with the now. Like radical politics, the body knows not gradation. There is safe and there is danger. There is inside and outside, friend and enemy, stay put or flee. I'm either on the verge of agoraphobia—I think—or a spiritual awakening.

Krupa Hotel, one star review entitled "It's a dump." Listen, I'm going to be frank. Surely, anything is better than this. I saw the city workers cleaning the sidewalk and I can assure you it is cleaner than this place. I now know why San Fran has a high suicide rate. I now know what poverty feels like. It's smells, you're surrounded by bugs and you feel like a rundown schmuck.

Weekly I google "San Francisco body parts suitcase," but since Shahwan was identified, there's been nothing new, it's been weeks. I know there's more to the story. I know there's plenty THEY're not telling us. Because THEY who feed us information are sneaky and secretive, because THEY believe nobody cares about old news, because THEY've got plenty of new stories. "Mom stored disabled daughter's body in duct taped suitcase, authorities say." "Chihuahua apparently climbs in owner's suitcase, rescued by TSA officials." "Former CEO of startup sentenced to two years for defrauding investors of more than $500,000." "Coroner says New Castle woman's body was found in suitcase, submerged in pond."

I walk past the Pork Belly Burgers surveillance camera, taking the same path as the suitcase, a short half block from where I saw the one-booted woman who started this whole cycle. Further down Lafayette a woman is carrying a comforter—huge and white and fluffy like a cloud—that drags on the sidewalk behind her. She sets it down and reaches up to a tree branch. Her blonde hair is short and randomly choppy. I walk down Natoma to avoid her, following the one-booted woman's path. After I'm home a few minutes I hear a man shouting. It's Trey. "Get out of here! You do not belong. Go! Go!" I step out onto the landing but I can't find him. He's watered the bottle brush tree so much it's grown gigantic, blocking my view to the right. "Don't take plants that don't belong to you," his voice yells. From behind the bottle brush tree the comforter woman emerges, holding a swatch of tree branch. She's nodding silently, feeling the ache of plants cramped in wine barrels and sidewalk panels, framed in the living wall at Twitter headquarters. She holds the branch upright like a wand. She plucked it because the tree loves her. The urban witch collects and rearranges; to be touched by her is a blessing. "Go! Go!" Trey shouts. "I know who you are. The next time I see you I'm going to kick the shit out of you." I'm sure the branch will show up later in the neighborhood, reconfigured as relic. From in front of the auto body shop, she picks up a milk crate full of stuff, piles the comforter on top and shuffles towards 11th Street. I go back inside and fume. I should have raced to the street and told him to shut the fuck up, I should have given her money, I should have called the cops and reported his threatened assault. Instead I say to Kevin, "You're right, it would have been better if *he* were in the suitcase." Before the body was identified we hadn't seen Trey for a few days, and we joked that it was he who was in the suitcase—"He's small so he'd fit in there easily." We said it was the revenge of the homeless for his asshole behavior. The urban witch taps her branch on 11th Street. Concrete buckles and blood bubbles in gutters. Pus vomit semen urine shit squish beneath Trey's feet as he screams in horror. The witch taps her branch. The Goodwill refunds the $327 million it received from developers and its future shrinks once more to two stories. Log cabin break rooms split apart, regain the log cabin integrity of their youth. The witch taps again. State asylum doors swing open, Bess walks out in fresh pink sweatpants and two Frye boots, and real feather-and-blood birds go TWEET TWEET TWEET. I'm hired by Twitter to develop the Tech Heart Institute. The witch taps. Street-cleaning hoses point skyward, transformed into fountains which nourish the earth, and every single person in San Francisco nestles at night full-bellied, enveloped in softness.

Acknowledgments

"Whistle While You Dixie" was commissioned and published as a chapbook by Susan Silton, in conjunction with a performance of the Crowing Hens at LAXArt on May 12, 2010. "When the Sick Rule the World" was previously published in *Bombay Gin* 38.1, 2012 (Boulder). "Rascal Guru" was previously published in *The Swan's Rag*, Issue 4, August, 2011 (Oakland). "Barf Manifesto" was previously published as the chapbook *Barf Manifesto* (Brooklyn: Ugly Duckling Presse, 2008). Thank you Anna Moschovakis for being such a wonderful editor and friend. "MLA Barf" was written for the panel "*Intimate Revolt*: Recognizing Liberatory Forms of Documentary and Life Writing," curated by Kass Fleisher and presented at the Modern Language Association Convention, Chicago, December 28, 2007. "CCA Barf" was written for the Graduate Lecture Series at California College of the Arts (San Francisco), and was presented on February 5, 2008. "Girl Body" was previously published in *Action Yes Quarterly*, Vol. 1, Issue 12, Winter 2010. "The Bandaged Lady" was previously published as the chapbook *The Bandaged Lady* (San Francisco: [2nd floor projects], 2008), commissioned as a catalogue essay for *Hanging Matters*, an exhibit of Tariq Alvi's art at [2nd floor projects], March, 2008. Thank you Margaret Tedesco for offering me the opportunity to write about the brilliant Tariq Alvi. "The Feminist Writers' Guild" was presented on "The Social" panel at *Feminaissance*, sponsored by CalArts, at the Museum of Contemporary Art, Los Angeles, April 28, 2007. It was also included in *Feminaissance*, ed. Christine Wertheim (Los Angeles: Les Figues Press, 2010). Thank you Christine for your continued support and affection. "Phone Home" was written for *Life as We Show It*, ed. Brian Pera and Masha Tupitsyn, (San Francisco: City Lights, 2009). An excerpt was published in *Apothecary*, Ether, 7/11/08 (Denver). "The Center of Gravity" was commissioned by the San Francisco Museum of Modern Art for FIELD WORK: *Mark di Suvero at Crissy Field—Poets Respond*, eds. Frank Smigiel and Kevin Killian, 2013. "Digging Through Kathy Acker's Stuff" was written to be performed in conjunction with "Kathy Forest," an exhibition of Kathy Acker's clothes I curated for at New Langton Arts, San Francisco, July 11–15, 2006; "Kathy Forest" was also presented at White Columns, New York, January-February, 2007. "Digging through Kathy Acker's Stuff" was previously published in *The Back Room, An Anthology* ed. Matthew Stadler (Portland, OR: Clear Cut Press, 2007). "July 4, 2011" was written for *Conversations at the Wartime Cafe: A Decade of War 2001–2011*, ed. Sean Manzano (Berkeley: CreateSpace, 2011). "The Beating of Our Hearts" was previously published as the chapbook *The Beating of Our Hearts* (Los Angeles: Semiotext(e), 2014). The first section of the chapbook was commissioned by the ICA in London, as a handout to accompany the exhibit *See Red Women's Workshop* (December 5, 2012–January 13, 2013). Thank for Anna Gritz for providing this opportunity to extend my range and for introducing me to the work of *See Red*. The final two sections of "The Beating of Our Hearts" were written about a poetry scene that has changed much since 2012. If I were writing about it now, I would produce a very different text. Thank you Andrew Kenower for still being there. "I Must Not Forget What I Already

Know" was commissioned in response to the *Reverse Rehearsals* exhibition, Southern Exposure, San Francisco; presented May 30, 2013 and published as part of an anthology to accompany the show. Thank you Michele Carlson for including me in such an amazing project. "In the Shadow of Twitter Towers" was written for this book. An excerpt was published online in *Fanzine* <www.thefanzine.com>. A bounty of thanks to Daphne Gottlieb for writing such a powerful chapbook, *Bess*, and for allowing me to quote from it. Thank you also to Ed Roberson for allowing me to quote from your stunning poem.

Thank you to Tariq Alvi, for gifting me the wonderful *Bandaged Lady* piece and allowing us to use it on the cover. Thank you to Margaret Tedesco for providing a high resolution image. Thank you Hedi El Kholti for your friendship, and being a dream editor. Thanks also to Chris Kraus and Sylvère Lotringer for publishing my collection. Thanks to my Spring 2015 students for being so patient with my craziness while I was finishing my manuscript— Somatic Engagement at CCA; MFA Fiction Workshop, Thesis, Directed Writing at SFSU. Thanks to Stephen Boyer for your biting and precise critique. Thanks to Kevin Killian for your endless availability to edit and critique my work.

ABOUT THE AUTHOR

Dodie Bellamy is an American novelist, nonfiction author, journalist, and editor.